MATTHEW LYON

MATTHEW LYON

"New Man" of the
Democratic Revolution, 1749–1822

Aleine Austin

Foreword by Richard B. Morris

The Pennsylvania State University Press
University Park and London

Publication supported in part by
a Research and Creativity Grant
from Western Maryland College

Library of Congress Cataloging in Publication Data
Austin, Aleine.
  Matthew Lyon, "new man" of the democratic revolution, 1749–1822.
  Includes bibliography and index.
    1. Lyon, Matthew, 1749–1822.   2. Alien and Sedition laws, 1798.   3. United
States—Politics and government—1789–1815.   4. Legislators—United States—Biography.
5. United States. Congress. House—Biography. I. Title.
E302.6.L9A95   328.73′092′4 [B]   80–281
ISBN 0–271–00262–X

Printed in the United States of America

To My Family————

who keep their faith with
"those who loved and fought before."

Contents

Foreword

The American Revolution, it is now generally recognized, was a complex phenomenon with far-reaching consequences. It achieved both independence and the bases of nationhood for the new United States. It built a durable constitutional order. It was also a people's revolution, which raised the level of political aspirations, made the new governments of the emerging states and nation more responsive to social inequities, and brought new men to power.

One of these new men, Matthew Lyon, is the protagonist of this sympathetic but critical biography. As Dr. Austin persuasively portrays him, Lyon was one of the new breed of upwardly mobile political figures, quick to profit from the expanding economy of the post-Revolutionary and early national years, yet caught up in the challenges of state and nation-building. If the American Revolution contributed to the displacement at least in some measure of the old "upper" class from the seats of power throughout the United States, as recent statistical studies have demonstrated, such evidences of upward mobility were especially evident in frontier areas, in future states like Vermont and Kentucky, in both of which Lyon would play a prominent role.

Matthew Lyon will never go down in history as the best-beloved American of his day. Rough-hewn, cantankerous, bullying if lily-livered, forthright yet duplicitous, and withal a transparent opportunist, Lyon is portrayed in this splendidly researched biography as a striking, if distinctly controversial, exemplar of the "new man" of the Democratic Revolution. Throughout his life he railed against the "Aristo-Tories," the same "monocrats" whom Thomas Jefferson feared and detested. The crude and ambitious Irish redemptioner, who started life in America at the very bottom of the social ladder up which white males might climb, Lyon, both in manner and substance, continually shocked the establishment, in his eyes embodied by the Federalist leadership, while contributing perhaps as much as any secondary political figure to democratizing the political system.

Never a man to allow his political career to damage his private interests, Lyon was a strident and colorful figure in each of his varied endeavors, as soldier, radical politician, land grabber, entrepreneur, and manufacturer. Indeed, the evidence Dr. Austin presents suggests that Lyon's private interests could and did influence his political stance. A supporter of American independence, he somehow was involved in the various Allen negotiations with the British for separating Vermont from the Union, negotiations entered into during the war and resumed long after. Lyon's Vermont-first position was not inconsistent with his intense localism and fear of a centralized Union. An ardent Jeffersonian Republican, and a prime mover in the formation of a Republican press and of the local Democratic societies in western Vermont, Lyon broke with his party over the war with England. A fire-eater toward the Indians, he became an apostle of enlightenment toward the aborigines in his closing years as Indian factor to the Cherokee Nation in the Arkansas Territory.

All in all, Dr. Austin has painted on a broad canvas a fascinating portrait with none of the warts removed. Lovable or not, Matthew Lyon, a principal victim of the Sedition Act, tenaciously holds his niche in the pantheon of lesser if notable Americans as a courageous upholder of First Amendment values.

RICHARD B. MORRIS

COLUMBIA UNIVERSITY

Acknowledgments

I wish to express my gratitude to many persons for their contribution to this study. First, the historians who read the manuscript, including the author of the foreword, Professor Richard B. Morris, who gave this study the benefit of his exacting scholarly and literary standards from its inception as a Ph.D. dissertation through its present stage of expanded coverage and interpretation. Dr. Alfred F. Young also has influenced the development of the manuscript over a number of years and has always been generous with his time and thoughtfully astute in his observations and concepts. I am also indebted to Dr. Ralph Levering, Dr. Eric L. McKitrick, and Dr. Robert Webb for their critical comments. To the extent that this study fails to live up to the quality of these scholars' critiques, the fault lies entirely with the author.

From scholars both inside and outside of the discipline of History, I have received assistance in thinking through the psychological implications of Matthew Lyon's personal and political behavior, which I discuss briefly in the concluding chapter. I owe particular thanks to an eminent Baltimore psychiatrist and internist, Dr. Ephraim Lisansky, for his insightful analysis of the clues to Matthew Lyon's personality that he observed through a close reading of the manuscript. In addition I wish to thank my fellow members of the PsychoHistory Seminar of the Washington School of Psychiatry for their observations and comments.

In a work of this sort, one inevitably is indebted to scholars who previously have written about the subject of the biography. In this respect, I wish to acknowledge the following partial studies which broke the ground for my present comprehensive study of Matthew Lyon's entire career: Hudee Z. Herrick, "Matthew Lyon, the Vermont Years" (M.A. Thesis); and George Lucien Montagno, "Matthew Lyon, Radical Jeffersonian 1796–1801" (Ph.D. Thesis). In addition, I am indebted to J. Fairfax McLaughlin, who wrote the first and only published biography of Matthew Lyon in 1900. Although this is a romanticized account of Matthew Lyon with many serious gaps and errors, this initial work uncovered much important information concerning Matthew Lyon's life and pointed the direction for future research.

To all the dedicated librarians and antiquarians of the libraries and local historical societies listed in the bibliography, I wish to express my deep appreciation of their services which resulted in my assemblage of a body of discrete and scattered manuscripts written by or about Matthew Lyon, which shed considerable new light on his career.

Another dedicated person who deserves my heartfelt thanks is Janet Himes, who not only typed several versions of the manuscript, but also made editorial corrections as well.

This work could not have come to fruition without financial assistance, for which I wish to thank the Louis M. Rabinowitz Foundation for a two-year research grant; the University of Maryland, Baltimore County, for a Summer Research Grant; and Western Maryland College for a Research and Creativity Grant to aid the publication of this work.

My appreciation also to *Vermont History* for permission to reproduce, in part, my article, "Vermont Politics in the 1780's: Emergence of Rival Leadership," which appeared in the Spring 1974 issue.

I have saved for last those to whom I have dedicated this book, and to whom I owe the most—my family.

Introduction: "New Man" of the Democratic Revolution

Matthew Lyon's claim to a place in history traditionally rests on his role as a civil liberties martyr, a victim of the Sedition Act of 1798 who scored a victory for freedom of speech by winning reelection to Congress from jail. On the surface he looms as a folk hero, who began as an indentured servant and rose to become a prosperous entrepreneur in frontier Vermont, where he emerged as the leader of the Jeffersonian Republican movement in the 1790's.

Closer scrutiny of his career invites a more sophisticated interpretation of his significance as a historical figure. Lyon was a complex man. Though dedicated to democratic principles, he was also an opportunist concerned with his own advancement. His emergence as a political leader signifies the entrance of a new breed into American political life after the Revolution; he is an early example of the self-made man who embraced the politics of democracy while challenging the control exercised by the social and economic elite. His career suggests that the phenomenon described by Richard Hofstadter as "liberated capitalism" had its beginnings in the Revolutionary era, with the opening of new opportunities to men of enterprise.[1] With economic opportunity Matthew Lyon sought political opportunity, and the unfolding of his early career in Vermont discloses why he helped forge the Republican Party in the 1790s as the outlet for his political aspirations.

Many currents fed into the mainstream of the Republican movement of the 1790s, and Matthew Lyon's career illustrates one of them. In presenting him as a case study of the "new man" in politics, I have drawn upon a concept that was widespread in postrevolutionary America. Alfred Young, in his study of the rise of the Democratic-Republicans in New York State, shows the outcries of the elite against the appearance of "new raw men" in that state's political life.[2] In another astute study of the ideological currents flowing out of the American Revolution, Gordon S. Wood gives numerous examples of lamentations over the appearance of new elements in the formerly restricted realm of politics. Take, for example, the complaint of John Jay to Alexander Hamilton while the Revolution was still in progress: "Effrontery and arrogance, even in our virtuous and enlightened days, are giving rank and Importance to men whom Wisdom would have left in obscurity." Similarly, respectable men of property were appalled to see those "whose fathers they would have disdained to have sat with the dogs of their flocks, raised to immense wealth . . ." The Revolution was causing the government to fall "into the hands of those whose ability or situation in life does not intitle them to it"; often they were "men without reading, experience, or principle."[3]

These outcries reflected the underlying premises of "deference democracy," which a number of historians have argued convincingly was the prevailing political ideology of colonial America. As briefly stated by Jack P. Greene, this tradition held "that government should be entrusted to men of merit; that merit was very often, though by no means always, associated with wealth and social position; that men of merit were obliged to use their talents for the benefit of the public; and that deference to them was the implicit duty of the rest of society."[4] In social terms, we may generalize that the majority of those who attained office in colonial society were men of inherited wealth who enjoyed prestigious family connections. Education, usually at a college level, accompanied wealth as an attribute of a gentleman worthy of office. The law was another avenue to political position, and most lawyers, because of their education and lucrative incomes, were regarded as belonging to the "better sort." According to Gordon Wood, the attitudes linking political office with social position carried over after the Revolution. Despite much lip service to the ideal of natural aristocracy, the traditional elite scorned men of new wealth if they lacked the refinements of education, style, and social connections.[5]

A "new man" of the postrevolutionary era, then, can be described as one who attained political office without the traditional social credentials. His family lacked status and influence; in fact, he may have come from the lower strata of society as in Matthew Lyon's case, although many of the new men originated from the ranks of the broad "middling" segment of colonial America. In financial terms, what set apart the new man from the old elite is that he acquired his wealth through his own enterprise rather than inheritance; he was a member of the nouveaux riches, an arriviste. Culturally he lacked polish. He was likely to be a man of rough exterior who had not acquired the refinements of manner or thought associated with a college education. Often, however, the new man was self-educated and widely read in the Enlightenment writings of the eighteenth century.

In exploring the personal and political development of Matthew Lyon, this biographical study seeks to discover the connection between his being a new man and his ardent involvement in the Jeffersonian Republican Party. Many local factors and personalities set the stage for his role as leader of the Democratic-Republican movement in Vermont, the details of which are developed in this study. Suffice it to say here that Matthew Lyon regarded the Federalists as "a set of gentry . . . who consider the science of government to belong only to a few families."[6]

The elite, in the newly settled Vermont frontier, did not consist primarily of wealthy families long entrenched in political office, but of men who enjoyed social status because of their family background and superior education. Graduates of Yale, Harvard, and Princeton who were members of the bar and clergy constituted the leadership of the Federalist Party in Vermont. In Lyon's view, these men threatened his opportunity for political advancement. The Republican movement that he led in Vermont was an instrument for keeping the avenues of opportunity open for himself and those like him, who lacked the social credentials on which the Federalists relied for their claim to political leadership. It is not without significance that he entitled his Republican magazine *The Scourge of Aristocracy*. In his eyes, the Federalists on both the local and national level favored the rule of the privileged. Lyon's Republican writings abound with appeals to the egalitarianism of the American and French Revolutions, as a means of combating the exclusivity of the Federalists in power. Because he identified the Republicanism of the French Revolution with that of the American, and was imprisoned, in part, for his attempts to avoid war with the new Republic of France, Lyon may be regarded as a defender of the broad democratic revolution of the eighteenth century.[7]

Matthew Lyon is not an isolated example of the new man in early American politics. Recent investigations into the Revolutionary era have disclosed numerous cases where individuals of modest origins suddenly emerged as members of the executive or legislative branches of the new state governments.[8] Similarly, a number of studies of the Democratic-Republican movement, particularly in the Northern states, reveal the emergence of self-made businessmen like Matthew Lyon, who embraced this movement as a means of challenging the entrenched elite of the Federalist party. A few examples of this phenomenon make the point.

In Salem, Massachusetts, Jacob Crowninshield, son of a deckhand who rose to head his own shipping firm, challenged the predominance of the long-established Derby family, who controlled the Federalist Party in the Salem area. By 1802, after the Crowninshields had fostered Republicanism throughout the 1790s, by financing a newspaper and organizing an effective political and social organization, the citizens of the district sent Jacob Crowninshield to Congress. Although described at the time as a victory of the many over the few, Jacob Crowninshield's election signified displacement of an old established commercial family by a new rising one.[9]

Leader of the new men in New York was George Clinton, who first

challenged the "great families' " traditional claim to political power as
Revolutionary governor of that state. His modest family background con-
trasted sharply to the social standing that had formerly been a prerequisite for holding office in colonial New York.

Although popularly regarded as the spokesman for the small farmers,
George Clinton became a prosperous member of the middle class by the
end of the Revolution. His rise stemmed largely from his speculation in
frontier lands and confiscated estates during and after the Revolution.
Hamilton accused him of accumulating "a large fortune," and this was
true not only of George Clinton but of many of the men who rose with
him to political power. Their ascendance has been described as representing a movement for opportunity versus privilege in New York State
politics.[10]

A recent study of the Democratic-Republican Party in Philadelphia indicates that its leaders "tended to be political newcomers, outsiders, ambitious economic types, and influential men tied to the state government."[11] One of their number, Congressman John Swanwick, is an interesting example of the influence of social factors on political affiliation.
Starting out as an apprentice in Robert Morris's counting house, he eventually bought out his senior partner and became one of the most prominent import-export merchants of Philadelphia, a director of the Bank of
North America, and a substantial holder of public securities. Nevertheless, his competitors, the well-established Quaker merchants who held
sway in the Federalist Party of Pennsylvania, ignored him both socially
and politically. In his Philadelphia gossip-sheet, William Cobbett jeered:
"Our Lilliputian, with his dollars, gets access where without them he
would not be suffered to appear."[12] As a self-made man, Swanwick had
little choice but to turn to the new Republican Party to fulfill his political
ambitions.

Blair McClenachan was another wealthy Philadelphian who won election to Congress as a standard-bearer of the Democratic-Republican
movement. Born in Ireland, he migrated to America at an early age, became involved in banking during the Revolution, lent substantial sums to
provision the army, and became one of Philadelphia's most prosperous
merchants. Ideologically, however, he consistently opposed the Federalist merchants of Pennsylvania. In 1788 he headed that state's Anti-Fed-
eral Convention, and in 1794 he presided over Philadelphia's Democratic
Society, parent of the so-called Jacobin Societies of the 1790s. Obviously,
factors other than economic interest influenced his political persuasion,
not the least of which were his "democratical" convictions and his Irish
origins, which automatically excluded him from Philadelphia's inner social and political circle.[13]

As these biographical sketches indicate, these new members of the
middle class, finding themselves excluded from positions of political influence by the "rich and well born Federalists," sought to enlarge their

opportunities through the Republican Party. Like Matthew Lyon, they too found in the democratic ideology of the American and French Revolutions a genuine justification of their claim to a share in political power. While these new men did not represent the main thrust of the Republican movement, they are one of its significant components. In certain respects they were the precursors of the self-made men who played so prominent a role in the ensuing movement for democracy during the Jacksonian era.

The following pages tell the story of the public life of Matthew Lyon, the most controversial of the new men of his era. His story, unique in the details of his personal experience, is nevertheless the saga of the evolution of a type, the "new man" of the eighteenth century's democratic revolution.

1

"By the Bulls that Redeemed Me!"

At the age of fifteen, in the year 1764, Matthew Lyon took leave of his native Ireland and commenced life in the New World as an indentured servant in the colony of Connecticut. Of his early years in Ireland only the barest facts are knowable; these are deduced largely from his unpublished memoirs. The only remaining traces of this autobiography are a few incidents imperfectly recalled by his grandson, Matthew S. Lyon, who found the original manuscript in the attic of the family homestead and read it before it was completely mutilated by mice and lost to posterity.[1] Lyon's youngest daughter, Elizabeth A. Roe, also wrote some recollections of her father's background. These two relatives are the only source of information about Matthew's youth.

Both descendants report that he was born in Ireland; Matthew S. Lyon specifically recalls from Lyon's memoirs that he was born in Wicklow County, Ireland. The date of his birth was probably July 14, 1749.[2] According to both accounts, he attended school in Dublin, where he received a basic education, including a rudimentary knowledge of Latin. His formal education could not have been extensive, however; in his early teens, he was apprenticed to a Dublin printer and bookbinder, according to his grandson's recollections. This information may well be authentic; it is supported by a facetious proposal Lyon made to the Kentucky journalist William Worsley, when Matthew was in his seventies and facing financial reverses: "I see you advertise for a youth capable of attending your book Store. Will an old man do for you? I was once the youth you call for and served an apprenticeship in part in a book Store."[3]

In 1764, at the age of fifteen, Lyon severed his apprenticeship and sailed to America as a redemptioner. At that time, European and Yankee shipowners were engaged in the prosperous trade of transporting redemptioners by the thousands, mainly from Ulster Ireland and Germany. The voyage, in the crowded hold of a ship packed with disease-ridden men, women, and children, was usually rigorous and debilitating. But for those who survived, a means of paying their passage awaited them

upon arrival. Potential employers would board the ship, select the ablest-
bodied among them for servants, and pay the captain the fare for their
passage. In return, the servants signed an indenture, agreeing to work off
their passage by serving their masters for a certain stipulated term, usually five to seven years, or in the case of children, until the age of twenty-
one.[4]

The legend of Lyon's voyage, as retold by his descendants, has all the
embellishments of a second-rate nineteenth-century novel. Where the
truth lies is difficult to ascertain, but the accounts have two threads in
common: they both describe the wrench that the youth experienced upon
leaving his family, and both indicate that he fell victim to the deceptions
of a high-handed Yankee captain.

According to Lyon's daughter, Elizabeth A. Roe, her father ran away
from a cultured, comfortable home in Dublin in search of adventure.
Her story continues:

> He had in his possession one guinea. But he made arrangements with the
> captain of a very fine vessel to be cabin boy for his passage. The vessel was
> to sail the next day. He told the captain he would have to secrete him, for
> his father would search every vessel at the wharf for him. The captain did
> so, and when his Father came to the vessel in search of him, he heard his
> voice calling, "Matthew, my dear boy, come to the embrace of your Father.
> Don't leave your parents and go you know not where." And Father would
> have gone to him, but that he was secured so he could not get to him. He
> was very sympathetic and affectionate.
>
> The vessel sailed next morning, and bore him out of port, and he never
> saw his parents again. He had such implicit confidence in the captain that
> he gave his guinea to him for safekeeping. But when he got to port the cap-
> tain indentured him just as he did the other boys and kept the guinea; only
> that as such a large, fine looking boy he passed him off on sale for eighteen
> years old. He let them go to the highest bidder. So he was only indentured
> for three years instead of five.[5]

The account given by Lyon's grandson, Matthew S. Lyon, differs in
several essentials from that of Mrs. Roe. According to his recollections, it
was not comfortable parents that Lyon left behind in Dublin, but an im-
poverished widowed mother. Nor did he sign up as a cabin boy, who was
later betrayed by the captain and sold into indentured servitude. Rather,
the deception of "the treacherous captain" lay in his urging the youth
"that his knowledge of his business could be turned to much profit, and
that when he had earned enough money he could pay him for the
passage." Despite the amusing romanticism of its style, this account is
probably closer to the truth, in view of the fact that it was recalled from
reading Lyon's manuscript memoirs. Particularly plausible is the following description of Lyon's wretched passage to America:

> He was attacked with a violent illness on the passage during which he was
> delirious for many days. When he recovered he found himself destitute from

the necessities he had brought with him. A change of clothing was absolutely necessary, and was furnished him from the wardrobe of some "abandoned" women who were all going to America and who turned to the instincts of their better nature (though lost and fallen [they] had kindly ministered to him in his illness when everyone else had deserted him, and when convalescent divided their scanty wardrobe with him. He mentions the incident feelingly and as a simple act of justice, although by the most frail and erring of the sex. . . . .)

At the point of debarkation he was together with a number of other immigrants indentured for a term in payment of his passage by the treacherous captain.[6]

That Lyon spent his first years in the colonies as an indentured servant in Connecticut, there seems to be little doubt. His descendants' statements that he was indentured are corroborated by several local historians of Connecticut towns.[7] Exactly who his master or masters were is a matter of dispute, however.

One claim is that upon his arrival in New York he was assigned to Jabez Bacon of Woodbury, Connecticut. Bacon is reputed to have been a dealer in pork and one of the shrewdest and most prosperous merchants of interior Connecticut. His "Red Store in the Hollow" was the center of trade for the surrounding farmers and backwoodsmen of Litchfield County, who used pork as "circulating medium" for the purchase of Bacon's shelf goods. Bacon apparently transported the pork to New York via the Derby Narrows and there, with the money he obtained for his product, bought up huge quantities of soft goods. In New York he gained the reputation of a shrewd Yankee trader, who had proven himself capable of manipulating the market to his advantage on more than one occasion.[8]

If indeed Lyon was the indentured servant of this enterprising merchant, his work could have been any of a variety of chores. He could have been a clerk in the store itself; more than likely, however, Bacon would have given a boy of fifteen more manual tasks to perform, particularly if he was of burly build, as Lyon was reputed to be. Possibly his chores were connected to the pork trade, which involved such operations as smoking hams, loading and unloading the sloops, and storing the merchandise brought back from New York.

Still standing in Woodbury today is the "Red Store in the Hollow." Behind it is a small shack, which local residents have conjectured once served as slave quarters. On the ground floor is a small room; attached to its walls are wooden slabs on which the slaves are presumed to have slept. In the center of the room is a staircase leading to an A-shaped attic where large iron hooks hang from the still charred ceiling. More than likely large hams once hung on these hooks, and this shack originally was a smokehouse rather than slave quarters. Matthew Lyon, rather than a slave, probably occupied the downstairs cabin and slept on one of its wooden slabs, if he was, in fact, the indentured servant of Jabez Bacon.

Whether Matthew suffered abuses or ran into serious difficulties with his master, the Litchfield County Court Records do not tell us.[9] That his life was circumscribed, however, is certain because of the strict legal codes devised by each colony, which governed the relationship between master and indentured servants. In return for his food, shelter, medical care, and "freedom dues," the indentured servant was obliged to obey the rules of the master and the colony. In general, indentured servants were forbidden to leave the master's premises, unless they were given special consent. They could not frequent taverns or engage in the local entertainments of billiards, games of chance, cards, and the like. They were not allowed to buy or sell; they were forbidden to congregate sinfully with others. If indentured servants violated these rules or if they attempted to run away from their master, their punishment usually consisted of an extension of their terms of indenture. In some instances, if a master did not wish to retain his indentured servant, he resold him for the remainder of his term; in New England this practice was widespread.[10]

Such seems to have been Matthew Lyon's fate, although the reasons for his transfer are not specified by his grandson, who stressed only that Lyon's master sold him for "A Yoke of Bulls." He not only recalled this incident from reading his grandfather's memoirs, but from stories told by his father (Lyon's son Chittenden), alluding to the "many bouts at fist cuffs he had when a boy, growing out of his being bothered by other boys in reference to it."[11]

Two Connecticut antiquarians corroborate this family legend of the "yoke of bulls" and elaborate upon it. They both concur that Lyon was assigned, for a pair of stags valued at £12, to Hugh Hannah of Litchfield, Connecticut.[12] The later taunts of Lyon's Federalist adversaries tend to substantiate these accounts. The following verse, written by Thomas Green Fessenden, is one of many examples of how Lyon's indentured status was satirized:

> Tis said that he brags
> How one pair of stags
>   Erst paid for his passage from Europe
> But the price of a score
> Would scarce send him o'er
>   And pay for his hangman a new rope![13]

Lyon apparently did not attempt to deny these charges. Instead, with typical bravado, he extolled the stags as his liberators, swearing, "By the Bulls that redeemed me!"[14]

A historian of Litchfield County gives us the following description of Lyon's years of indenture to Hugh Hannah:

Matt was then a lad of fourteen years [sic], unusually green, full of life and energy, but rough, untutored, independent, and often impertinent. In those days the "rod" was very generally regarded as an efficient instrument of discipline, and Hannah is said to have had even more than ordinary faith in its virtues. The young "redemptioneer" spent several years in this town, attending the district school for a specified term each winter, and making remarkable progress in his studies but often manifesting a most unmanageable temper. His indentures were at length violently sundered. In an altercation between them, Matt threw a mallet at the head of his master, and fled.[15]

Exactly how many years Lyon served out his indentures is uncertain. His daughter's version of how he liberated himself differs considerably from Kilbourne's account. According to her, Lyon was originally indentured for only three years, and after working out part of his time, "he bought the rest of it, and commenced life for himself."[16]

From these scattered accounts of Lyon's youth one obtains some clues regarding his personality. His basic decision to emigrate to America alone, at the age of fifteen, is a self-evident indication of an adventurous nature bolstered by strong ambition. His decision to run away from home may also suggest that he was a rebellious youth who harbored more than the average anger against one or both of his parents. His rebelliousness is further evidenced by the story of how he broke his indentures by throwing a mallet at his master and running away. Though this story may be a legend, his future conduct jibes with it. From the information regarding his youth, we should not be surprised when we find Lyon, the man, to be ambitious, adventurous, resourceful, angry, and rebellious.

The first official record of Lyon's residence in Connecticut appears on June 22, 1772, in the Town Records of Cornwall, Connecticut. By that time Lyon was twenty-three years old and apparently sufficiently independent to purchase one hundred acres in the south part of the township. A year later, on June 23, 1773, he reached another milestone when he married Mary Horsford.[17]

His twenty-two-year-old bride was the daughter of Samuel Horsford, an early pioneer of the settlement of Litchfield, who later moved with the frontier to Cornwall. There he died in 1757 leaving a modest estate worth £244, of which Mary inherited £24 and 6 shillings.[18]

Mary's mother had previously been married to Daniel Allen, brother of Ethan Allen's father. Although the relationship is somewhat remote, it is perhaps significant, in the light of Lyon's later career, that Mary's family kept some ties to the Allen clan. During Mary's childhood and early womanhood, the Allens had pursued their fortunes in the woods, mines, and lands of Cornwall and the neighboring towns of Salisbury and Litchfield. An indication that the Horsfords and the Allens were fairly closely associated is the fact that both families simultaneously transferred their religious affiliation from the prevailing Congregational Church to the dissenting Episcopalians. On March 26, 1764, both widow Mary Horsford and widow Allen were discharged by Reverend Thomas Davies to the "dissenting collector" for Episcopalians.[19] This means that after they had indicated their desire to disaffiliate themselves from the Congregational Church, the minister discharged them from paying their taxes to the Congregational Church collector and, in accord with the provisions of Connecticut's rate bill, he assigned them to pay their church taxes to the Episcopalian collector.

That Lyon chose a wife who was one of the disaffected Congregationalists of Connecticut is not without significance. Mary Horsford's family and the Allens, to whom they were related, were representative of the small settlers of back-country Connecticut whose discontent with the established Congregational Church was widespread.[20] Ethan Allen's father, Joseph, was one of the outspoken dissenters against Calvinist doctrines as early as 1740; by 1754 he had succeeded in converting his Congregational minister to Episcopalianism.[21] Ethan Allen went beyond his father in rejecting Calvinism. Influenced by the rationalist teachings of his friend, Dr. Thomas Young, he eventually expressed this philosophy in his famous treatise, *Reason the only Oracle of Man*, one of the first attacks on revealed religion to emanate from America.

While the "Oracles" did not appear in print until 1784, the intellectual and social currents that influenced Ethan were operating in back-country Connecticut at the time Lyon resided there from 1764 to 1774.

Throughout the rest of his life, Matthew Lyon harbored deep-seated hostilities toward the Congregationalists, who were among his most virulent Federalist enemies. When one of them, Congressman John Allen of Connecticut, questioned Lyon's American blood in 1797, Lyon contemptuously replied: "He could not say, it was true, that he was descended from the bastards of Oliver Cromwell, or his courtiers, or the Puritans who punished their horses for breaking the Sabbath, or from those who persecuted the Quakers, or hanged the witches."[22] This vehement antipathy to the Congregationalists was shared and expressed by many New England Republicans in the 1790s. Indeed, it seems more than a coincidence that many of the most active Republicans in Connecticut and Vermont, including Matthew Lyon, were members of the Episcopal Church (see chapter 10).

Whether Lyon was born an Episcopalian is difficult to state with certainty, since there are no records of his birth extant in Ireland. (The Public Records Office in Dublin was destroyed in 1922.) There are records, however, which reveal the existence of an Irish Protestant family by the name of Lyon, some of whom were descendants of Bishop William of Cork, who was appointed by Queen Elizabeth to head the Anglican Church in Ireland in 1583.[23] In Matthew Lyon's native Wicklow County, the names of several members of a Lyon family appear often in the records of the (Anglican) Church of Ireland.[24] Combining this information with the fact that Lyon later actively participated in Episcopal Church Conventions in Vermont (see chapter 7), it is quite conceivable that he was an Episcopalian by birth. His formal religious affiliations notwithstanding, Matthew Lyon was typical of the many Connecticut migrants to western Vermont who subscribed to the rationalist Deism espoused by Ethan Allen.[25]

The Allen brothers had an even more direct influence on the life of Matthew Lyon and his fellow settlers in back-country Connecticut, as land speculators in the New Hampshire Grants. In advertisements in the *Connecticut Courant*, they extolled the opportunity for acquiring land cheaply in this northern frontier territory that lay between New Hampshire and New York. From the Salisbury-Cornwall region alone, hundreds migrated to the Grants seeking a new start in a new territory.

All around him, Matthew Lyon saw men buying up land at bargain prices and moving to the Grants. Realizing, no doubt, that in Connecticut his opportunities were circumscribed, he too took his chances. In February 1773 he drew lots and thereby purchased his first piece of property in the Grants, in the township of Wallingford.[26] From that date on, all his activities were directed toward that southwest corner of the Grants.

In March 1773 he sold the hundred acres he had purchased in Cornwall the year before.[27] In June he married Mary Horsford, and together they must have made plans to start their new family on their new land. Mary was already pregnant when they made their arduous journey by wagon train along the Housatonic, through the Berkshire Hills of Massachusetts, and into the Green Mountain country beyond. Passing through the frontier town of Bennington, they pushed on through the wilderness another fifty miles and finally reached Wallingford. It was little more than a clearing in the forest, with a few rough log huts scattered in the surrounding woods.

On January 14, 1774, Lyon purchased an additional ninety acres of Hampshire Grant land for the nominal sum of £20.[28] He was behaving like a family man, and for good reason. Six days later, Mary bore him a daughter, whom they named Ann. After ten years of wandering, Matthew Lyon had finally made himself a home. His future was rooted in the Hampshire Grants.

2

Fighting the Revolution

For Colonial Independence

Lyon arrived in the Grants in 1774 at a crucial juncture of history, when Britain's Coercive Acts brought the first Continental Congress into existence. Between 1774 and 1776, when the American Colonies ultimately declared their independence, Lyon joined the settlers of the Hampshire Grants in waging a battle for their own independence not only against the government of Great Britain but also that of New York. During the course of this dual rebellion, Lyon was instrumental in bringing into existence the state of Vermont.

As the owner of land bearing a New Hampshire title, Lyon found himself involved in a controversy that had a complicated history.[1] In the colonial period, the territory that lay north of Massachusetts, east of Lake Champlain, and west of the Connecticut River was claimed by two colonies, New York and New Hampshire. The royal governors of both provinces had been making conflicting grants of land in this region for many years; but after the French and Indian War ended in 1763, land speculators rushed into this region, and rival claims to titles became acute.

In 1764 the controversy was submitted to the King's Privy Council, which ruled that the territory in question came under the jurisdiction of the Province of New York. While the governor of New Hampshire ceased granting new titles after 1764, the land bearing the old New Hampshire titles became the object of great dispute. New York claimed that all former grants made by the governor of New Hampshire were invalid and required holders of the New Hampshire grants to surrender them and purchase confirmatory New York patents. When the settlers in general and the speculators in particular refused to comply with these regulations because they considered them costly and unjust, the governor of New York proceeded to issue grants to the lands already held by Hampshire grantees, thereby sowing the seeds of discord that Ethan Allen soon reaped.

Allen assumed the role of defender of the rights of the Hampshire

Grants settlers. In time, he organized them into the celebrated Green Mountain Boys. This vigilante-type militia of Hampshire Grant settlers stood ready at a moment's notice to descend upon any Yorker sheriff, surveyor, or settler who dared to lay claim to their lands or threaten eviction.

As a Hampshire grantee, who had a vital stake in having his title recognized, Lyon immediately threw in his lot with Ethan Allen's Green Mountain Boys, determined to defend his property by force if necessary. Implicitly he subscribed to Ethan Allen's philosophy that the natural rights of property supersede the laws of men.[2]

In later years he described how in 1774 he went about organizing his local unit of the Green Mountain Boys: "I laid before the youngerly men in my neighborhood, in the country now called Vermont, a plan for armed association which was adopted. We armed and clothed ourselves uniformly. We hired an old veteran to teach us discipline, and we each of us took command in turn, so that every one should know the duty of every station."[3]

In the midst of their military preparations against the Yorkers, the Green Mountain Boys were called into action against an entirely different enemy in 1775. According to Ethan Allen, after the British made their "first systematical and bloody attempt at Lexington, to enslave America,"[4] the Hartford Committee of Correspondence commissioned him to mobilize his Green Mountain Boys for an attack on Fort Ticonderoga.

Matthew Lyon and twenty of his company were alerted during the night of May 9 by Gershon Beach, a Rutland blacksmith who spent the night rousing the Green Mountain Boys of the surrounding territory. Lyon was one of two hundred men who poured into Hand's Cove, the rendezvous headquarters one mile north of the promontory of Ticonderoga. He was there when Benedict Arnold arrived in his scarlet uniform and asserted that he was commissioned by the Cambridge, Massachusetts, Committee of Safety to lead the attack, and he undoubtedly participated in the row that ensued. The Green Mountain Boys threatened to go home unless they were led by their own officers. In the end a compromise was reached; Allen and Arnold marched together at the head of the column that stormed Fort Ticonderoga on May 10, 1775. Silently, in the grey preceding the dawn, Lyon followed the two commanders of the column to the gate of the fort. There a sentry suddenly awoke. Seeing the two uniformed officers, followed by a motley-clad troop of backwoodsmen rushing toward him, he pulled his trigger in terror and ran. Lyon and his fellow militiamen broke ranks. With war whoops and cheers, they pursued the fleeing sentry and rushed to capture the barracks. In the meantime, Commanders Allen and Arnold obtained the surrender of the fort's commandant, Captain De la Place.

The conquerors "tossed about the flowing bowl," which consisted of ninety gallons of Captain De la Place's rum, and in high spirits toasted "the liberty and freedom of America."[5] Lyon discovered a group of Royal

Irish soldiers among the prisoners and persuaded some of his former countrymen to join the American rebellion against the British. He claimed that many of them "afterwards distinguished themselves in our cause."[6]

Later that day, Lyon joined Captain Seth Warner's expedition to take possession of Crown Point. This was easily done, the entire British garrison there consisting of one sergeant, eight privates, and ten women and children. More difficult was the problem of salvaging the one hundred cannon and other munitions, which were in serious disrepair. Lyon addressed himself to this task with ardor and in later years bragged of his exploits on this occasion. "For the purpose of taking an armed sloop in the Lake," he wrote, "it was necssary to mount two heavy pieces of ordnance at Crown Point. Our European artilleryists said it could not be obtained without a ruinous delay. With the assistance of a few backwoodsmen, and some timber readily procured, I mounted them and put the match to the first cannon ever fired under the auspices of the American Eagle, whose reknown has spread far and wide."[7]

Carried away by this victory, Lyon soon volunteered to join Ethan Allen in an expedition to capture the British garrison at St. John's, Canada. Arnold had warned Allen of the foolhardiness of this undertaking, and, as he predicted, British regulars from Montreal were quickly dispatched to reinforce the St. John's garrison. When the British troops were only two miles away from their encampment, Allen ordered a retreat, probably much to the relief of Lyon and his fellow soldiers. By this time they were exhausted from three days of rowing, little food, and barely any sleep. They clambered into the boats and sailed across the Sorel River to St. John's, where some of the men didn't even bother to land, but remained in the boats to sleep.

At dawn Lyon and his companions were awakened by shots from the British across the river. Again beating a hasty retreat, they jumped into the boats and shot at the regulars, while the oarsmen hastened to get them out of gunshot range. It was a gloomy finale to what had started out as a glorious victory. However, Lyon could take solace in the fact that the Green Mountain Boys' accomplishments did not go unrewarded. The Continental Congress passed a resolution to pay their Ticonderoga expedition as if it had been part of the Continental Army. When Ethan Allen and Seth Warner appeared before that body on June 25, 1775, it ignored the price upon their heads and passed on to the Provincial Congress of New York a recommendation that the Green Mountain Boys be formed into a separate regiment. In addition, it conceded to them the unusual privilege of electing their own officers.

At their ensuing convention, the Green Mountaineers elected the ever-reliable Seth Warner as Lieutenant Colonel of their regiment, thus rebuffing the impetuous Ethan Allen as a military leader and shattering his dream of leading them on another expedition into Canada. His zeal for making Canada a part of the United States led him to accept General

Phillip Schuyler's offer to take him along on the Canadian expedition, launched in 1775. He was the only Green Mountain Boy to join this ill-fated expedition, which eventuated in his capture in September 1776.[8]

Meanwhile, even before that expedition was launched, Lyon and the rest of the Green Mountain Boys turned their attention to protecting the settlers on the Grants. Immediately upon his return from St. John's in June 1775, Lyon was made adjutant of his militia regiment.[9] The following year Lyon concerned himself more with domestic than with military matters. Life seemed to return to normal; Lyon devoted himself to his neglected farm and family, the responsibilities of which increased when Mary gave birth to their second child, James, on April 15, 1776.[10] But this domestic tranquility was short-lived. By July, pandemonium reigned. The British had defeated the American expedition in Canada; the American Army was retreating. The northern frontier lay virtually unprotected. In the meantime the Continental Congress adopted the Declaration of Independence, and the Colonies were officially at war with Britain.

Lyon immediately entered the Continental Army and was commissioned as second lieutenant on July 19, 1776.[11] His first assignment ended in a debacle, the repercussions of which were to haunt him in his later career. His company, under the command of John Fassett, Jr., was ordered to Jericho, in the abandoned northern frontier region, to protect a blockhouse where wheat was stored. The men resented this assignment, according to Lyon's story, not only because they were completely isolated and exposed to the enemy just north of them in Canada, but also because they believed they were placed there to protect the interests of wheat speculators.[12] Lyon claimed he opposed these rumors with all the arguments in his power and urged the men to submit to the authority of the general, who could not be expected to be omniscient. However, when a scout reported sighting five or six hundred Indians on the shores of Lake Champlain only twelve miles away, "all entreaties were ineffectual." The men mutinied. Threatening the officers with violence if they refused to take refuge from the Indians by crossing the river, the men forced the officers to submit. According to Lyon, he "expostulated with them long and earnestly" and "urged them to stay in the event of a battle"; but when "the other officers, which were two Captains and one Lieutenant seemed willing to go . . . I did not think it my duty to resist alone."

The following morning Lyon was dispatched to headquarters to inform General St. Clair of what had transpired. "But some of the wheat speculators had arrived before me," Lyon explained, "and so exasperated the General that when I arrived, he was enraged to the highest pitch." He ordered a court-martial, which sentenced all the officers, including Lyon, to be cashiered, or dishonorably discharged from the army. The soldiers were sentenced to corporal punishment.

General St. Clair's action was a necessary form of military discipline, regardless of the extenuating circumstances. At the time it was essential to control the general chaos that accompanied the retreat of the disintegrating Northern Army. Several months later, however, General St. Clair saw fit to ignore the court-martial's sentence and recommended Lyon to General Phillip Schuyler for a responsible post in the Continental Army. General Schuyler, who was then in command of the Continental Army's northern campaign, in turn promoted Lyon to the rank of captain and appointed him as paymaster to Colonel Seth Warner's regiment.[13] He took this action on July 15, 1777, thirteen days after Burgoyne's northern expedition began its invasion of the Colonies from Canada. In his new capacity Lyon spent part of this time "rideing express" during the trying months of Burgoyne's invasion. He also acted as guide and rifleman in the Northern Army, as it locked horns with the enemy along the line of retreat.[14]

Conditions for civilians in the besieged territory were beyond endurance. Homes were burned to the ground, settlements left in rubble. In certain areas a Tory underground collaborated with the enemy, compounding the devastation. With fear and hunger stalking the villages, Lyon sent his family back to Cornwall, Connecticut, while he continued to combat both the internal and external enemy.[15]

General James Wilkinson, in his memoirs, has left an account of the type of service Lyon rendered during these dark times:

> The night of the 7th (July, 1777, the night after the battle of Hubbarton,) being extremely dark and rainy, one of the guards took up and reported to head quarters a young man suspected of being a spy. I visited the guard, and found the prisoner to be a Lieutenant Lyon (since Mr. Matthew Lyon of Congress) of the militia, who had joined us to offer his services as a guide, of whom we stood in great need, being strangers to the country, which was in general a wilderness. . . . Lieutenant Lyon, an active, ardent young man, was extremely zealous, and accompanied us as long as his services were useful.[16]

At Saratoga, in the final clash between Burgoyne's troops and the Continental Army, Lyon served as a volunteer in Warner's regiment. For almost a month the two armies had been arrayed against each other along the Hudson, in the wooded region outside Saratoga. Finally, in the second fierce battle of Freeman's Farm, the Continentals crippled Burgoyne's forces beyond repair. With casualties numbering almost 700, compared to the patriots' 150, Burgoyne was forced to retreat. Several days later his army was surrounded at Saratoga. Further retreat was impossible, and Burgoyne was forced to surrender. On October 17, Matthew Lyon "had the honor and pleasure of seeing his army pile their arms."[17]

Burgoyne's defeat marked the turning point in the American Revolution. The victory at Saratoga brought France into the war as an ally of the patriots. The remnants of Warner's regiment were ordered southward for future engagements with the British in the spring of 1778. At this juncture Lyon resigned his commission in the army to turn his attention once again to the military and political problems that confronted the war-ravaged people of his Green Mountain region.

For Vermont's Independence

Even during his years of military service, Lyon played an active role in the political upheaval taking place in the Grants. On July 24, 1776, when the American army was retreating from Canada, Lyon represented his town of Wallingford at the Second Dorset Convention. Here he voted for the momentous resolution to form the Grants into a separate district (or state).[18]

The "unhappy disputes" with the "monopolizing Land Traders of New York" was the reason given for not placing the Grants under New York's jurisdiction "in such a manner as might be detrimental to our private property."[19] This daring movement to free the Grants from New York's authority was originated by Ethan and Ira Allen. As large land speculators, holding in excess of 60,000 acres, they had a great deal of private property at stake, but Lyon and the small settlers who participated in the conventions found common cause with the Allens because they too were concerned about protecting their holdings. The Allens were shrewd enough to enlist the small settlers in their battle as speculators by appealing to the whole series of accumulated political and economic grievances that the small settlers had harbored against the colonial Province of New York. Among these were the feudal quitrents, the high property qualifications for voting, the lack of adequate representation in the New York Assembly, the refusal to recognize local town governments, the abuses of New York sheriffs and courts, and the political and economic power that the eastern seaboard merchants exercised over the back-country debtors.[20]

What seems to have turned the tide in the Hampshire Grants decisively against New York were the conservative features of the constitution passed by the Revolutionary government of that state in April 1777.[21] This document perpetuated some of the most serious abuses of the provincial government of New York; among them were the property qualifications for voting and the continuation of such feudal institutions as primogeniture and entails. The Grants inhabitants were particularly dismayed by the inadequate representation the new constitution provided for their back-country region. Of the seventy seats in the Assembly they were allotted only nine, and only three of the twenty-four seats in the Senate. Thus the combined economic and political grievances of the

Grant folk eventually consummated in their forming their own independent, democratic, state government.

July 2, 1777, was the date set for the Constitutional Convention that would officially launch the new state. Another six months was to elapse, however, before the Grant settlers could establish a permanent government. Just as the Constitutional Convention's deliberations began to get under way, word came of Burgoyne's advance on Ticonderoga. With the enemy at their doorstep, the delegates quickly appointed a Council of Safety to govern the territory during the siege and then disbanded the Convention. The Council of Safety was to serve as a temporary substitute for a state government during the emergency.

In all probability, Matthew Lyon was a member of this key governing body.[22] As such, he was involved in an epoch-making event, the formulation of Vermont's constitution. This document reflected the revolutionary democratic aspirations of Lyon's fellow back-country settlers; it incorporated the most advanced political ideas of the American Revolution.

An influential figure in guiding the thinking of Lyon and his colleagues was Dr. Thomas Young, who resided in Philadelphia at the time and was an enthusiastic supporter of the "radical" constitution of Pennsylvania's Revolutionary government. When agents sent by the Grants' convention failed to win recognition of their proposed new state from the Continental Congress in January 1777, they sought advice from Dr. Young. In a subsequent letter to the "Inhabitants of Vermont," he enclosed the revolutionary directions given by Congress in May 1775 "to all such bodies of men as looked upon themselves as returned to a state of nature, to adopt such governments as should in the opinion of the Representatives of the peoples best conduce to the happiness and safety of their constituents in particular and America in general." Reminding them that Congress had prepared these instructions when it was about to declare the Colonies' independence, he assured them, "You have as good a right to choose how you will be governed, and by whom, as they had."[23] All that was legally necessary was to present to Congress a constitution democratically accepted by representatives of the constituents of the territory.

Matthew Lyon and his colleagues on the Council of Safety readily accepted Dr. Young's revolutionary advice. They collaborated with Ira Allen in drafting a constitution that incorporated most of the provisions of the radical constitution of Pennsylvania, also made available to them by Dr. Young.[24] In fact, the Vermonters went beyond the Pennsylvania constitution in extending democracy. By providing for universal manhood suffrage, theirs was the first state constitution to divorce property or payment of taxes from the voting qualification. It also placed exclusive and supreme legislative power in a single assembly and made this body responsible to the electorate by providing for annual elections.

In contrast to the New York constitution, which was based on the theory of separation and balance of powers, the Vermont constitution sought to make the power of the legislative branch outweigh that of the executive branch, which consisted of the governor, lieutenant governor, and twelve annually elected council members. This branch was given advisory power only in the legislative process; it could not veto laws but had only the power to postpone action until the next session of the Assembly heard its recommendations or amendments. The function of the executive was to carry out the laws passed by the Assembly.

Probably the most advanced feature of the Vermont constitution was that it prohibited slavery, the first state constitution to do so. Of even greater immediate significance to the formerly unrepresented settlers was its provision for one representative in the Assembly for every town of less than eighty persons and two for towns of more than eighty. Little wonder that the back-country settlers of Vermont embraced this document as the fulfillment of their aspirations. They adopted it overwhelmingly at the Constitutional Convention held at Windsor on December 24, 1777.[25]

That Vermont should have adopted the most democratic constitution of all the newly independent states is one indication that the Revolution was carried to the extreme in that state. After ties were sundered with New York, a vacuum of power existed in Vermont. There was no governmental machinery in operation with remnants of the colonial elite wielding power. The men who gained control of the political power were "new men" in the sense that they lacked the social status generally considered a prerequisite for political office in the colonial period. In order to maintain office, they relied not on the deference of their electorate but on carrying out policies that reflected the popular will, such as the liberal constitution of 1777.

Thomas Chittenden, Ira Allen, and Matthew Lyon are examples of the social upthrust of the Revolution in Vermont, which elevated new men to the highest political offices of the state.

The first governor of Vermont, Thomas Chittenden, started life on a small farm in Guilford, Connecticut, and obtained no more than a common school education. At twenty he moved to the frontier settlement of Salisbury, Connecticut, and during the twenty-four years he remained there, he became a moderately prosperous farmer and a leading citizen of the town. He represented Salisbury six years in the Connecticut legislature, served in many local offices, and enjoyed the rank of colonel in the militia. At the age of forty-four, these were probably the limits to which he could aspire in Connecticut. Lured by the opportunities which the Hampshire Grants offered, he and a neighbor bought several thousand choice acres from the Allen brothers and made a new home in the wilderness bordering Lake Champlain.[26] Though by no means a poor man by the time he was elected governor, Thomas Chittenden was a man on the rise, who was selected for his rare qualities as a trusted leader, rather than by the traditional social and educational criteria that qualified men for holding office before the Revolution.

Similarly, Ira Allen had nothing in his social background to recommend him for the important office of treasurer of Vermont. He too was the son of a farmer and grew up in the back country of Connecticut with the barest rudiments of education.[27] By the time the Vermont settlers chose him as a member of the Revolutionary Council of Safety, he had proven himself as a shrewd and prosperous land speculator and a political leader of the movement against New York's jurisdiction. He probably benefited also by the reflected glory of his brother Ethan, who had been captured in Canada in 1776 and therefore was not available to continue to serve the cause of Vermont.

Had the Grants remained under the jurisdiction of New York, opportunities for high political office would scarcely have been within the reach of a man of Matthew Lyon's humble origins. Under the Revolutionary circumstances prevailing in Vermont, however, Lyon stepped into the openings at the top levels of government. Apparently he had natural leadership abilities, which his fellow settlers recognized by continually electing him to office. In 1778 he held the following positions: Councilman, Deputy Secretary of the Governor and Council, Clerk of the Court of Confiscation, and Assistant Treasurer (to Ira Allen). In 1779 he served as Secretary of the Board of War and Clerk of the Assembly. This year marked the beginning of his role as legislative leader in the Assembly; the town of Arlington annually reelected him as their representative throughout the war years.[28]

In these various capacities Lyon was involved in making and executing policies concerning the complex problems facing Vermont during the war. From within, Vermont confronted a Loyalist opposition; from Canada, the ever-present possibility of British invasion threatened her borders, the defense of which Vermont would have to shoulder herself in view of the Continental Army's commitment in other areas. Perhaps most crucial of all, Vermont needed, and constantly sought, recognition of her statehood from the Continental Congress.

While Lyon played an active policy-making role on all these issues, his major activities centered around the Tories and the problems of financing the defense of Vermont. The two, in fact, were interrelated. Lyon vigorously advocated and implemented a policy whereby Vermont raised its war revenue by selling both confiscated Tory property and ungranted lands. This policy created wide public support for the leaders of Vermont's Revolutionary government, the Allen-Chittenden bloc, of which Lyon obviously was a member. It enabled the state to raise revenue without resorting to the heavy taxes upon which most of the other state governments relied. While thus serving the public interest, Lyon utilized this policy to serve his private interests as well.

Lyon's earliest activities against the Tories were centered in the town of Arlington, which was inhabited by a number of devout and prosperous Episcopalians, who remained loyal to the Crown. These Tories formed a military band under the leadership of Dr. Samuel Addams and were in active communication with Burgoyne. Lyon's first encounter with them occurred shortly after the Battle of Hubbarton, when he led a company of men in an attempt to prevent the Tories from delivering a drove of cattle to Burgoyne. In the ensuing skirmish between the two companies, Addams killed one of Lyon's men. So enraged were the patriots that they suspended Addams in a chair from the Bennington Tavern signboard, as a warning of the punitive measures they were prepared to carry out against all Loyalists. Shortly afterwards Addams fled to Canada, but his nest of Arlington Tories continued to supply the enemy with provisions and information.

Determined to put an end to this type of Loyalist intrigue, the Vermont Council of Safety authorized the formation of local Committees of Safety. Lyon served on the most crucial of these committees in the Tory stronghold of Arlington, along with the leading members of Vermont's Revolutionary government: President Thomas Chittenden, Secretary Ira Allen, and Jonathan Fassett, an ex-officio member of the Allen-Chittenden political clique. The committeemen made their headquarters in three confiscated Tory homes; between Lyon's and Chittenden's houses they dug a long vault, sided it with timber, and converted it into a jail. They sat as a Court of Sequestration and followed the procedure laid down for Vermont's local Committees of Safety: to hear evidence against those persons "inimical to the American Cause," to jail and banish those they found guilty, and to order their property "seized and sold at public vendue to support the army and prosecution of the war."[29]

As a result of his militant opposition to the Arlington Tories in 1777, Lyon was elected clerk of the first statewide Court of Confiscation on April 23, 1778. This body, appointed by the governor and council, examined the evidence and pronounced decision on persons accused of "Notorious and Treasonable Acts." Lyon's records show that the trials were swift and ruthless. For example, the first examination upon which he sat heard proofs concerning 158 persons from seventeen towns who were either inhabitants of the state or had interests therein. Lyon's minutes state that "after Several Adjournments from day to day haveing maturely considered the several proofs," the Court found "Each and every one of them" guilty, and ordered "the whole of their Real and Personal Estate" to be confiscated.

Nine months later, Lyon purchased one of the estates he was instrumental in confiscating during that first trial in April 1778. It was a large parcel of the property of the prosperous Arlington Tory Isaac Brisco, which Lyon bought for £530 from the Commissioner of Sales, Jonathan Fassett, his confederate of long standing.[30] Governor Chittenden had issued strict instructions to the Commissioners of Sale to "make known that you have such lands to sell," and they generally followed these instructions.[31] However, Lyon was in a particularly advantageous position to acquire inside information about the availability of choice property and to act swiftly to acquire it. His purchase of the Brisco property in 1778 is his first recorded venture in land speculation; he was to engage in this pursuit much more avidly after 1780. Among his other shrewd transactions that year, he placed £400 as security with the Court of Confiscation, which in turn directed the Commissioner of Sales "to sell to Capt. M. Lyon any farm or farms in his district" up to that amount.[32] In this way Lyon acquired seventy more acres of Isaac Brisco's coveted property. For the two farms involved in this transaction, he paid £300.[33]

These two purchases, in 1778 and 1780, are the only ones Lyon made directly from the Commissioner of Sales of Confiscated Land. Compared to others listed in the commissioner's account, his purchases were moderate. For example, the lowest figure in this account was £75, while Governor Chittenden topped the list with a £3,000 acquisition.[34] There is nothing to indicate that Lyon bought these properties at less than the going rate. While he paid £300 for seventy acres, for instance, another purchaser, Jesse Sawyer, paid £350 for one hundred acres, or about the same rate per acre.[35] The records do not indicate, therefore, that Lyon was guilty of corruption in his transactions in confiscated estates. What Lyon's purchases signify is that he was insensitive to the notion of conflict of interest (more developed today than in his time, to be sure), and that he used his official position and inside knowledge to acquire some choice property for future speculative gain. To the extent that his means allowed, Lyon seized the opportunity for economic advancement offered by the confiscation of Tory property.

The granting of townships is another area in which Lyon's policy making for Vermont's public welfare redounded to his private welfare. In March 1780, as a member of the Committee to Defend the Northern Frontiers, he recommended to the General Assembly that it grant "four, five or six townships of land" as a means of raising additional revenue for prosecuting the war.[36] In this report he also recommended that the state issue loan certificates, offering an annual interest of 6 percent, to supplement the "avails" from the sale of grants. If the commissary could not obtain sufficient provisions from the revenue raised by these two methods, Lyon's committee made the egalitarian recommendation that the commissary "take the provisions where they can be found in the hands of any person over and above the wants of his family . . . paying such person the current price in money or certificates."[37]

When Lyon's committee made this report, Vermont's commitment to the continental cause was still firm. The committee recommended these strong measures in order to wage an effective campaign against the anticipated British attack on their northern frontier. On June 20, 1780, the Continental Congress launched an attack of another sort. It again refused to recognize Vermont's independence and asserted that the self-constituted state had no authority to make grants of land.

In defiance of this resolution, Vermont put itself on an independent war footing. The policy of raising revenue by selling ungranted lands, which Lyon advocated on a modest scale in March 1780, now became a major source of the state's income, second only to the sale of confiscated Tory property.[38]

At this juncture Lyon began work on a crucial committee, set up in October 1780, to determine "what lands can be granted, and what persons will most conduce to the welfare of this State to have such grants."[39] Translated, this meant that Vermont would sell portions of its ungranted land to persons who could exert their "good offices" in behalf of the new state. Lyon and his shrewd associates on the committee, such as Ira Allen, Jonathan Fassett, and Jonas Fay, made sure to offer to men of influence throughout the New England states opportunities to pick up Vermont's land grants at bargain prices. Their purpose, of course, was to win support for Vermont's independence in these states, and thus eventually in the Continental Congress.[40]

Lyon and his colleagues worked at fever pitch to capitalize on the advantages offered by Vermont's virgin lands. Between October 1780 and the following March, it recommended the granting of over fifty townships.[41] Lyon petitioned for two of these townships and, as a member of the committee, was not embarrassed about voting for himself as one of the grantees, or proprietors.[42]

This was neither the first nor the last time that Lyon exploited the opportunities offered by the new townships. In 1779 he had signed petitions for three of the first townships to be granted by the state.[43] Since the charters required grantees to cultivate at least five acres of land and build a house within a five-year time limit, Lyon could not have intended to remain a proprietor of the five townships he helped charter between 1779 and 1780. His payment of the proprietor's fees for these various townships was another form of speculative investment. Apparently Lyon, like so many luminaries of the Revolutionary generation, had been bitten by the land speculation fever. Moreover, as assistant treasurer to Ira Allen, he had profited from exposure to a master speculator in action.

But speculation was not Lyon's main objective; he merely acquired his initial capital in this fashion. His primary goal was to stake a large claim in a new township that offered fruitful opportunities for future entrepreneurial undertakings. The township that fulfilled these requirements most closely was Fairhaven, the one which Lyon had petitioned for first in 1779.

In 1780 Lyon began laying the foundations for his future plans. In

December of that year, when the survey of Fairhaven was completed, he located the first and second division of his rights on the land around the falls of Castleton River. To increase the amount of acreage he controlled, he bought the rights of two other grantees.[44] By January 1781 he had possession of over four hundred contiguous acres rich in iron, lumber, and water power, resources that kindled Lyon's enterprising imagination. Years later, Lyon proudly acknowledged, "I had so attended to my affairs in the more advanced stages of the war, and towards its close, that I was able under the most favorable auspices to set a going a number of mills and manufactures which made me rich."[45]

Lyon's experience is an illustration of the important role that Vermont's Revolutionary land policies played in giving rise to members of a new middle class. Lyon's acquisition of property is a specific demonstration of J. Franklin Jameson's thesis that the Revolution brought about redistribution of property into new hands. He rose from being an impecunious back-country farmer to become a middle-class proprietor and entrepreneur, by acquiring both the confiscated estates of affluent Tories and the ungranted lands formerly possessed and controlled by the Crown. Had Jameson been searching for an individual to document his statement that "the raising of the Colonies to the position of independent States brought with it the promotion of many a man to a higher order in the scale of privilege and consequence,"[46] he could not have uncovered a better example than Matthew Lyon. By taking advantage of the open opportunities for power created by the Revolution in Vermont, Lyon and his associates in the Allen-Chittenden bloc used the Revolutionary governmental machinery they controlled to redistribute property formerly belonging to the British Crown and its Tory supporters.

Lyon's active land deals in the Arlington area are a further example of how he "attended to his affairs" and accumulated the capital necessary for his future Fairhaven enterprises. According to the Land Records of that town, in the single month of May 1781, Lyon purchased fourteen deeds of land ranging from one acre to one hundred acres in size, and from a minimum of 5 shillings to a maximum of £⅓ in price. In all, he acquired a total of 353 acres for less than £10.[47] The indications are that Lyon and others were able to acquire land at such absurdly low prices as a result of Vermont's first land tax. When the landowner (usually an absentee or Tory) neglected or refused to pay the tax, the sheriff collected the money due the state by selling the land at vendue.[48]

Several years later, between 1783 and 1785, Lyon became an active seller of Arlington deeds. His selling price ranged from 18 shillings to £137, although most of the sales ranged from £5 to £15.[49] Although Lyon's exact profit from his acquisitions of May 1781 is difficult to ascertain (since these future sales included deeds that he purchased on other occasions and for higher sums), the pattern of his activity is clear.

Wherever possible, he acquired land at its lowest selling price and sold it later at a handsome profit.

In May 1782, Lyon also purchased at vendue "for the payment of the public land tax" the farm of the notorious Arlington Tory, Dr. Samuel Addams.[50] Although Lyon bought this farm as another speculative venture, he and his family settled on it temporarily, since the uncertain circumstances of war precluded their moving to Lyon's new uncultivated lands in Fairhaven. Two years before Lyon took over Addams's farm, in November 1780, the Vermont legislature had passed the conciliatory Redemption Act, entitling the Tories to return to their former possessions.[51] Samuel Addams did not lay claim to his farm immediately after the act's passage, but to Lyon's chagrin, he did so shortly after Lyon had acquired title to it. Consequently Lyon entered into a vigorous correspondence with Addams's son, negotiating the terms on which he would redeem the farm. "I cleared considerable on the farm, and have at this time Eleven acres of Wheat on it, which was a piece of Choice Mowing and was exceeding heavy bad Clearing," he wrote to Colonel Andrew Addams on October 9, 1782. "If you mean to get present possession you will pay me for clearing, fencing, etc."[52]

Here Lyon took a position that he later fought for in the Vermont Assembly. In the heated controversy over the Betterment Acts, Lyon took the side of the small settlers against the Tory claimants. Based on his own experience, he maintained that the Tories should repay the settlers for their effort and toil in improving the farms, which their former owners had left neglected and undefended.

In his later correspondence with Colonel Andrew Addams, Lyon shrewdly pointed out that although the "farm was in miserable condition when I came on it . . . I have now 20 acres of grain in the ground and make no doubt of being able to winter between 30 and 40 head of cattle next winter." Because of his plans to move to Fairhaven, he continued, he would consider capitulating to Addams's claims "on honorable terms, that is to say pay for betterments . . . and something handsome for my legal title."[53] After more than a year's dickering, on April 22, 1784, Lyon finally returned the deed to Andrew Addams for the "handsome" consideration of £5.[54]

This transaction indicates Lyon's drastic change of attitude toward the Tories since the early days of the Revolution. His conciliatory conduct toward the Loyalists stemmed from a broader policy of conciliation with the British, which the leaders of Vermont adopted shortly after June 20, 1780, when the Continental Congress firmly rebuffed Vermont's demand for recognition as an independent state. As a member of the inner circle of the Allen-Chittenden bloc, Lyon was instrumental in formulating this new policy; by this time he had a large stake in Vermont's independence. In addition to his political position, he ran the risk of losing his extensive holdings in Fairhaven, should New York reassert its authority over the Grants. New York therefore loomed as an adversary as threatening as Britain to Lyon and his ilk. They were caught between Scylla and Charybdis: the Yorkers in the Continental Congress, who threatened their property claims, and the British on their northern borders, who threatened their very existence. Recognition from the Continental Congress would have resolved the Vermonters' conflict and aligned them on the side of the other thirteen American states against the British. However, once it became apparent that support from this body was not forthcoming, a turning point was reached in Vermont's revolutionary diplomacy. Lyon was one of the new state's leaders who was prepared to align Vermont on the side of Great Britain, in order to preserve the social changes wrought by Vermont's rebellion against New York.

General Frederick Haldimand, Lieutenant Governor of Quebec, was well aware that "the Insurgents of Vermont under Allen continue to give umbrage to what is called the New York Government."[55] He communicated this information to Lord Germain, British Secretary of State for Colonial Affairs, who agreed in 1779 that "much advantage might be derived" by the British from Vermont's separation from New York. Therefore Germain had "no objection to giving them reason to expect the King will Erect their country into a separate Province."[56] Haldimand adopted this strategy in his attempt to woo Vermont away from the Continental cause, and Vermont's leaders proved amenable to entertaining his proposals.

Lyon participated in this cagey flirtation with the British from the seemingly innocent beginnings of the Haldimand negotiations. On October 31, 1780, as a member of the assembly, he voted to approve the continuation of a correspondence between Governor Chittenden, Ethan Allen (whom the British had recently released as a war prisoner), and General Haldimand "for settling a cartel for exchange of Prisoners."[57] Ostensibly, the exchange of prisoners was the sole object of the Haldimand negotiations. However, Vermont's appointed agent, Ira Allen, entered into negotiations of a much broader scope during the eighteen days in May 1781 that he spent with Haldimand's representative on the Ile aux Noix in Canada. Specifically, he discussed the possible terms on which Vermont might consider aligning herself on Britain's side. He did so with the knowledge of only a trusted few. That Matthew Lyon was one of this elite group, there can be no doubt; Allen specifically designated him as one of the "eight gentlemen" in Vermont to whom Haldimand's messenger could "make himself known."[58]

Unfortunately for the inner circle, Lyon proved too garrulous a personality to serve as guardian of their secrets. Possibly while declaiming to some tavern companions, he revealed the main elements of the Vermont leaders' strategy in the Haldimand negotiations. A British spy, sent to Bennington to ascertain the contents of Ira Allen's profoundly secret report on his negotiations, reported that he overheard Captain Lyon say "that Governor Chittenden would settle with the British if the present leading Men in Vermont were allowed to continue such under Britain, their old and new Grants confirmed—the East and West new Territories confirmed—all their Laws and Acts confirmed, and nothing revoked."[59] Lyon insisted that these "were the only Terms Vermont would agree to, and if General Haldimand would not agree to them, it was the business of Vermont to spin out this Summer in Truces, and in the meantime fill their Magazines as fast as possible with arms, ammunition and provision by which, with the continued increase of the Inhabitants, he hoped to be able by next Summer to defend Vermont against invasion from Canada."[60]

These remarks of Lyon's further excited the British spy's suspicions that Ira Allen was probably merely stalling for time. It is doubtful, however, that Ira Allen, Matthew Lyon, and Vermont's other "leading men" viewed the Haldimand negotiations purely as a device to postpone and possibly prevent the British from invading Vermont. Their main concern was to strengthen Vermont in her struggle for independent self-government. Although they desired union with the other American states, they were prepared to hedge their bets and become an independent British province if the Continental Congress continued to refuse to recognize their legality as an independent state. This Congress again refused to do, in no uncertain terms, on March 1, 1782. Immediately thereafter, Ira Allen intensively renewed his negotiations with the British. General Haldimand actually drew up a proclamation, recognizing Vermont's territorial claims and granting her political privileges similar to the former self-governing colony of Connecticut. According to Ira's plan, Haldimand, accompanied by troops, would deliver his proclamation to the Vermont Assembly in October 1782.[61] By setting the date for October, Allen apparently was delaying for time to determine the effect of Cornwallis' surrender the previous Fall. His tactics were vindicated by September 1782, when formal peace negotiations began and recognition of the new United States seemed assured.

Vermonters were exultant, and Lyon himself considered the final victory in 1783 an act of Providence. Despite Vermont's failure thus far to consummate her independence from New York, the threat of another British invasion and further brutal warfare was now at an end. Fifteen years after the peace treaty was signed, Lyon recalled with emotion the desperation that accompanied the seven long years of the American Revolution in Vermont: "I very well knew, although that war was a war of necessity, and had for its object, on our part, our very existence as a nation, as well as the saving of the lives and properties of those who had taken an active part in it, that many were tired out with its troubles and perplexity to that degree, that nothing but the seeming interposition of a kind Providence could have brought it to a favorable issue on our part."[62]

3

Lyon as Entrepreneur

With the termination of the war, Lyon at last was free to develop the enterprises he had long envisioned in Fairhaven. Just what inspired him to become an entrepreneur, rather than ply his former trade as farmer, can probably be surmised. By temperament he was dynamic, imaginative, ambitious, and ever responsive to new challenges. Thus he must have realized that in the virgin territory where he had shrewdly amassed the titles to four hundred acres, the incoming settlers would require essential services. He therefore assumed the initiative and built the establishments providing these services, before the settlers arrived.

While still in Arlington, in 1782, he set in motion adroit plans to build a sawmill and gristmill on the Castleton falls, where he carefully had located his Fairhaven property. First Lyon made arrangements with an Arlington associate, Silas Safford, to house and feed the men who would build the mills. As a premium for housing his employees, Lyon offered Safford eighty acres of his Fairhaven property. To supervise the building of the mills, Lyon engaged the services of an Arlington millwright, Agur Hawley, giving him a one-third interest in the mills when they were completed.[1]

Thus Lyon overcame the depreciated currency problems of the postwar period and laid the foundation upon which he would build the future town of Fairhaven.[2] Safford, Hawley, and the work crew of twenty-five men comprised the town's first settlement. Arriving by covered wagon in 1782, they built a log cabin near the river, and while Mrs. Safford cooked their meals, they gradually constructed Lyon's first two mills.[3]

These undertakings represented the first step in Lyon's entrepreneurial career, but only in a very limited sense did they reflect the opportunities to advance the level of economic pursuits that the Revolution had unleashed. It is true that the Revolution had made it possible for Lyon to acquire cheaply this unsettled property formerly belonging to the Crown and thus provided him with the opportunity to become an entrepreneur.

But his first undertakings did not represent a significant advance over the economic practices of the Colonial period. Small gristmills and sawmills were commonplace throughout the colonies, the most primitive costing only between £500 and £1,000 to construct—or little more than a farmer's home.[4] Had Lyon stopped at this stage, his entrepreneurial career would have had little significance. However, these first mills were merely the foundations upon which Lyon gradually built a thriving manufacturing town.

After the mills were built, sometime in the latter part of 1783, Lyon brought his family to Fairhaven, where their prospects for future happiness seemed assured.[5] Tragedy, however, accompanied this new move. Lyon's wife Mary, who had borne four children amid the hardships of war, died in April 1784. Lyon had her buried in the churchyard of the St. James Episcopal Church in Arlington. Her tombstone bears the following inscription, which he, in all likelihood, composed:

IN MEMORY OF

Mrs. Mary Lyon the amiable consort
of Colonel Matthew Lyon who died in
Arlington April 29 in AD 1784
Aged 32 years & 6 Months
Ah shes gone Shes took her flight
Beyond this Hemisphere of night
Gone to enjoy her Christ above
In the eternal world of love[6]

His wife's death compounded Lyon's personal problems. As a widower, he now had the sole responsibility for rearing his four young children, the oldest of whom was only ten. Grief-stricken though he may have been, Lyon recognized what steps had to be taken. Although in later years he was to complain of being "a football of dame fortune," fate was rather benevolent to him on this occasion.[7] Among the eligible young widows of the area was Governor Chittenden's twenty-year-old daughter, Beulah, whose husband had died recently, leaving her with an infant son, Elijah Galusha. What could be more opportune for Lyon than to rescue her from widowhood and at the same time acquire for himself a wife of means and status? As he himself commented later about his relationship to the Chittenden family: "I had powerful connections attached to me by long riveted confidence, as well as matrimonial affinity."[8]

It should not be surmised, however, that the governor's daughter lent an air of aristocratic elegance to Lyon's marriage. Governor Chittenden, after all, was a product of the back-country frontier life, and so indeed was his daughter. According to the recollections of a contemporary, Beulah was "very intelligent, but somewhat masculine and coarse in her manners and accent."⁹ From another account it seems she was also something of a flirt. Lyon's "connubial relations would have been quite unsatisfactory to a 'Yankee,' " comments this nineteenth-century reporter. "But," he continues, "my informant says that he never heard Col. Lyon say anything or saw anything that led him to suspect that Mrs. Lyon's flirtations occasioned him any uneasiness. I have heard some *remarks* of hers *repeated* that would not do to be *written* so near the close of the Nineteenth (19th) Century as Fifty Eight (58). Nevertheless she was a woman of great benevolence ever ministering to the wants of those around her."¹⁰

With Beulah as his helpmate, Lyon began anew his life as founding father of Fairhaven. Operating his sawmill and gristmill occupied most of his time as entrepreneur until 1785. In that year he branched out into a new and much more significant field of enterprise, the manufacture of iron products. While the production of pig iron was widespread in the northern colonies before the Revolution, manufacturing iron products was a venture in a new direction for American entrepreneurs; and because it was, a detailed analysis of Lyon's iron undertakings will be postponed until after his more traditional enterprises have been surveyed.

One of these establishments was the tavern that Lyon also built in 1785, using one wing as his family's residence.¹¹ This enterprise satisfied simultaneously Lyon's gregariousness and his business interests, for in keeping with the frontier customs, the tavern served as the center of the townsmen's social life. Lyon gives us a glimpse into the manner in which he ran his tavern in the following answer to a political attack accusing him of dispensing free liquor to the electorate: "My house (which was always open to the needy, and to my false and true friends) has been very much rid of one class of people, who were previously fond enough of my wine, rum, brandy, or even the whisky they make verses about, and a share of whatever else Providence had blessed my table with."¹²

Despite his open-handedness, the tavern must have been a profitable venture. Indeed Lyon considered the tavern so valuable an establishment that when he later sold portions of his land to other entrepreneurs, he stipulated in the contract that he maintain the exclusive privilege of "operating a public house of entertainment" on the property.¹³

In 1792 Lyon again stipulated his exclusive right to operate a tavern in a contract with Boyle and White, to whom Lyon sold the "little red store" he had built and operated in 1791.¹⁴ This sale indicates that Lyon decided to concentrate his energies on the productive mill operations rather than combine the harassing problems of both entrepreneur and merchant. It is apparent, however, that Lyon performed many of the services of a merchant in the course of delivering his manufactured articles to his customers.

In later years Lyon was to state that he had been a merchant all his business life,¹⁵ an assertion borne out by several of his Vermont business letters. For example, in 1786 he wrote to Levi Allen, merchant, of St. John's, Canada: "I have received yours concerning the Hatters Wool and have this to say—that my Waggon had but just returned from new City —I had sent them to Albany for some Hatters Wool among other things for a Hatter here, and they could not get there for the floods." In addition to the difficulties of transportation and climate, this letter indicates that Lyon was harassed by the currency problems common to the Confederation period: "It is impossible for me to send you cash now. . . . I shall not want the other things I spoke to you for cash grows scarcer every day."[16]

It was in the field of paper manufacture that Lyon evidenced his greatest entrepreneurial inventiveness. Indeed the indications are that he deserves a belated place in the annals of American manufacturing, as the first American to use wood pulp for the manufacture of paper. Around 1790 he added a paper mill to his numerous undertakings, in order to produce his own supply of paper for the Republican newspaper he was about to launch.[17] Originally Lyon followed the prevailing and ancient practice of producing paper out of finished cloth. Like papermakers the world over, he found this commodity increasingly difficult to obtain and sought assistance from his subscribers through ads such as the following:

> clean cotton, linen & cotton & linen
>
> RAGS
>
> will be received in pay for paper,
> at a penny half penny per pound,
> by all the Posts who ride from
> this Office.[18]

His difficulties in securing cloth spurred Lyon to explore other raw materials out of which he might manufacture his paper. He finally succeeded in his quest. On October 28, 1794, his newspaper announced: "We have the pleasure here to present to the public, a specimen of printing paper, manufactured from the bark of the BASSWOOD TREE, together with an equal proportion of common coarse rags:—This is a new discovery made by Col. Lyon of Fairhaven, and promises fairly to accelerate the paper making business in this country, as the cost of the Bark, which abounds in great plenty, is not more than one third as much as the cost of rags."[19]

The article points out that the paper on which this issue was printed was made "by the hands of the Editor," who did not possess a knowledge of the papermaking craft. Therefore the paper was sized only with alum and water. The editor, James Lyon, expressed complete confidence, however, that in the future, under the supervision of a skilled papermaker, good quality paper would be made from the bark alone.

While Lyon was not the first to discover that wood could be used for papermaking, this theory was a recent one, first proposed in a scientific treatise in 1719. It was not until the 1780s that the first isolated experiments with wood paper were made in England and France, and by the 1790s this process had not yet been adopted by commercial papermakers. According to Dard Hunter, a leading authority on the history of papermaking, "The first commercially made paper in the Occident" was made by Matthias Koops, who in 1801 built "Europe's first paper mill in which materials other than linen and cotton rags were to be extensively used."[20] Actually it was Matthew Lyon—who manufactured paper out of basswood bark in the 1790s and thus preceded Koops—who more correctly deserves the credit of producing the first commercially made wood paper of the Occident.[21]

Hunter was not unaware of Lyon's paper mill but, lacking the evidence previously cited, states, "According to Joel Munsell . . . Lyon manufactured paper from the bark of the basswood tree, but this statement cannot be verified and is most doubtful."[22] One reason Hunter may have considered this statement doubtful is that it took almost another half century before this process was again adopted. It is generally accepted that until the middle of the nineteenth century, paper in Europe was made almost entirely from rags and that the manufacture of paper from wood pulp dates from the invention of the wood grinding machine by a German, Friedrich Keller, in 1840.[23] It was not until 1867 that the first ground wood paper mill in the United States was founded by Albert Pagenstecher.[24]

That Lyon has never received the credit for being the first commercial manufacturer of wood paper is probably due to the fact that he declined patenting his invention. In this instance his conduct as an entrepreneur seems to have been influenced more by eighteenth-century Enlightenment values, which stressed the well-being of the community, than by the later entrepreneurial emphasis upon individual self-interest. He magnanimously announced in the *Farmers' Library*, "If this discovery should prove advantageous to mankind we shall be glad to bid the world—welcome to it, without the selfish reserve of an exclusive privilege or patent right."[25] Therefore Lyon promised to insert the directions for peeling and curing the bark into his 1795 Almanac, which was then on the press. True to his word, he squeezed these instructions into the last page of the Almanac, thus making his discovery available to the public.[26]

Lyon's imaginative technological contribution to the manufacture of paper illustrates his innovative mind as an entrepreneur. His establishment of the mill itself, however, cannot be regarded as an innovation in the development of American manufactures. Paper mills had existed in the colonies since 1690, and by the 1790s Hamilton could report that "manufactories of papers are among those which are arrived at the greatest maturity in the United States, and are most adequate to national supply."[27]

Lyon's undertakings in the area of iron manufacture, on the other hand, represented a new economic thrust. His complex of iron works marked a significant advance over the level of colonial activity in the area of iron production and were a reflection of the impetus which the American Revolution gave to the domestic manufacture of iron.

As early as 1785, Lyon built a dam on his forty-foot falls in order to provide the water power necessary for his projected iron establishment.[28] Eventually his iron works consisted of three plant components: the forge, the slitting mill, and the blast furnace. Had Lyon erected these plants before the Revolution, all but the most rudimentary forge would have been in violation of the Iron Act of 1750, which proscribed the erection of any mill or other engine for slitting or rolling of iron, any plating forge to work with a tilt hammer, or any furnace for making steel. At the time of the Act, the number of such establishments, as reported by the colonial governors, was four slitting and rolling mills, ten plating forges working with tilt hammers, and three steel furnaces. Although the colonists built more such iron works after 1750, in defiance of the Act, Britain nevertheless remained the chief source of supply of manufactured iron articles until the Revolution. It was only then, when the rebellious colonies were cut off from their source of supply, that many new iron works and small manufactories were called into existence.[29]

Lyon's slitting mill for the manufacture of nails is an example of the trend of American entrepreneurs after the Revolution to continue to produce articles formerly imported from the mother country and to elevate these manufactures to the technological level achieved in Britain. In October 1785 Lyon submitted a petition to the Vermont Assembly "to Encourage the Building of a Sliting Mill." In it he requested the "Laying a Duty of two pence on each pound of Nails brought into the State," explaining that he "thinks it is possible to supply this State with Nails of its own manufacture which Article is one of the most costly of any of the Importable Necessarys for which almost all the Circulating Cost is Constantly Carried out of the State[,] yet the building of a Slitting Mill—will be of such Great Cost that possibly . . . nails could be imported cheaper than they can be made at home (although not so much to the Public benefit—) unless the Honorable the legislature should think proper to Encourage the Building of a Sliting Mill."[30]

Lyon's proposal for the encouragement of an infant industry expressed the common needs of the new iron manufacturers. Most of the enterprises they had established during the Revolution were ruined at its close, when Britain flooded the American market with her cheaper iron products.[31] Since the Continental Congress had no power to lay tariffs under the Articles of Confederation, the problem of protecting the infant domestic industries devolved upon the separate state legislatures. The Vermont Assembly, however, did not see fit to grant protection and encouragement to Lyon's slitting mill, possibly because the concept was too new and the problems of manufacturing too unfamiliar to members of this agrarian state. One could make a fair inference, however, that the Assembly denied Lyon's petition because of political animosity toward him and toward the Allen-Chittenden faction with which he was associated. The author of the motion to defeat Lyon's petition was Beriah Loomis, a member of the Chipman-Tichenor faction, which at this juncture of Vermont politics was engaged in a bitter controversy with Lyon and his allies over their debtor-relief policies.[32]

Six years after Lyon submitted his petition to the Vermont Assembly, Alexander Hamilton made the following recommendation to Congress regarding the manufacture of nails: "The expediency of an additional duty on these articles is indicated by an important fact. About one million eight hundred thousand pounds of them were imported into the United States in the course of a year, ending the 30th of September 1790. A duty of two cents per pound would, it is presumable, speedily put an end to so considerable an importation."[33] The similarity between Lyon's position and Hamilton's is striking; were economics the only factor to determine political affiliation, Lyon should have become a Federalist. Why he joined Hamilton's Republican opponents to achieve his ends is one of the significant features of his career, and it will be explored throughout the next four chapters.

Despite the Vermont Assembly's refusal to grant Lyon's petition, he proceeded with his plans to build a slitting mill. As a farseeing entrepreneur, he recognized that this method of manufacturing nail rods promised to be profitable despite the high cost of the machinery. Technologically the slitting mill represented an advance over the prevailing method of producing nails during the colonial period, whereby each individual nail was carved by hand from a massive roll of bar iron. In the slitting mill, on the other hand, the bar iron was reduced into long, thin rods, whose thickness was no wider than a nail. With most of the work having been done by machinery, all that remained to be done by hand was to slice the individual nails from the rod and shape their heads and points.

It has been estimated that an average slitting mill, such as Lyon's, would produce enough rods to keep three hundred nailmakers constantly employed.[34] Exactly how many nailmakers Lyon employed is not known, although it has been estimated that "a large number of men were employed" in his entire complex of iron works.[35] Many of his nailmakers may have worked in their own homes rather than in the mill, as was the case with Richard Beddow, a British blacksmith and nailer who had been a soldier in Burgoyne's army but either deserted or was taken prisoner during the Revolution. After the war Beddow settled in

Fairhaven and worked in a shop on his farm making nails for Lyon, who supplied the nail rods and paid Beddow for his output.[36]

The domestic system of nail manufacture became widespread immediately after the Revolution. According to Hamilton, "a great proportion of boys whose early habits of industry are important to the community" were employed in this fashion.[37] Although Lyon was a firm advocate of the Republican principle of educating the young, his entrepreneurial interests led him to practice the Hamiltonian principle of making children "more especially useful" by employing them in the simple operations of nail manufacture. While there is no evidence that he directly employed children in his mills, it is recorded that he supplied iron rods to the families of the town, and that "each family returned its output of finished nails to him, and was paid accordingly."[38]

If Lyon had been typical of America's earliest manufacturers, he would have been an advocate of cheap labor. It comes as no surprise, therefore, that his political adversaries charged him with saying in 1786 that "it would never be good times, until the common people were forced to beg employment at six-pence per day."[39] Lyon denied this charge vociferously, stating, "no such idea was ever in my brain, or such assertion passed my lips; neither was it ever my opinion, that the public suffers any loss at the current wages for laboring men, *mechanics* especially. I have always asserted, contrary to the opinion of many, that the wages given to mechanics, is not the great obstacle to the growth and prosperity of our manufactures. The gradual increase of the manufacture of nails, in this State, and of other matters in the Eastern States, daily confirms the opinion."[40]

Lyon made this statement in 1793, by which time his slitting mill probably had proven to be a wise investment. Several business letters of the period show that Lyon's nails were in great demand, which contributed to "the gradual increase of the manufacture of nails" Lyon describes above. In July 1787 Ira Allen wrote to his brother Levi, "In consequence of Col. Lyon's Works stopping for Cole etc. I am Disappointed of Nailes." He then requested Levi to secure from Canada the nails he had intended to order from Lyon: "ten pounds of shingle Nailes and five thousand of Ten Pound Nailes."[41] This was not an excessively large or atypical order. Allen wanted the nails "to secure my Wheat and Hay," in other words, to build a hayloft, a typical need for nails of the farmers of Vermont.

Just how independent Lyon could be about the price of his nails is indicated by the following letter, which he wrote in 1786 under the insignia Matthew Lyon, Ironmaster: "I have sent you Eight thousand of tenpenny Nails of my own make they are dear I cannot afford them under 22s–6d per thousand. If you don't choose to keep them Squire Safford who carries them will bring them back."[42]

One reason that nails were in scarce supply was that Lyon owned the only slitting mill in western Vermont.[43] Another reason, as Ira Allen's letter indicates, was that Lyon's mill periodically went out of operation. The necessity of furnishing the hearths with a new supply of coal was the most frequent cause of such stoppages. While some iron works used mined coal, many made their own charcoal, as Lyon most likely did, since he owned the primary factors of production: an extensive tract of timberland and a sawmill to cut the logs out of which the charcoal was made. The making of charcoal was a hazardous and difficult process, consuming eight to ten days and requiring extreme vigilance to prevent the burning stacks of logs from oxidizing and bursting into flames. One can readily visualize Ironmaster Lyon, black with char-dust, supervising every phase of this critical operation which, if carelessly handled, threatened his surrounding enterprises and property. In fact, he experienced several such disasters during his years as entrepreneur in Fairhaven. His iron works and his paper mill burned to the ground on four separate occasions.[44]

The difficulties encountered in maintaining and operating the machinery could also account for the temporary stoppages of Lyon's slitting mill. According to one authority on the early iron industry, breakdowns were commonplace because of difficulties in keeping the slitters and rollers in adjustment.[45] Since the construction and operation of slitting mills had been a well-guarded secret before the Revolution, Lyon was forced to go through the usual trials and errors involved in using new and unstandardized machinery.[46]

A stroke of good fortune enabled Lyon to overcome many of the mysteries of his machinery. In 1786 David Erwin, a nailer trained in England, came to Lyon seeking employment. Lyon, ignorant of Erwin's skilled background, at first engaged him at low wages in the unskilled capacity of blower and striker at the forge. Erwin soon revealed his superior knowledge and training by outdoing Lyon's chief workman at the forge, and within a short time Lyon made him superintendent of the slitting mill. The workmen nicknamed Erwin "The General," probably because of the authority with which he ran the mill. So valuable were his services that Lyon took "The General" with him when he moved to Kentucky.[47]

The source of Lyon's machinery is revealed by a reliable Vermont historian, who states that much of it was brought, with great labor and expense, from Lenox, Massachusetts.[48] As for the iron, another scholar surmises that Lyon obtained most of it from New York.[49] This speculation is supported by a letter that Lyon wrote in 1785 to Oliver Platt, founder of the town of Plattsburgh, New York. Lyon explained that although there were two valuable bodies of ore within two miles of Fairhaven, his "dependence was on the ore of Lake Champlain," for which he was prepared to pay "one half dollar per tun."[50] Platt replied: "I and my associates have obtained a law to be passed in our favour for takeing as much ore out of the ore bed belonging to the people of the State of New York near Crown Point as we shall have ocation of or can manufactor in the township of Plattsburgh for the term of ten years . . . and altho I should be happie to Serve and oblige you yet you will se by the Inclosed minits that it is not in my power."[51]

The reason Lyon preferred the Lake Champlain iron was that the magnetic and specular ore from these beds was purer than the brown hematites from the local ore beds of Rutland County, which yielded only one-sixth to one-quarter iron.[52] Despite the increased transportation costs of the Lake Champlain iron, Lyon considered it more efficient for his manufacturing purposes and eventually succeeded in obtaining it, according to several informed sources.[53]

Another component of Lyon's iron works was a pair of forges in which two types of iron production took place, one traditional and one advanced. The traditional one was the production of bar iron from old cast iron and scraps. In 1785 Lyon petitioned the Assembly for "mortar, broken cannon, etc. carriage wheels on Mt. Independence" for the production of bar iron, which request was granted on October 15.[54]

The second type of iron production, the manufacturing of implements, represented an advance over the prevalent level of technology of the colonial iron forges. This type of iron manufacture took place in a plating forge, equipped with a tilt hammer, which fell into the category of proscribed forges under the Iron Act of 1750. An advertisement appearing in the *Vermont Gazette* in 1788 reveals that Lyon's forge produced axes, hoes, and various agricultural implements.[55] Other types of iron articles he manufactured are indicated in the following letters: "I send three hundred and ten pounds of Iron including two pair Slayshoes and two Crow bars," Lyon wrote a customer in 1786. From this letter we also learn that he manufactured plate iron, out of which iron machinery was manufactured. "My light hammer is froze fast, therefore I could not get any plates Iron for Addams," he apologizes.[56] Writing to Ira Allen in 1789, Lyon discusses deliveries of graphins and anchors, which he designed for Allen's shipbuilding undertakings: "I have sent out two Graphins and one anchor to the bay. . . . I have one more Anchor here Wt 22£ which I designed for you but it is impossible to get a team to move from here at present."[57]

Lyon's blast furnace, the third component of his iron works, was by far the most advanced of his plants, both technologically and financially. The manufacture of iron products in his forges involved the timeworn direct process by which wrought iron was made directly from the ore. On the other hand, the blast furnace involved the more efficient though more complicated indirect process, by which the ore was first smelted in the furnace and cast into the form of pigs and sows. Then these cast-iron pigs were brought to the forge, where they were more efficiently wrought into iron products. The second advantage of the blast furnace was that it made possible the production of hollow ware, which was done by ladling the liquid mass of iron from the furnace crucible and pouring it into clay molds, shaped in the forms of such articles as kettles, stoves, and anvils.

While possessing many advantages over the direct process of iron manufacture, the indirect process required a much heavier investment, since the construction of a blast furnace was much more elaborate than a forge. Made of concrete and stone, the average blast furnace was about twenty feet high and required fairly complicated masonry in the construction of its interior workings. In addition, it involved construction in timber and leather, including a massive wooden bridge and two huge leather bellows.[58] These bellows were the lungs of the blast furnace; they produced the blasts that caused the heat of the furnace to rise to the extreme temperatures required for smelting. This was an elaborate undertaking as the following description, written by a contemporary of Lyon's, indicates:

> The blast was produced in the manner of that day by two huge bellows, 22 feet long and 4 inches width, producing alternate blasts by a water wheel 25 feet in diameter. Two or three blasts, of 16 or 18 weeks each, were made in about 6 months, in which time 360 tons of hollow ware and other castings were produced, estimated at 1,200 lbs. per nominal ton of all sizes.[59]

Dr. James Thacher, the author of the above passage, was one of the proprietors of the Federal Furnace, erected in Carver, Massachusetts, in 1794. In this same letter, he has left posterity one of the few itemized lists of expenses involved in operating a blast furnace such as Lyon's, which was constructed in the same decade:

EXPENSES

2,130 cords of wood, converted into 1,420 loads of charcoal at $2.50	3,550.00
726 tons of ore, at $6	4,356.00
Two sets of stone for hearth	153.32
Compensation to the founder at $1 per ton	360.00
Ditto to the Moulders and other workmen	331.00
Total	10,750.32

Among the 350 tons of hollow ware and other castings that the Federal Furnace produced semiannually were such items as "rolls for slitting mills cast in iron cylinders, potash kettles, stoves, fire backs and jambs, plates, gudgeons, anvils, large hammers, cannon shot of all kinds, machinery for mills in great variety."[60]

As early as 1788 Lyon recognized the advantages of producing such items on the large, efficient scale that a blast furnace made possible. In the same advertisement in which he listed the iron farm implements he was making, he announced that he was getting ready to manufacture hollow ware and pig iron.[61] This was a most ambitious project for an individual entrepreneur, as the foregoing information indicates. The construction of a blast furnace required a large capital investment, as Hamilton also indicated in his "Report on Manufactures" under the subtopic "Hollow-wares": "There are respectable capitals, in good hands, embarked in the prosecution of those branches of iron manufactories, which are yet in their infancy." He added that although hollow wares were beginning to be produced in considerable quantity, "the business of castings has not yet attained the perfection which might be wished."[62]

Just how Lyon raised sufficient capital to construct and operate his blast furnace is a mystery, but it is nevertheless well established that early in the 1790s he "erected a furnace for casting all kinds of hollow iron ware."[63] From the reminiscences of a Fairhaven resident, we learn that he procured many of his castings from B. Erskine and Company.[64]

Lyon was well aware that, "engaged in so Weighty a matter," it was "his business to look on every hand for Resources."[65] From 1789 to 1794 he met with one frustration after another in his attempts to devise some method of raising the requisite capital for this comparatively advanced undertaking. The story of that attempt is worth recounting in some detail, for it reveals the problems of the entrepreneur in the tentative stages of American manufacturing. In many ways Lyon's attempts to solve these problems were in advance of his time and anticipated the direction of the future.

In October 1789 Lyon submitted a petition to the Vermont legislature "For State Aid in the Construction of a Blast Furnace." By way of preamble, he stated that this "Important piece of business," when accomplished, will be a "great acquisition to the state of Vermont." Emphasizing the "advantage of the Patronage of the legislature to a bussness of this kind," he reminds the Vermont Assembly of the "attention paid by the Legislatures of all free states to every bussness that tends to make their Constituents independent of other Countries."

His petition included a request for a loan of £800, for which he offered security and promised repayment with interest in two years. He added that he would consider the loan merely as a "Reserve in the Rear to be brought in if necessary." His other request was equally if not more urgent; it was for the state to sell him a portion of land, owned before the Revolution by the Society for the Propagation of the Gospel and now the property of the state. The particular piece of land Lyon desired adjoined his Fairhaven property in the neighboring town of Orwell. Lyon had leased one hundred acres from the town of Orwell until 1792, the term allowed by state law, but he explained that this time limit "was too short to answer his purposes as all the Necessary permanent Buildings such as houses barns & other surrounding Accomodations are to be set on Sd lot."[66]

Lyon had first evinced his consuming interest in the SPG lands in 1786, when he signed a petition with leading Vermont figures, including Nathaniel Chipman, to turn the lands over to a society that would use them for "promoting Arts, Learning and Christian Knowledge."[67] After the Assembly rejected that petition, Lyon submitted the above petition to personally purchase these coveted lands for his blast furnace. That portion of his petition was rejected in October 1790.[68] Lyon, however, did not desist from his activities in behalf of the SPG lands. In 1792, as a delegate to the Episcopal Church Convention in Vermont, he signed a petition of that body for the transfer of the SPG lands to the Vermont Episcopal Church. While his actions in this last instance had wider political implications (see chapter 7), his persistent determination to release these lands from the public control is striking. Undoubtedly he hoped to acquire the Orwell lot as his private property from whatever agency ultimately gained control of the SPG lands. This ambition was never fulfilled, however, for in 1794 the Assembly voted "that they be disposed of for the use and benefit of the common schools."[69]

From 1789 to 1791 the Vermont Assembly deliberated over the other request Lyon made in his petition for a loan of £800 to aid him in the construction of a blast furnace. In 1790, after Lyon presented his case to the committee considering his petition, it resolved that the House go into a Committee of the Whole to discuss the weighty new considerations involved. After full discussion, the Committee of the Whole recommended that the state grant a loan for this project, leaving to the committee the details of the amount and terms of the loan. The question then went back and forth, from Committee to Assembly, from Assembly to Committee, until January 21, 1791. On that day, when the final vote was tallied, Lyon lost by one vote.[70]

Among those who voted "yea" appear the names of Lyon's old associates, the Allens and Chittenden, as well as names of men who would soon be prominent in Vermont Republican circles, such as Robinson, I. Smith, and Tolman. But men who would soon be numbered among Lyon's bitterest Federal opponents—such as the Reverend Dr. Samuel Williams and Chipman—also voted in favor of granting Lyon the loan for the blast furnace. Perhaps it is no coincidence that they all hailed from western Vermont, where the blast furnace would be of immediate benefit to the region's economy. It is particularly noteworthy that future Federalist and Republican leaders in Vermont were in agreement over the issue of state aid to encourage manufacturing in 1791, when party lines were beginning to be drawn in that state. Apparently this issue was not a basic cause of conflict between the two divergent political factions.

Frustrated in his appeals to the state for aid, Lyon resigned from the Committee for Promoting Useful Manufactures in 1790. He saw state aid as an important means of "promoting useful manufactures," as indeed did other state and even colonial legislatures, when from time to time they granted public loans to new industries requiring a large initial investment.[71] Lyon's statement in his petition regarding "the attention paid by the Legislatures of all free states to every bussness that tends to make their Constituents independent of other countries" indicates that he was probably familiar with the recent encouragements given to new manufacturing enterprises by the surrounding states of Massachusetts and Pennsylvania.[72]

Lyon's resentment of the Vermont legislature did not deter him from seeking new means of raising the requisite capital for his blast furnace, however. Two years later, in 1793, he initiated a new petition to that body, not for a loan but for a charter of incorporation as the Vermont Manufacturing Society. This move marks Lyon as one of the more forward-looking entrepreneurs of the period. At the time he applied for the charter, there were only four manufacturing corporations in existence in all of Massachusetts, New York, Connecticut, and New Jersey; by 1800, the number had increased to only eight.[73]

Charging that the "poor, low and Despicable State of the Manufactures of this Country" may be ascribed to the "want of Sufficient Capital and Legislative Encouragement," Lyon's petition for incorporation, while primitive in language, contained sophisticated legal concepts slightly in advance of his time, such as corporate entity and perpetuity.[74] In the same petition Lyon and his associates sought permission to set up a Lottery to raise an additional $500 annually for "Experiment and Unforeseen Accidents." This old device for raising funds for charitable and public services had recently been sanctioned in other states for aiding manufacturing enterprises needing large amounts of capital.

Again Lyon's attempts to realize his ambitious iron manufacturing plans teetered on the brink of success and then failed. At one juncture the Committee of the Whole recommended chartering the corporation for a limit of thirty years rather than "forever";[75] but when the signers of the petition were disqualified from voting on the measure, it was defeated.[76] This time Lyon's political foes, Chipman and Williams, were among those who voted against chartering the corporation, which raises the possibility that they opposed Lyon's corporation for political rather than economic reasons.[77]

Whatever the reasons, the action of the Vermont legislature was contrary to that of other states during this period when American corporations were making their tentative beginnings. As Joseph S. Davis, a leading authority on American corporations, states, "Certainly the failure [of eighteenth-century manufacturing corporations] was not due to lack of encouragement by the legislatures. I have seen no evidence of refusal to grant charters which were seriously sought for this purpose."[78] Apparently Davis was unaware of Lyon's Vermont experience.

One of the striking features of Lyon's entrepreneurial personality was that despite repeated defeats, he continually rose to the challenge of new opportunities. By 1795, when the Vermont environment proved to be politically hostile and economically constricting, his eyes began turning "to the Westward." In a letter to Oliver Phelps, one of the country's largest land promoters, Lyon proposed to sell his property in Vermont in order to found a copper manufacturing town in the Lake Erie region. He outlined the following ingenious plans for mining the ore, building a settlement, raising capital, and marketing the copper:

> No doubt the Indians might be employed to bring the Ore until some better method could be fell upon. . . . A company would easily be found in Philadelphia to unite a capital sufficient to set a business on foot; Congress would give the Ore Assist about Roads, and give a right to Coin Cents, in order to encourage the business; you easily can form to yourself an idea how much such a piece of business would promote the settlement of the country. . . .
>
> I should like to own one third of the Township where the business could be done best—that must be good lands for raising provisions for man and beast with good Streams of water and falls in a healthy situation as the Climate will admit; before much can be done at Manufacture provision must be raised in plenty & Roads cut from such a place.[79]

Absentee ownership, public improvements, federal patronage, and planning a company town are some of the future trends that Lyon projected in this letter of 1795. He modestly added, "My Experience & Genius in Mechanism might be of eminent service in an Enterprise of this kind." This particular scheme of Lyon's never materialized, but it was the forerunner of his later operation in Kentucky and indicates the extent of his imagination, daring, shrewdness, and perhaps delusions of grandeur, as an entrepreneur and town founder. Fairhaven, Vermont, considered in the 1790s "the most flourishing manufacturing town in the state," fully attested to these qualities.[80]

4

Lyon versus the Lawyers: Confederation Period Conflicts

A significant feature of Vermont politics during the 1780s was the conflict between the "new men" who had risen to leadership during the Revolution and the lawyers who challenged their policies throughout the decade. Lyon's Republicanism was forged in the political crucible of these Confederation years. One cannot understand his estimate of the Federalist-Republican conflict of the 1790s as a "struggle . . . between the aristocrats and democrats"[1] without first examining his political contests in the 1780s with the men who later emerged as his Federalist foes.

Chief among Lyon's adversaries was the young attorney Nathaniel Chipman. Son of a comparatively prosperous farmer in Salisbury, Connecticut, he was afforded an education at Yale University, a privilege shared by few of his back-country neighbors. His religious upbringing also reinforced the sense of cultural and social superiority that accompanied his education. Raised as a strict Congregationalist, Nathaniel Chipman embraced the traditional and elitist values inherent in orthodox Calvinism.

During the Revolution, Nathaniel Chipman served one year in the Continental Army, and in 1778 commenced his legal studies in Litchfield County, perhaps under the tutelage of Tapping Reeve, whose ideal of paternalistic government molded the political philosophy of a number of his future Federalist colleagues in Congress.[2] By 1779 he was ready to practice law in the Hampshire Grants, where his parents had settled in 1775.[3]

Chipman arrived in Bennington fired with ambition. His optimism is captured in the following letter: "I shall indeed be rara avis in terra, for there is not an attorney in the state. Think, Fitch, think what a figure I shall make, when I become the oracle of law to the state of Vermont." A few months later, with accurate prophecy, he wrote of the political heights to which he planned to soar:

Ha ha ha! I cannot but laugh when I think what a flash we shall make, when we come to become members of Congress. And then again I am vexed when I think how many steps there are by which we must mount to that pinnacle of happiness. Let's see: First, an attorney, then a selectman, a huffing justice, a deputy, an assistant, a member of Congress. Is that not a little vexing? However, we must make the best of it.[4]

Chipman correctly appraised the unique position in which his legal training would place him among the frontier lawmakers of Vermont. He reports that shortly after he arrived in the state, "the House of Representatives requested me, though not a member, to examine and report my opinion concerning certain debts due from persons whose estates had been confiscated."[5] This episode occurred early in the year of 1780, soon after Vermont had entered into the Haldimand negotiations and reversed its former policies toward the Tories. Chipman's statement indicates that the question at issue involved the amount of money that the expelled Tories should pay to recover their confiscated property from those who had bought and settled it.

Over this issue of confiscated estates, Lyon immediately clashed with Chipman, who championed the property rights of the original holders. Lyon was doubly involved on the side of those who had bought and settled the confiscated property. He was a purchaser of Tory property, and he held the position of Clerk of the Board of Confiscation. Therefore, during the course of Chipman's report to the Assembly, Lyon rose and "took offense." Several days later, meeting Chipman face to face at Stephen Bradley's law office, Lyon charged that "no man with a spark of honesty" could have reported as he had done. Retorting "in a passion" Chipman branded Lyon "an ignorant Irish puppy." Thus the first lines of battle were drawn between Chipman, the educated lawyer, and Lyon, the "ignorant Irish" indentured servant. Quite literally, the two came to blows on this occasion. Lyon flew into a rage at the insult and seized Chipman by the hair, breaking his comb. Chipman grabbed a pen and attempted to stab Lyon with it. In the end Bradley and Chipman took Lyon by his hands and feet, dropped him into a corner of the room, and returned to their seats "laughing very merrily at the scene." After recovering his composure, Lyon forced a laugh and left the room exclaiming, "Damn it, I will not be mad—."[6]

Ludicrous as this episode appears, the economic and social issues which divided the two men ran deep. For the next five years Lyon and Chipman stood as adversaries over the question of paying settlers for "betterments," the subject matter of Chipman's controversial report. What was at stake was the confirmation of the original land titles of two groups of landholders: Tories, whose property had been confiscated and sold; and absentee landlords, mainly from New York, whose estates had been sold at vendue for failure to pay taxes. If the English Common Law precedents were followed, the courts merely would have restored the land to their previous owners without requiring extra compensation to the many small settlers who, acting on the assumption that their purchased titles were legal, labored to cultivate the abandoned land and added considerably to its value.

In his own private transactions, it will be recalled, Lyon had insisted on being paid for "improvements" before returning the land's original title to the Tory, Samuel Addams. Lyon's position was supported by the leading spokesman for the small settlers, Governor Thomas Chittenden, who advocated this policy of betterments in a message to the Assembly, urging it to pass resolves "as will in equity quiet the ancient settlers."[7] Commenting on Chittenden's position, Nathaniel Chipman's brother, Judge Daniel Chipman, later stated that Chittenden "knew nothing of the niceties of the law" and therefore pursued "that course which was dictated by the principle of natural justice."[8] Taking the same rule as his guide, Lyon fought actively in the Assembly to obtain legislation to protect the rights of the small settlers. He was on the committee that prepared the first Betterment Act in 1781 and was a leading member of the committee that proposed the controversial Betterment Act of 1784.[9] The preamble of the Act, which bears the stamp of Lyon's style, fully states the intent of its sponsors:

> whereas, many persons who have purchased the aforesaid vendue and voted titles, and other supposed titles while the real title was obscured . . . have taken possession of such lands and have by their extraordinary exertions, with others, been the means, (under Heaven) of supporting and defending the title of the land under which the legal owners now claim, against the avaricious and unreasonable claims of a neighboring government, and thereby together with the large improvements made thereon by their labors and industry, have raised the land in general, to their present value. And whereas if the strict rules of law be attended to, such persons will be turned off from their possessions made at great labor and expense, and others, who have neglected both the defense and settlement of the land, will unjustly enjoy the benefits of their labors: which manifest evil and injustice to prevent, be it enacted . . .[10]

that the settlers should recover "so much money as the present true value of the farm or estate exceeds what was its real value, (after deducting the interest of such real value at six per cent per annum,) at the time when such settlement was begun."[11]

Along with a number of other lawyers, Chipman raised a storm of protest against this Act. Their objection to it, according to Daniel Chipman, was that "the law makes every man a trespasser who enters on the land of another without license, and subject[s] him to damages; instead of this you would compel the legal owner to pay him a bounty for this trespass."[12] Following this line of reasoning, Chipman and the other lawyers in the Assembly led a determined opposition to the Betterment Act proposed by Lyon's committee in 1784. They succeeded in bringing about the bill's defeat by a vote of 45 to 33.[13]

The strong popular feeling on this issue forced the bill's opponents to accede to a resolution that sent the bill to the state's towns for a referendum vote. The results of the towns' balloting were 756 for the bill, 508 against. Despite this popular mandate, the opponents of the bill again succeeded in defeating it in the Assembly by a vote of 31 to 29 in June 1785.[14] Under popular pressure, however, they were forced to agree to a compromise bill. Nathaniel Chipman devised amendments that substantially reduced the amount recoverable by the "ancient settlers." Instead of recovering the full increase of value they had added to the property, as Lyon's committee had proposed, Chipman's amendments provided that the settlers receive one-half "of what such lands had risen in value."[15] Thus amended, the second Betterment Act was finally enacted into law in 1785.

A careful analysis of the vote that defeated the more liberal Betterment Act of 1784 reveals significant data concerning the nature of the alignments in Vermont over domestic issues during the Confederation period. The most obvious factor that emerges in studying the 78 votes cast is their geographic distribution. Twenty-three of the 33 votes favoring the bill came from western Vermont; in contrast, eastern Vermonters cast 36 of the 45 votes opposing the measure.[16]

To understand the significance of this geographic division it is necessary to return once again to the conflicts in the Hampshire Grants that led to the formation of the state of Vermont. There was a marked difference between the history of eastern Vermont and that of the region west of the Green Mountains. The settlers east of the mountains tended to be law-abiding Congregationalists who duplicated the institutions of Massachusetts and Connecticut whence they had come and from which they were not far removed.[17] Because of their respect for law and religion, they originally did not join their brethren west of the mountains in the insurgent movement against New York. In fact, some eastern towns actually obtained confirmatory patents for their New Hampshire land titles and operated under charters granted by New York prior to 1777. Even after Vermont established its jurisdiction over the eastern counties, there remained a vociferous body of residents, particularly active in the southernmost county of Windham, which vigorously resisted the new state's authority and insisted upon recognizing only New York's jurisdiction.[18]

The western Vermonters, by and large, were a more unrestrained group of settlers. Observers of the times commented that "in the place Religion is much out of style" and estimated that one-quarter of the inhabitants were deists.[19] Respect for the law was also less rigid in western Vermont, where the settlers defied New York's legal jurisdiction over their territory and participated in an insurgent movement that eventually resulted in the establishment of the state of Vermont.

Little wonder, then, that the significant differences in composition and history of eastern and western Vermont should be reflected in different voting patterns. Eastern Vermonters, who generally did not share the experience or the ideology of the insurgents of western Vermont, were not inclined to be sympathetic to those settlers who had acquired land titles arising from western Vermont's strife with either Yorkers or Tories.

Another striking feature of the division over the Betterment Act was the consolidated position taken by the lawyers and judges who, with only one exception, cast their votes against the proposed bill of 1784.[20] In the category of attorneys belong Nathaniel Chipman, Isaac Tichenor, Stephen Bradley, and Nathaniel Niles, and among the judges were John Strong, Luke Knoulton, Samuel Mattocks, Jacob Bayley, and Samuel Knight. While these men represented only approximately one-sixth of the legislators who opposed the Betterment Act, they formed a unified group of leaders who commanded considerable influence.

The fact that these lawyers and judges aligned themselves on one side adds both a social and an ideological dimension to this early division in Vermont politics. Socially their higher education set them apart from the self-made men who led the opposing side. Not only did attendance at Harvard, Yale, and Princeton signify superior training; it was also a symbol of social status reflecting a middle- or upper-class family background.[21] Moreover, two of the members of this group, Luke Knoulton and Samuel Knight, had been loyalists during the Revolution and were identified with the wealthy Yorker and Tory landholding interests.

The ideological division between the two sides is based largely on their divergent attitudes toward legal precedents. Take, for example, the grounds upon which these legal spokesmen based their almost unanimous opposition to the Betterment Act. In the statement quoted above, Daniel Chipman stressed that the law traditionally punishes a person occupying another's property, instead of which the Betterment Act "pays him bounty."[22] The lawyers and judges insisted upon following past legal precedent; they advocated strict adherence to legal tradition regarding the protection of property rights. Their approach was a rigidly legalistic one, in contrast to the flexible, pragmatic attitude adopted by the adherents of the act, who favored making new laws to meet the requirements of a new situation.

In the future party conflicts of the 1790s Matthew Lyon categorized lawyers as "aristocrats," basing his accusations partially on their attitude toward the Betterment Act. In 1794, at the height of his protracted fight against Nathaniel Chipman, Lyon reminded the small settlers of the role lawyers had played in the 1780s: "It is not yet grown out of memory, that these professional gentry, by their intrigues, their cabals, and their plausable speeches, kept back the Legislature many years from passing a law to secure the ancient settlers their betterments . . . ," he asserted. These "law characters" were oblivious to the rightful claims of those who "ventured themselves and families in a wilderness, but late the hunting ground of savages, without clear ground to raise their bread on, or mills to grind their corn when raised, without bridges to cross the rivers, or roads to find their neighbors houses; poor people . . . many of them soldiers and sufferers in the late British war as well as in the troubles with New York,—but all this would not move them; their books and their rich clients told them that the Common Law of England knew nothing of paying for betterments of labor." In conclusion, declared Lyon, "it is well known that nothing but the firmness of the people of good common sense in not suffering the law to be opened until provision was made to secure this meritorious class of citizens has saved them from being a prey to their voracious enemies."[23]

Legislative relief for debtors was another Confederation period issue that Lyon utilized to substantiate his attack on lawyers as "voracious enemies" of the small settlers. Following the policy of granting new townships inaugurated by the Revolutionary government of Vermont in 1780, the land-hungry settlers of the Grants had bought much of this coveted property on credit. The terms of the charter bound each proprietor to build a house and cultivate five acres of land within three years or forfeit his land. By 1786 time had run out for many of the settlers. Simultaneously the creditors deluged the courts with lawsuits, demanding payment. But the debtors, "distressed and harassed by the war," were "destitute of a supply or provision."[24] They inundated the Assembly with petitions for relief, protesting, among other things, the "needless coast [cost]" of lawsuits because of the "present latitude granted to attorneys and law sheriffs deputies."[25] These petitioners were referring to the prevailing practice that held the debtor responsible for paying all legal costs including the high attorney's fees and the deputy sheriff's four-cents-a-mile traveling expenses for serving writs on the debtors. As elsewhere, the Vermont debtors faced the distress of the postwar depression, the chief symptom of which was a scarcity of money.[26] In addition, many proprietors who had not yet settled and cultivated their land because of the uncertain war conditions prevailing until 1783 sought an extension of the time limit provided in the original charters.

As in the case of the Betterment Acts, a sharp cleavage developed in the state legislature over the adoption of relief measures. Lyon's bloc stood behind the program of Governor Chittenden, who, in an effort to "ease and quiet the people," reluctantly recommended a state bank, which would issue paper money.[27]

Drawing upon his legal training, and fortified by his sense of professional responsibility to his creditor clients, Chipman led the opposition to this and other debtor relief measures proposed in the 1786 Assembly. According to Daniel Chipman's account, Nathaniel, "being extremely anxious to devise some means by which these evils might be averted,"[28] called together a caucus of the few members of the Assembly who were sympathetic to his point of view.[29] "They unanimously agreed that the popular current was too strong to be resisted . . . and that they could therefore do nothing to any good purpose unless they could devise some means by which the proposed measure might be postponed until the passions of the people should have time to cool." The means they devised was a resolution calling for a referendum of the people on "what is the best mode of relief." On October 31, 1786, the Assembly followed Chipman's leadership by voting to submit the various proposals for debtor relief to a referendum vote of the towns.[30]

The Assembly's action gave the spokesmen for the creditors extended time to continue their arguments in the press against the "depravity" of avoiding debts and contract obligations.[31] Moreover, their warning against the "licentiousness" and lawlessness of the debtor class seemed to be borne out by debtors' riots in Rutland and Windsor counties, which occurred shortly before the referendum, in November 1786. By the time the question of paper currency came to a vote in February, the state bank proposal was defeated by a vote of 2,197 to 456.[32]

Again the leadership bloc with which Lyon was associated adopted a pragmatic attitude toward solving the problems of economic distress, while the Chipman approach was a legalistic one, concerned with strict adherence to the terms and conditions of contract obligations. The conflict was waged on an ideological level, but its consequences were economic. The "new men," who were by no means small farmers themselves, nevertheless sought to relieve the debtors' distress by being flexible and issuing paper money through the state bank. Whether they did so out of conviction or political opportunism is a matter of conjecture; conceivably both factors played a role. Coming from this background themselves, they were inclined to identify with the problems of the frontier farmer; certainly they also realized that in order to stay in power they needed the support of the agrarian population.

Nathaniel Chipman, on the other hand, countered their program by appealing to the voters' sense of "unerring rectitude" regarding "contracts made by parties," and opposed "obliging persons to accept of a fluctuating paper currency or other articles of less value than was originally agreed upon."[33] In short, Chipman defended the claims of the creditors on ideological and moral grounds that won the support of the electorate.

Both the negative vote on the state bank and the riots that preceded it dealt a serious blow to Lyon and his political colleagues. Indeed the Chittenden faction felt it necessary to quell the riots with dispatch, and Lyon made a point of officially congratulating the militia, headed by his political ally Colonel Isaac Clark, for restoring order in Rutland. Lyon's resolution expressed the Assembly's "hearty thanks" to "the officers and soldiers whose spirited exertions crushed the late daring insurrections against the Government in the counties of Rutland and Windsor."[34]

While thus aligning himself with the forces of law and order, Lyon took the debtors' side on ensuing legislative issues. He came into direct conflict with Nathaniel Chipman on "a bill to prolong the time in which the Grantees of land chartered by this State are obliged to settle the same." In addition to giving relief to the settlers, this bill touched on the question of the validity of the land titles granted by Vermont's Revolutionary government. Lyon challenged the wording of the section "ascertaining the time in which the Grants of land made by the King of Great Britain shall vest in this State." He moved "to erase the words 'made by the King of Great Britain or any of his servants' and insert instead 'issued by the Governor of New Hampshire.' "[35]

The central point at issue was New York State's conflicting claim to jurisdiction over the Hampshire Grants. The purpose of Lyon's motion was to protect the validity of the charters that Vermont's Revolutionary government had granted, by denying New York's jurisdiction over this territory and insisting that the Crown lands were formerly under the jurisdiction of the Royal Government of New Hampshire, rather than New York. Here again Lyon and Chipman were on opposite sides, and Chipman's supporters defeated Lyon's motion.[36]

Legally Chipman was correct; the Royal Proclamation of 1764 had placed the Grants under New York's jurisdiction. Whatever the legalities, however, Lyon and his confederates in the Chittenden-Allen camp were determined to preserve the redistribution of property that the Vermont insurgents had carried out during the Revolutionary period.

Chipman's pro-Yorker position explains, at least in part, why Lyon identified his legal opponents as representatives of the "aristocrats." "Experience has taught the people of Vermont that these professional gentlemen are inclined to stand up for the claims of landlords, landjockies and over-grown land jobbers in preference to the poorer sort of people," he declared in a lengthy diatribe entitled "Twelve Reasons Against a Free People's Employing Practitioners in The Law as Legislators." In this article Lyon gives the following explanation of how the British Common Law trains lawyers to protect the property of the privileged class:

> 1stly, The rudiments of their professional education leads them to be conversant with the world in the feudal state of things, and to pore over the transactions of the times of vassalage, when English lords transferred the tillers of the ground with the land they tilled . . . as portions to their sons and daughters. . . .
>
> 2ndly, Those gentlemen pedantically deduced their maxims from reports and decision, of those, and still more modern times, when orders and

distinctions among mankind, lay the foundation of what is by them called civil polity. . . .

3rdly, They are early taught to revere the opinions of, and look up to ancient British Judges, for their authorities and presidents who have derived their greatness and sucked their principles from the very poisonous breast of monarchy itself.[37]

Although Lyon wrote this article in 1794, his attitudes are traceable to the conflicts of the 1780s over both domestic and foreign issues. On the key domestic questions, such as betterments and debtor relief, Lyon joined battle with many of the men who were to become his Federalist opponents in the 1790s, men who, he believed, were intent upon protecting the privileged social and economic position of the few. Falling into this category were lawyers, Yorker landholders, former Tories, and ministers.

Chipman was joined in his leadership of this group by another attorney, Isaac Tichenor. Dubbed "Jersey Slick" by his opponents, Tichenor was a graduate of Princeton who settled in Vermont during the Revolution.[38] Although he bought his land under Hampshire Grant title, he "was a strong friend of Yorkers both within and without Vermont."[39] Firmly attached to the "cause of order," Tichenor, like Chipman, held fast to the conservative concept of a graduated society.[40] Another ally of this faction was Luke Knoulton, previously a member of the loyalist Yorker group that sought restoration of Vermont to both New York and Great Britain. Other of Lyon's opponents during the Confederation period who became prominent Federalists in the 1790s included Samuel Williams, editor of a future Federalist newspaper; Charles Marsh, the prosecuting attorney at Lyon's trial for sedition; and Jabez Fitch, Lyon's future jail keeper.[41] The Yorker, Lewis R. Morris, who arrived in Vermont in 1785 to look after the vast property holdings of his father, Richard Morris, also became a leading member of the Chipman-Tichenor faction and a bitter opponent of Lyon in the 1790s.

Underlying the conflicts that led to the tentative beginning of factions over domestic issues in the 1780s were two fundamentally different attitudes concerning the relationship of law to property rights. To summarize, Nathaniel Chipman reflected his training in the law by placing his emphasis upon the inviolacy of property rights. Thus he favored full restoration of the Loyalists' confiscated property by the "trespassers" of the Revolution, and insisted upon a "standard of unerring rectitude" in regard to meeting contractual obligations during the monetary crisis of the Confederation period.

In contrast, Thomas Chittenden and Matthew Lyon were not influenced by preconceived limitations of the law, but responded to the pressure of events. In their view, the necessities of the Revolution justified confiscation of Tory property as a punitive policy. Therefore those settlers who acquired the property were not trespassers, but persons who deserved compensation for their improvement of the property value, before returning it to the original owners. A similar pragmatism characterized Thomas Chittenden's paper money policy. Debts should be honored, to be sure, but since the shortage of currency was a reality, the issuance of paper money was an expedient measure to enable the debtor to meet his obligations.

The Council of Censors, a body set up by the Vermont constitution to review and criticize the state's legislation, made a scathing report in 1786 castigating the Assembly for "casting aside all restraints of law in their decisions." It charged that the legislators "were to determine every cause, without being shackled by rules, but by their crude notions of equity." In extenuation, the introduction to the report explained that "a few husbandmen, unexperienced in the arts of governing," assumed the helm of state during the Revolution.[42]

This last statement points to the nub of the conflict between the lawyers and the Revolutionary leaders during the 1780s. The Revolution had thrust into positions of leadership men who lacked the traditional prerequisites for holding political office. While neither Thomas Chittenden or Matthew Lyon was a simple husbandman by the 1780s, both were self-made men who could claim neither family background nor education as qualifications for holding office. They were a new breed of political leader, who based their claim to office not on their background but on representing the popular will. Guided by "crude notions of equity," they sought to make policies that responded to popular needs.

By attacking these policies, the lawyers, led by Nathaniel Chipman, challenged the right of such men to hold public office. The failure of the populist-style political leaders to be influenced by the "restraints of the law" reflected their lack of training. Inherent in the conflict of the 1780s was a bid on the part of the lawyers for a return to deference politics, by which men were accorded political office in recognition of their social origins and education.

It is not by accident that in the following decade, when political parties emerged, Vermont's leading Federalist officeholders, Senator Nathaniel Chipman, Representative Nathaniel Niles, and Governor Isaac Tichenor, were lawyers who had been educated at Yale, Harvard, and Princeton.[43] Matthew Lyon, the self-made leader of the Republican Party in Vermont, branded them as representatives of aristocracy, while he claimed to be the standard-bearer of democracy. Other issues contributed to the development of these partisan ideological categories, but the conflicts of the 1780s laid their foundations.

5

Lyon's Brand of Antifederalism

The New York-Vermont land dispute was central to the conflict between Lyon's faction and Chipman's throughout the 1780s, and led to two diametrically opposed foreign policies. The direction of the bloc to which Lyon was attached was set during the wartime Haldimand negotiations, when Vermont's leaders, fearing loss of jurisdiction over their lands to New York State, entered negotiations directed toward union with Great Britain and Canada. As major property holders in the Champlain Valley, Thomas Chittenden and Ira Allen were further impelled toward a connection with Canada by their desire to enhance the commercial prosperity of their region, which was isolated from connections to American markets, while its situation on the Champlain River made Canada a natural outlet for their trade.

The Chipman-Tichenor faction, essentially pro-Yorker in its socioeconomic outlook, came from the southwest section of Vermont, which also was linked geographically and commercially to New York and the Hudson River market. Lacking both the political and economic motivations for linking Vermont to Canada, this group vehemently opposed the foreign policies of the faction in power and sought instead to unite Vermont with the other American states. In time Chipman and Tichenor headed a coalition of diverse elements from the southwestern and Connecticut Valley regions of Vermont, which opposed the Allen-Chittenden bloc's foreign policies on similar grounds.[1]

At first Chipman was embarrassed in directing his attack on the Haldimand negotiations by the fact that he himself had participated in the intrigue when the Revolution's prospects were at their lowest ebb in Vermont. In October 1781, at Governor Chittenden's request, he doctored a British dispatch which revealed that the Vermont leaders had reached a secret armistice with the British.[2] Nevertheless, shortly thereafter Chipman, in conjunction with Tichenor, became a formidable leader of an opposition movement to reverse the separatist policies of Lyon's associates in the Allen-Chittenden bloc and to wrest control of the state government from their hands.

One of Tichenor's first triumphs occurred as early as February 1782, when he succeeded in pushing through a resolution in the Assembly to dissolve the East and West Unions. Lyon had played an active role in annexing these territories from New York and New Hampshire, and his faction was intent upon retaining these territorial acquisitions as a bargaining lever to pry the most favorable terms of union from either Britain or the United States. Tichenor, convinced by resolutions of the Continental Congress that it would admit Vermont as an independent state if she repudiated these annexations, succeeded in persuading the Vermont Assembly to pass his resolution "to redress the injuries of the people of the East and the West Unions."[3] This was a tremendous victory for the nationalist forces over the separatists, but their hopes for union with the United States were short-lived. On March 1, 1782, the Continental Congress, under pressure from the New York delegates, voted 7 to 4 against admitting Vermont to the Union.[4]

Undaunted in their determination to unseat the state's revolutionary leadership, Chipman and Tichenor continued to lock horns with its key spokesmen. Despite the original popularity of these leaders, their opponents were aware of the small settlers' growing restiveness over their increased economic and political power. In particular, the inhabitants were beginning to question Ira Allen's handling of funds derived from the sale of confiscated estates.[5] In 1782 Tichenor seized upon this inflammatory issue as a means of discrediting the group in power. Charging Allen with embezzlement, and hiding his Treasurer's accounts from the public, Tichenor succeeded in making the sale of confiscated lands an issue of public debate and scrutiny.[6] Lyon came to Allen's defense on this occasion, certifying that as his assistant in 1779, "I did examine the account of the Treasurer of this State, and found regular accounts of debt and credit cheerfully exhibited by the Treasurer."[7]

Although Allen partially succeeded in clearing himself by submitting all available accounts to Tichenor for an audit, he acknowledged that he did not have in his possession all of the receipts from the Commissioners of Sales and Sequestration. This left the question of misappropriation of confiscation revenue open to further investigation. Although Lyon was never a Commissioner of Sales, as Clerk of the Court of Confiscation he became the next candidate for public scrutiny. For some reason, the opposition waited until 1785 to demand his records. In that year, when the Betterment Act controversy was at its height, a large number of the adminstration's opponents obtained seats on the Council of Censors.[8] This body censured the legislature and council for "continuance of persons in office of great public trust, who did not keep regular books; by which means (we conclude, from the information of those auditors who have taken an active part in the business) several public accounts of a very important nature, can never be properly adjusted; and the defaulters of uncounted thousands will probably reserve for themselves and their families."[9]

Apparently the Council of Censors was pointing its finger not only at Allen but at Lyon, for in October 1785 it ordered him to turn over his records of the Court of Confiscation. Lyon, in a characteristic action, disregarded the order; he appeared at the state legislature and participated in its activities as if nothing had transpired. Then suddenly, on October 15, while attending the Assembly, he heard a bill read from the Council of Censors "impeaching Colonel M. Lyon for refusing to deliver to the order of this Board."[10] Lyon claimed to be dumbfounded by this action and, in extenuation, gave this explanation of why he had failed to turn over his records to the Council of Censors:

> In March, 1778 the General Assembly of Vermont resolved that the Governor and Council, or such persons as they might appoint, should be a Court of Confiscation. The Council divided themselves into two courts one on each side the mountain; Paul Spooner Esq. was appointed clerk of the court of the east side and myself on the west. I had a book for my records; he had none for his. Some time after, the Council resolved themselves into one Court and I was appointed clerk. Mr. Spooner's records were sent to me on loose bits of paper. I applied to the Governor, who was President of Court to know if I should transcribe them into my book. After several applications I received for answer—Wait until the Council meets at Windsor in October and take direction from them. A few days before the Governor and Council were to meet, in Oct. 1785, I think, I received an order from the Council of Censors (who were sitting at Windsor) for the records of the Court of Confiscation. Considering it improper to let the records out of my hands in the situation before mentioned, and not being ready to go that moment to carry them, I wrote for answer, that I meant to resign the office and the records to the Court who appointed me; and as I was going the next week to Windsor, to attend the General Assembly, of which I was a member, I would bring them with me. This I accordingly did, and lodged the records in the Council Chamber, informing the Governor of what had passed and of my determination to resign the office; also reminding him of the State of Mr. Spooner's records, which were in a bundle laid into the book, and of my willingness to transcribe them into the book, if the Court should so direct. The Governor answered me that the business would be attended to at some convenient time, and I thought no more of the matter, until a day or two after, as I sat in my place in the House of Assembly, I heard an order from the Council of Censors read for my impeachment.[11]

Lyon maintained this facade of innocence throughout the ensuing impeachment trial, which was conducted by the governor and the Council. Ordinarily Lyon might have counted on the support of Thomas Chittenden, but because the governor was Lyon's father-in-law, he was disqualified from presiding at the trial. Instead the trial was conducted by the lieutenant governor, who happened to be Paul Spooner, the very man whom Lyon had blamed for the disorderly state of his records. Israel Smith, who later ran against Lyon in several Congressional elections, served as prosecuting attorney.[12]

On October 19 the Court handed down its verdict of guilty and ordered Lyon to deliver his records to the Council of Censors immediately. Lyon interrupted the Court's reprimand, protesting that "his cause had not been rightly understood and defended," and moved for a new trial by jury.[13] The court so ordered, setting the following Friday for the new trial. No such trial was ever held, according to the *Records of the Governor and Council* as well as Lyon's account of this episode. He states that he merely turned over the records of the Court of Confiscation "in the state they were," and the matter was dropped.[14]

Nevertheless, one can hardly accept Lyon's profession of innocence at face value. Why, for example, did he wait until 1785 to be concerned about transcribing Paul Spooner's records? The Court of Confiscation had ceased its activities when the Redemption Act pardoned the Tories in 1780; in 1782 the opposition forces had raised the issue of missing confiscation records. With Ira Allen under fire, Lyon surely could have seen the handwriting on the wall and sought advice from the Council about transcribing Spooner's records at that date. True, there is overwhelming evidence that important records of Vermont were carelessly kept in the early war years, and this part of Lyon's story is most likely accurate.[15] The question arises whether concern over the loosely kept records was the real reason why Lyon neglected to turn them over to the Council of Censors. Reading between the lines of Lyon's account, it appears that he and Chittenden deliberately planned to defy the investigation instigated by their opponents on the Council of Censors. Lyon, assured by the governor of his protection, attempted to sidestep the Council of Censors by delivering his records into the safekeeping of the governor and the Council, and belatedly resigning as Clerk of the Court of Confiscation.

Exactly what Lyon was trying to hide is difficult to determine, since his records dealt with the trials, decisions, and directives of the Court of Confiscation, and not with the sales and purchases of confiscated land, which were the province of the Commissioner of Sales. It is possible, however, that Lyon had something to hide and that the misappropriation of revenue from the sale of confiscated estates may help account for the launching of his career as an entrepreneur. This, however, is a matter of conjecture; what appears more conclusive from Lyon's account of this episode is that he and Chittenden deliberately schemed to resist the Council of Censors' investigation. Possibly this was a maneuver to curb the growing power of their political opponents. If it was, it obviously failed. Lyon's tactics played into the hands of the opposition by further undermining the public's confidence in Vermont's original leaders. This may have been the Council of Censors' major motive for impeaching Lyon. Once they obtained his records, they brought no damaging information to public light, and somehow Lyon survived the ignominy of his impeachment. In the following year, the citizens of Fairhaven reelected him as their delegate to the 1786 Assembly.[16]

It was not until 1789 that the opposition succeeded in unseating Lyon as well as the other leading members of the Allen-Chittenden bloc. The Chipman-Tichenor faction was able to assume control of the state in 1789 by unearthing a scandal which revealed that Chittenden had granted Ira Allen the charter to the town of Woodbridge without the Council's consent. The disillusioned Vermonters cast out of office their founding governor and his colleagues and elected in their stead members of the Chipman-Tichenor coalition.[17] The citizens of Fairhaven replaced Matthew Lyon with a rival entrepreneur, Simeon Smith,[18] and the citizens of Vermont replaced Governor Chittenden with the southwesterner from Bennington, Moses Robinson.

The Woodbridge exposé could not have occurred at a more propitious moment for the nationalist coalition. If it had failed to achieve power in that auspicious year of American history, Vermont possibly might not have become the fourteenth state of the Union. There is substantial evidence at hand to indicate that in 1789 the Allen brothers were on the verge of committing Vermont to a commercial and political alliance with Britain and Canada. While the Allens engineered this plan behind the scenes, key members of their faction, including Lyon, Chittenden, and Isaac Clark, appear to have supported them in their separatist designs. There is no indication, however, that the Vermont populace was aware of these negotiations, or that they would have followed their former leaders had they succeeded in arriving at a separate alliance with Britain and Canada.

Lyon's chief motive was probably political rather than economic, since his political fortunes were inextricably linked with those of the Allen-Chittenden bloc. Economically, as a resident of southwest Vermont engaged in the manufacture of iron products, Lyon's commercial links to New York and New England were equally if not more important than those to Canada. Nevertheless, other of his undertakings, although of secondary importance to his iron industry, tied him commercially to the Allens and the Canadian trade. This is borne out by his dealings with Levi Allen, the self-avowed Tory of the Allen family, who shortly after the Revolution established himself as a merchant in the Canadian port of St. John's, located on the northern shore of Lake Champlain. Lyon's active hauling "waggon" kept him in close contact with Levi throughout the 1780s. Levi frequently sailed his schooner "Mary," laden with merchandise from Canada, down Lake Champlain to a landing in Vermont, where Lyon met him and exchanged goods. On several of these occasions Lyon also served as the bearer of letters from Levi to Ira Allen.[19]

In one of these letters, written in 1784, Levi indicates that Lyon was engaged in the sale of staves to the prominent Quebec timber firm of

Fraser and Young, commenting that "his connection with A. Fraser . . . turned out much worse than I expected."[20] Years later, Lyon wrote a letter to President James Monroe that confirms the implication of Levi's letter. In it Lyon explicitly states, "I have been Conversant with Ship builders, timber getters and ship owners for many years. I followed getting Ship timber on Lake Champlain for the London market."[21]

While this sale of lumber was merely a sideline of Lyon's, Ira and Levi Allen sought to make their fortune out of the sale of Vermont timber to British shipbuilders. Ira had developed a thriving lumber industry in Colchester, where his sawmills cut the timber from his extensive lands into planks for ships.[22] He floated these planks up Lake Champlain to brother Levi, who negotiated their delivery and sale to the Quebec firm of Fraser and Young. These merchants eventually reexported the timber to London, making the usual middleman's profits. Quite naturally, the Allens desired to eliminate the necessity of dealing through the middleman at Quebec. Their aim was to establish free trade between Vermont, Canada, and Great Britain by securing a commercial reexport agreement that would allow Vermonters to ship their timber via Quebec to London under the same customs regulations that applied to the inhabitants of that British province.

The Allens reasoned that Vermont, as an independent state, was free to negotiate trade agreements that would exonerate her from duties imposed on exports from the United States.[23] The political implications of such a reexport agreement are clear. Vermont would enjoy the same commercial relationship to Britain as Canada; in return Vermont would owe Britain some form of political allegiance. While Ira and Ethan Allen conceived of such a Vermont-British alliance as one between "equal and sovereign states,"[24] Levi, the consistent Tory, aspired to form lower Canada and Vermont into a separate British province.[25] Writing to the Reverend Dr. Morrice, Secretary of the Society for the Propagation of the Gospel in Foreign Parts, in May 1789, Levi stated: "Vermont is an independent republic, unconnected with Congress and ever have been, and wish to remain so, or come under the British Government, to which they are well disposed, they are tied to their local interest to Canada and Great Britain."[26]

Apparently the Allens shared their thinking on these matters with Lyon as early as 1784. "It is vastly satisfactory to meet with Such a man as Col. Lyon to whom one may speak with freedom," wrote Levi to Ira, in the same letter in which he mentioned Lyon's disappointing dealings with A. Fraser.[27] That same year Lyon confirmed Levi's confidence in his comprehension of the Allens' free trade aims by serving on a committee that prepared a bill "to obtain license for inhabitants of Vermont to pass by the waters leading from this state into and through said Province, with their lumber, and to barter or exchange commodities on terms reciprocal."[28] The Assembly passed the bill on October 27, 1784, illustrating the general desire of Vermonters to eliminate the trade barriers that separated them economically from the country that adjoined them territorially.

Lyon, at a later date, graphically described the close link between the residents of his Congressional district and their Canadian neighbors. "A very great number of my Constituents have brothers, Sons and fathers who have moved into that territory. . . . There have been large and generous locations to my Constituents in the territory adjacent to the district I represent, the lands on the line are cultivated for many miles together, it is good and about as thick settled on both sides as any part of Vermont, and thousands from Vermont have already moved over."[29]

This proximity of Vermont to Canada was a matter of grave concern to such astute leaders of the United States as Washington and Hamilton. Warning the New York Assembly that if it refused to acknowledge Vermont's independence, the people of that region would "provide for their own safety, by seeking connections elsewhere," Hamilton pointed out that these "connections have already been formed with the British in Canada."[30] Hamilton's object in so addressing the New York Assembly in 1787 was to expedite Vermont's admission into the United States before it became inextricably connected to Canada and Great Britain. Motivated by the same desire, Nathaniel Chipman and Lewis Morris contacted Hamilton in July 1787 to discuss possible terms of settling the New York claims to Vermont lands.[31]

The Allen brothers saw the handwriting on the wall and intensified their efforts to attain a treaty of commercial and political alliance with Great Britian. Levi acted as their representative and hastened to London in January 1789 to accomplish this delicate diplomatic mission. Working furiously and making contacts at the political, economic, and ecclesiastical levels, Levi eventually succeeded in realizing the commercial goal of his mission. An Imperial Statute, which went into effect on July 1, 1790, legalized the reexport of Vermont goods from Quebec without the payment of duties imposed on other United States exports.[32]

Perhaps Levi might have been equally successful in achieving his political aims of allying Vermont to Britain either as a province or an independent republic, had the Woodbridge scandal not erupted and forced the separatists out of power in Vermont. As soon as the nationalists gained control of the State Assembly, they set the wheels in motion to secure the admission of Vermont into the United States. As the first step in this direction, the Assembly voted to negotiate the land dispute with New York State, appointing as commissioners Nathaniel Chipman, Isaac Tichenor, Stephen Bradley, Ira Allen, Elijah Paine, Stephen Jacob, and Israel Smith.[33] Chipman had already laid the groundwork for a settlement with Hamilton the previous winter,[34] and the New York-Vermont Commission agreed to a formula by which Vermont would be obliged to pay a sum of $30,000 to indemnify the holders of Vermont lands under

New York grants. Considering New York's years of intransigency on this subject, the settlement constitutes a remarkable feat of diplomacy on the commissioners' part. The success of their negotiations may be partially explained by the generous grants of Vermont land that the Vermont Assembly later made to Yorkers who were influential in winning recognition of Vermont's independence in 1789.[35]

With the major obstacle to Vermont's joining the union removed, the only task remaining to the Vermont nationalists was to secure the ratification of the new United States Constitution. The composition of Vermont's ratifying Constitutional Convention, held in January 1790, practically guaranteed that the nationalists would emerge victorious in their aims. Lyon, for example, was conspicuously absent from this convention. Chittenden and Ira Allen were practically the only members of the old regime among the 109 delegates.[36] Instead of Lyon, the representative from Fairhaven was Simeon Smith, a delegate who reflected the general composition of the Convention, described by one authority as the "more substantial citizenry of Vermont."[37] Smith, for example, was a successful entrepreneur, a judge, and a man of considerable personal wealth whose estate was valued at $80,000 upon his death in 1804.[38]

Whether Lyon would have voted for ratification, as Chittenden and Ira Allen eventually did, is a matter of speculation; but that he opposed the Federal Constitution as an antifederalist there can be no doubt. Levi Allen listed Lyon as one of the leading opponents of union with the other American states in the following frantic letter to Ira from London: "I hope in the name of——you will not join congress. Governor Chittenden, yourself, our deceased brother, Gen. Keyes, Erne, Pearl, Clark, Col. Lyon, Spafford, Hitchcock, Ebenezer Allen, Coit &c. all being fully determined to the contrary when I left you."[39] This letter implies that Lyon opposed ratifying the Constitution because he supported the Allens' separatist policy of remaining an independent sovereign republic, allied to Britain and Canada by commercial and political treaties.[40] Indeed Lyon's activities in the Episcopal Church between 1793 and 1795 tend to confirm this interpretation, for even after Vermont joined the United States, Lyon was involved in activities related to a similar separatist project (see chapter 7).

There was a link between Lyon's separatism and his antifederalism; if Vermont remained an independent republic, linked to Britain only by commercial and political treaties, she would retain complete control over her own state government. Lyon, like many of the antifederalists in the other American states, was a localist par excellence. Having risen to a position of influence in Vermont politics, he feared above all that a strong federal government would put an end to local control of state politics. He foresaw with alarm the increased taxes that a federal government would impose and identified a strong central government with the monarchies of Europe, whose entourage of public officeholders squandered the peoples' money in luxury and ostentation.[41]

By January 1790, when the Constitution came before Vermont for ratification, the question of the public assumption of the states' debt had just become a national issue. Lyon vehemently opposed Vermont's adopting the Constitution on these grounds in particular, since Vermont had effectively financed its own war debt by selling confiscated Tory property and the ungranted Crown lands. Under the pseudonym "Independent Spectator," Lyon later summarized his own antifederalist position while writing as a political follower of Col. Lyon:

> At the time of adopting the Federal Constitution, the Colonel was an anti-Federalist; that is, he was not at that time for coming into the Union thinking it better, if possible, to settle some leading preliminaries, that we might obtain some credit for our expenditure in the war. In this he was not alone, but many of the worthy free men, and also many respectable characters in our Convention, these were endeavored to be brow-beat out of their reasoning by those thirsting after the emoluments of federal offices–What should we have lost, had we not been so hasty (the claim of New York was settled). And what have we gained, but a set of useless salaried-men and pensioners, and earlier participating in the public debt, without a six-pence credit for our expenditures in the war, and assuming the payment of that of other states; pompous titles, pompous parade, and empty show.[42]

In describing the advocates of the Constitution as "those thirsting after the emoluments of federal offices," Lyon unmistakably was referring to Nathaniel Chipman, who was appointed Federal District Judge, and Lewis Morris, who was made U.S. Marshal for Vermont as soon as Vermont entered the Union in 1791.[43] These appointments confirmed Lyon's fears that the adoption of the Federal Constitution threatened his political career. Far from despairing over his opponents' victory, however, Lyon, the resilient politician, merely joined battle with them in the wider political arena. With characteristic brashness, he made the first move to act on the ratification he had opposed by urging the legislature to immediately "appoint senators to represent this state in Congress."[44] This motion foreshadowed Lyon's future political direction. From 1791 on, he set his sights beyond the local politics of Vermont. His ambitions now embraced the Congress of the United States.

6

Lyon Runs for Congress

In 1791 Lyon entered Vermont's first Congressional race, announcing himself "the representative of the commercial, agricultural, and manufacturing interests in preference to any of their law characters."[1] He was referring to the three lawyers who opposed him in the election: Isaac Tichenor, Samuel Hitchcock, and Israel Smith. While these candidates ran as individuals and not on political platforms, Lyon made their status as lawyers a campaign issue by accusing them of protecting the privileges of wealthy men of property.[2] In contrast, by presenting himself as the representative of agricultural, manufacturing, and commercial interests, Lyon sought to identify himself with those who labored productively. Throughout the 1790s, Lyon employed such appeals to class cleavages as that reflected in the following letter:

> As we find that education gives a strong turn or bias of mind in favor of the particular class of people one belongs to, and as the great bulk of the people in this district are laborious hard-working farmers; then a person from that class would more properly represent them.
> . . . If a man has been used to labor and industry himself . . . this will teach him to be saving and frugal of the public money, and not to lavish enormous sums on useless officers and pensions. . . . If a person has judgment and prudence to lay out and plan his own business to good advantage, it may be expected and presumed he will use the same wisdom and economy when he comes to manage public affairs.[3]

While Lyon's campaign slogan of 1791 foreshadows the ideological populist content expressed in the later Republican-Federalist conflict, the campaign of 1791 was primarily a contest over power. Lyon specifically wrote that his aim was "to emancipate this country from the domination of a set of men who assumed all appointments upon themselves."[4] There can be little doubt that Lyon was alluding to Nathaniel Chipman, whose recent appointment to the position of federal district judge was an alarming indication of his Federalist faction's increasing influence over Vermont's politics. Although Chipman himself was not a candidate in the

Congressional election, he and his brother, Judge Daniel Chipman, actively backed the candidacy of Israel Smith. Lyon wrote Ira Allen that, if necessary, he would back either of his other opponents in order that "the Chipmans shall know they are not to carry every point."[5]

Lyon's purpose in writing to Ira Allen was to turn to "Natural Allies for Assistance" in his campaign to defeat Israel Smith. He reported that the results of the first balloting in Rutland, where the Chipmans and Israel Smith resided, were encouraging: Lyon received 598 votes, Israel Smith 573, Isaac Tichenor 472, and Samuel Hitchcock 355. In order to procure support from Allen's Lake Champlain region in the runoff election, Lyon proposed a complex political deal to Ira in a letter replete with innuendo. He wrote that "although the Chipman family is at the highest pitch of Rage and madness against me in the business one of them has ventured to point out his wishes to me in case of Success. . . . There has been another proposal to me which I need not Mention or hint at you must guess for yourself." Although Lyon left the matter to conjecture, he implies that the Chipmans' proposal involved exposing Ira Allen. Using this veiled threat as a bargaining lever, Lyon assured Ira that if he supported Lyon, "it will fix the business and leave me void of obligations to others that have or may make proposals."

The main thrust of Lyon's proposition to Ira involved securing support from the Allen-Chittenden forces in the Lake Champlain area. Lyon's competitor in the Congressional race from that region was Samuel Hitchcock, Ethan Allen's son-in-law, whom Levi Allen had identified with the Allens' separatist, antifederalist faction in 1789.[6] "If you and he join with my friends in your quarter," Lyon wrote Ira, "I am willing to throw those matters sought for into his hand." The implication is that if Allen could persuade Hitchcock to withdraw from the race, Lyon would throw his weight behind Hitchcock for another office he desired. As far as Allen was concerned, Lyon promised to "pull every string" in the General Assembly to secure the appointment of Ira's father-in-law, Revolutionary War hero General Roger Enos, as senator from Vermont. Lyon also suggested that his "numerous friends" in the coming election would provide Ira with the opportunity of "slipping into the Council again."[7]

Whether Ira complied with Lyon's proposals is uncertain; several informed sources claimed he did not support Lyon in the election.[8] They base this conclusion on the impression that Lyon and Ira Allen became estranged and jealous of one another during the 1790s. This is supported by Lyon's own words, written to Secretary of State Timothy Pickering in 1797:

> He [Ira Allen] is the only surviving brother (save one) of the celebrated Ethan Allen; more sly, more cunning than the others he has contrived to get into his possession almost all the property of four deceased brothers who had each a pretty considerable share of Vermont. . . . By this means he has become the greatest Landholder in our State. He has by building works,

Mills et cetera and by carrying them on without Economy become embarrassed in his Affairs and therefore projected going to Europe to sell some of his lands for property to pay his debts.[9]

Despite Lyon's expression of hostility to Ira, the chief purpose of this letter of 1797 was to aid Ira by lifting the cloud of international suspicion which hung over him because of his procurement of French arms, allegedly for the Vermont militia. Several months after Lyon submitted this letter, he wrote to Ira's wife, "I am happy to find that my exertions to serve General Allen when at Philadelphia have been some service to him." Then, as an ironic reminder of his past loyalties, he concludes: "There are but few that have been more Steady in their friendship and Attachment to Ira Allen than Madam your very humble sevt—M. Lyon."[10]

If it were indeed true that Lyon broke with Ira Allen during the 1790s, his assertion of independence might well modify the earlier image of him as an opportunist and set his crusade for Republicanism in a more principled light. As tempting as it might be to reach this conclusion, however, the general pattern of Lyon's political career indicates that he combined principle with opportunism throughout his life. Indeed opportunism may have been an essential aspect of his Republicanism, a reflection of his conviction that men of humble origin should be able to advance, regardless of the means used. His vacillating relationship with Ira Allen is only one of many examples of his willingness to collaborate with men of dubious principle in order to achieve his goals. In the election of 1791, the possibility remains that Ira complied with Lyon's political bargain and persuaded Hitchcock to withdraw from the race in Lyon's favor. In all events, Hitchcock's name did not appear on the ballot in the runoff election of 1791.[11]

Other circumstantial evidence suggests that as early as 1791, the opposing political factions attempted to unify their efforts around one candidate. Writing Ira Allen at this time, Lyon stated that the Chipmans "talk largely of uniting the two parties against me but they cannot effect it as they have nothing to give Tichenor for the Sacrifice he must make and they have no idea of Giving Smith up for him."[12] While Tichenor did not withdraw from the election, he received only 85 votes out of the 3,785 cast. Since he had received 355 votes in Rutland alone, in the first balloting, the indications are that the word was out to throw Tichenor's votes to Smith. Thus Israel Smith and Matthew Lyon emerged as the major contestants in the runoff election of September 1791. The Chipman forces behind Smith proved stronger than those Lyon could muster; Smith won the election by a vote of 2,588 to Lyon's 1,112.[13]

Since Lyon continued to oppose Smith as his major contestant in the ensuing Congressional elections of 1793 and 1795, it is of interest to analyze the nature of the early political differences between these two candidates in order to gain insight into the origins of the nation's first party battles between the Federalists and the Republicans.[14] What makes this question particularly complex is that although Lyon emerged as the leader of the Republican movement in western Vermont, Smith also moved into the Republican ranks in Congress during the controversy over the Jay Treaty in 1796, and even Lyon described him as a Republican, grown "luke-warm."[15]

It appears that local issues were at the root of the conflict between Smith and Lyon in 1791. Essentially, Israel Smith represented the Yorkers in Vermont.[16] As early as 1778, when Vermont declared its independence of New York by adopting its own constitution, Israel Smith joined a group of Loyalists residing in western Vermont and instituted meetings to protest the organization of the new Vermont government.[17] Shortly afterward Smith attended Yale College and then went on to study law in Bennington with his brother, Noah Smith. After being admitted to the Vermont bar in 1783, he served four terms in the General Assembly, his most significant post being that of commissioner on the joint body that settled the Vermont-New York land dispute. Then, in 1791, he participated in the victory of the nationalist faction as a member of Vermont's ratifying convention.[18]

Obviously Smith fits into the pattern of the followers of Nathaniel Chipman up to this stage of his career. As far as Lyon was concerned, his real enemy was Chipman rather than Israel Smith; and in the following election campaign of 1793, it was Lyon and Chipman who directly confronted each other in a series of vituperative articles appearing in the *Vermont Gazette* and the *Farmers' Library*.[19] Although Chipman was not a candidate, Lyon equated him with Smith, and the controversy they engaged in reveals the key political issues around which the Federalist-Republican alignments began to form. Although the articles are rife with personal abuse, when one wades through the mud slung by each of the adversaries, one discovers that the issues over which they were at variance were no longer limited to the local scene but were of nationwide proportions. (See Note 19 for explanation of *FL* dates.)

The brunt of Lyon's attack upon Chipman was that he was "the means of adding one more to that majority in Congress . . . who have consented to every measure which has been proposed to burthen these states with unequal taxes" (*FL*, June 10, 1793). In short, Lyon made the Hamilton Funding System the central political issue of the 1793 campaign. He charged that the new fiscal policies were "the measures of a set of aristocrats who every day strengthen the undue influence of that part of the federal government who have the distribution of the money picked out of the hard-earnings of the industrious part of the community" (*FL*, June 10, 1793).

Pointing to the "unequal burthen" of the salt tax and whiskey duty, Lyon accused "the Secretary of Treasury and the other nabobs" of

"screwing the hard earnings out of the poor people's pockets for the purpose of enabling the government to pay enormous salaries" and in other
ways "vie with European Courts in frivolous gaudy appearances" (*FL*,
June 10, 1793). Particularly abhorrent to Lyon was the Hamiltonian
system of financing the public debt by means of interest-bearing public
securities. Claiming that this system benefited commercial interests at
home and abroad at the expense of the American farmer, Lyon asked
Chipman, "Why did you not shew the people the advantage that has
arisen to them from the appreciation of the domestic debt, from 2s 6 on
the pound, in the hands of our people at home[,] to 20s on the pound,
great part in the hands of foreigners who get 6% per annum out of the
hard earnings of the American farmers, and this very debt, which once
might have been redeemed with little more than is now paid for two
years interest" (*FL*, June 10, 1793).

This argument is characteristic of the attacks that the emerging
Republican faction was making against the Federalists both in Congress
and in local election contests. Chipman, in fact, accused Lyon of forming
a connection with the Clinton antifederalists in New York "with a view
to render yourself the consequential head of a party" (*FL*, May 13,
1793). He charged that Lyon collaborated with General Williams of
Salem, New York, an unscrupulous politician, according to Chipman,
and a "tool of Clinton, whom, with all his party, you reckoned among
your Friends" (*FL*, May 13, 1793). Lyon denied these connections,
claiming he had not seen Williams in six years and that Williams, even
"had he influence in Vermont, and a disposition to use it for me . . . has
had no opportunity, as he has been in New York nearly the whole of the
five months that have preceded this" (*FL*, May 13, 1793).

If Lyon's denial is true, Chipman nevertheless forecast the future
interstate party connections between Lyon and the New York antifederalists who evolved into Republicans. Writing retrospectively to Albert
Gallatin in 1803, Lyon took the credit for restoring Williams's seat in
Congress, by converting the voters of this New York district to the Republican principles that Lyon espoused in his newspaper from 1793 to
1797.[20]

Although it is uncertain that Lyon had organizational links with his
political counterparts in New York State in 1793, both he and Chipman
were well aware of their identification with the parallel political groups
being formed in that and other states. While Chipman attempted to
malign Lyon by identifying him with the Clinton antifederalists, Lyon
retaliated by charging Chipman with courting the favor of the "Jay party
in New York and Philadelphia" (*FL*, May 13, 1793).

Lyon and Chipman did not confine their dispute to a discussion of
political issues and alignments, however; the electioneering tactics of
both were on the lowest level of personal vilification. Chipman, for example, opened his attack on Lyon with this statement: "In examining

your conduct I will not endeavor to 'pursue you through all the mazes of your unexampled turpitude.' It forms a labyrinth almost inextricable: nor will I attempt to rouse your conscience with the horrors of a guilty conscience: your political conscience is too callous for compunction" (*FL*, May 13, 1793).

Chipman may have had in mind Lyon's reputation for politically dominating the residents of the town he founded. An offended townsman reported of Lyon:

> I have known him to have the vanity and impudence to come into the annual freemen's meeting in the town, and make open proclamation, that it was his right to represent the town of Fairhaven in the General Assembly, and that no man ought to think otherwise; for they were all indebted to him for the existence of the town—he had been the making of it, and it was his right to represent it as long as he should please. (*FL*, June 17, 1793)

After accusing Lyon of gross corruption and opportunism, Chipman took the occasion to point out the connection between Lyon's "political villainy" and "the country from whence you sprung" (*FL*, May 20, 1793). Lyon in turn accused Chipman of betraying principle for "pecuniary emolument" and of currying favor with the ruling aristocrats "in hopes of gaining by it the next *sinecure* appointment" (*FL*, May 13, 1793). Each accused the other of making heavy campaigning expenditures and employing others to conduct intensive electioneering activities (*FL*, May 20, 1793). The indications are that both conducted the type of aggressive organized campaign characteristic of two-party politics by the election of 1793.

Despite his strong exertions, however, Lyon again failed to defeat the Chipmans' candidate, Israel Smith, in the runoff election held on March 4, 1793. Smith won by the narrow margin of 298 votes. The final election returns were:

Israel Smith	1,928
Matthew Lyon	1,630
Isaac Tichenor	161[21]

Two years later Lyon came tantalizingly close to winning the Congressional election of 1795. The results of the February 1795 balloting were 1,783 votes for Lyon and 1,804 for Smith; Lyon lost by the slim margin of only 21 votes.

The extent of Lyon's frustration can be measured by the lengths to which he went to contest Smith's victory. The day after the Fourth Congress convened, on December 8, 1795, Lyon presented it with a petition "complaining of an undue election and return of Israel Smith, to serve as member of the House for said State."[22] In this petition Lyon charged that the sheriff of the towns of Kingston and Hancock had failed to notify the citizens of these towns of the election, thus depriving them of the opportunity to vote. He further maintained that there were fifty voters in these towns, a sufficient number to change the results of the election.[23]

The House referred Lyon's petition to the Committee on Elections, the chairman of which was the Virginian Abraham Venable, a staunch supporter of the "Madison Party" in the factional alignments that had formed in the previous two Congresses.[24] On the surface it might appear that Venable and his faction would welcome the opportunity of winning a seat in the House for so ardent a supporter of their policies as Matthew Lyon. From the debates on Lyon's petition, however, there is no evidence that the Republican faction in Congress was aware of Lyon as an ardent exponent of Republicanism in Vermont. On the other hand, there is abundant evidence that the "Republican interest" looked upon Smith as their ally and supported him in his fight to retain his seat.

On February 4, Venable's Committee on Elections reported "that they are of the opinion that Israel Smith is entitled to take his seat in this House."[25] The committee rejected Lyon's petition on the grounds of "ex parte" evidence, which was inadmissable. Ironically, William Smith, ardent leader of the Federalist faction from South Carolina,[26] supported Lyon and charged that his unadmitted evidence indicated that "there was an enmity" between Mr. Lyon and the sheriff, "who failed to notify the towns," and argued that this type of malpractice "cuts up by the roots the rights of elections."[27]

Israel Smith himself participated in the debate and gave the House a detailed description of "the nature of carrying on elections in Vermont." He assured the House that "he did not believe the petitioner had any expectations of gaining a Seat in the House at present, but that he took these measures only to influence the people in his favor at the next elections." John Swanwick of Pennsylvania supported Smith, arguing that the towns in question had only thrown in fifteen votes in the previous election; and although the petitioner claimed they would have come forward with fifty votes on this occasion, there was no evidence they would have done so.

On the following day, leading Republicans and Federalists argued bitterly over whether to recommit the committee report in order to give Lyon an opportunity to submit further evidence. Atypically, Massachusetts' Federalist, Theodore Sedgwick, buttressed the "rights of election" argument with a ringing appeal for the rights of the "insignificant." Attacking the opposition for calling the two disenfranchised towns "insignificant," he warned, "they might go from towns to men and say that such and such men being insignificant, their rights were not worth attending to."

Prominent Republicans, ordinarily identified as strong advocates of democracy, accused the opposition of "straining the business of elections too far," since few elections for members of the House were "perfect."[28] Taking this side of the argument were such staunch Republicans as Giles,

Nicholas, and Venable of Virginia and Varnum of Massachusetts. Gallatin summarized the Republicans' position by arguing that Lyon's evidence was insufficient and that Vermont law set the date of elections;
therefore notification by the sheriff was a mere matter of form. Of the
Republicans, Madison alone conceded that more information was desir-
able. Eventually the House reached a compromise whereby, instead of
recommitting the report of the Committee on Elections, it voted to postpone consideration of the report, in order to allow the committee time to
obtain further evidence from Lyon and other sources in Vermont.

Three months later, on May 28, 1796, the Committee on Elections
came forth with a new report, reversing its former position. The new
evidence it had obtained buttressed the position of the Federalists on the
committee, whose leading spokesman, Zephaniah Swift of Connecticut,
explained to the House the latest decision of the committee. It had ascertained that the townships of Kingston and Hancock contained seventeen
and nineteen voters respectively, and that the sheriff, by accident, had
not notified the voters of the election in question. Therefore the committee concluded "that as there appears to have been a sufficient number of
qualified voters in the towns of Hancock and Kingston to have changed
the state of the election, Resolved that Israel Smith was not duly elected,
and is not entitled to his Seat."[29]

Again vigorous debate ensued, with Harper, Sitgreaves, and William
Smith defending the report, while the Republican spokesmen, Venable,
Gallatin, John Nicholas, Giles, and Findley, vehemently opposed it. In
the conclusion, the Republicans won their point. Gallatin proved that
Lyon needed 21 votes to have tied with Israel Smith in the contested election, but that he had been able to produce only 20 certificates showing
votes in his favor; 7 additional certificates showed votes favoring Smith.
Therefore, since Lyon still would have lost the election by 8 votes, the
House voted 41 to 28 in favor of seating Smith. Thus ended Lyon's six-
month battle to unseat Israel Smith. The Republicans defeated him,
although he was the most outspoken representative of the Republican
position in Vermont, while Israel Smith was the representative of the
local Federalist faction. What is the explanation of this apparent
contradiction?

To understand the Congressional Republicans' support of Smith, we
must turn to the issues around which party alignments were being
formed in Congress at this time. When the Fourth Congress convened in
December 1795, the Republicans were aware that their major challenge
over the coming months would be the defeat of the Jay Treaty. From the
opening days of the session, they made intensive efforts to win to their
side members of the House who had been independent of party ties in the
past.[30] Israel Smith fell into this category. He had supported Madison on
only twelve out of thirty-five key measures in the Second Congress and
voted against the Republican faction on their most fundamental resolu-

tions attacking Hamilton's Treasurer's Report and the financing of the public debt.[31] On the issue of the Jay Treaty, however, Smith joined the Republican side and eventually voted not to implement the agreement when the crucial contest came to a head on April 29, 1796. There is little reason to doubt that Smith made his position known in the beginning of the session, when the Republicans were furiously attempting to assess their strength and line up their supporters.[32]

When the battle over Israel Smith's seat is seen against the background of the party contest in Congress over the Jay Treaty, the seeming contradictions of Federalist support and Republican opposition to Lyon become resolved. In order to retain the Republicans' new adherent in the House, Lyon's staunchest supporters in the future, such as Gallatin and John Nicholas, opposed his petition. On the other hand, men who were to become Lyon's bitterest adversaries in the Federalist camp, such as Sedgwick and Harper, ardently supported Lyon's petition in their desire to reduce the Congressional Republican faction's strength.[33]

These contradictions also reveal the limited state of party organization at the time; the embryonic parties had not approximated organization on a national level. Although the "Republican interest" had formed a bloc in Congress by 1795, the members of this bloc were out of touch with the local political and organizational developments outside of their own states and apparently were unfamiliar with such strong local advocates of their policies as Matthew Lyon. There is the possibility, of course, that Smith may have familiarized his Republican colleagues with Lyon's activities in Vermont, but that his description was a deprecatory one. Nevertheless Lyon had the political backing of the Republican sympathizers in Vermont, and it was he and his supporters who built the organization that eventually emerged as the Republican Party of 1800. In this sense, the evolution of the Republican Party in Vermont did not follow the pattern of "organization from above" by members of Congress, which was characteristic of many other states, according to Noble Cunningham's observations in his astute study of the process of development of the new Republican Party in the 1790s.[34] It was not Smith, the Republican member in Congress, who gave impetus and direction to the development of Vermont's Republican organization, but Matthew Lyon, Smith's longstanding local rival. Undoubtedly it was Smith's previous identification with the Federalist faction in Vermont state politics that precluded his assumption of the leadership of the Republican movement in Vermont. Lyon had already assumed that initiative in 1791. It was not until the election of 1796, however, that his concerted efforts bore fruit.

At this juncture in Vermont politics, the Federalist faction was in control of the State Assembly. Their main strength came from eastern Vermont, which had always reflected the conservatism of the Connecticut Valley region in contrast to the popular democracy prevalent in western Vermont. Lyon's newspaper (see chapter 7) teemed with accusations of "electioneering" on the part of the State Assembly, charging it with "declaiming against Democrats, and extolling the American Aristocracy."[35] Documenting these charges, the *Farmers' Library* pointed out that the Assembly "passed over the Patriotic Governor Chittenden for elector of President and Vice-President" and passed election laws "for the sake of depressing one and setting up another."

The latter accusation referred to the fact that during the course of the election of 1796, after eastern Vermont had reelected its former representative to Congress, the Assembly passed a law changing election procedures. Under the law in existence at the time the election commenced, if no candidate received a majority of the votes cast, a runoff election was held between the leading candidates. Whoever then received the plurality of votes won the election. The new law provided that there would be "no election until one person should have a majority."

Lyon's *Farmers' Library* charged "that to alter the law in the present situation of things would appear like pointing at an individual, and would be going into the principle of electioneering on the great scale; that it would have a tendency, by repeating election after election, to wear out the best disposed part of the community, they would neglect the meetings and leave it in the power of designing persons, eventually to decide the election."

Lyon had reason to believe the Assembly was "pointing" at him, as can be seen by the following results of the first balloting:

Matthew Lyon	1783
Israel Smith	967
Samuel Williams	322
Nathaniel Chipman	310
Isaac Tichenor	287 [36]
Gideon Olin	198
Enoch Woodbridge	188
James Galusha	147
Daniel Chipman	85
Samuel Hitchcock	52

Despite the fact that Lyon led the field with 816 votes more than his leading contender, Israel Smith, he was faced with the formidable task of winning a majority of the total 4,304 cast among ten opposing candidates.

As in earlier elections, however, the competing candidates made coalitions, so that in the runoff election of December 1796 only three leading contestants emerged: Matthew Lyon with 1,625 votes, Samuel Hitchcock with 841, and Israel Smith with 775. The remaining fifteen candidates polled a total of only 224 votes.[37] Despite his large plurality, Lyon still lacked the majority required by the new election law.

The significant phenomenon of this December runoff election was the meteoric rise of Samuel Hitchcock as the second leading contender in the election, after receiving only 52 votes in the first balloting. Hitchcock, formerly attached to the Allen-Chittenden bloc, had risen up the legal ladder in Vermont to the position of Judge of the U.S. District Court and was now allied to the Federalist Chipman-Tichenor faction.[38] This group, disenchanted with Israel Smith for joining the Republicans in Congress on the Jay Treaty vote, transferred their solid support to Samuel Hitchcock. Thus Hitchcock, rather than Smith, became Lyon's leading Federalist opponent in the final runoff election.

Shortly before the election took place, Lyon published the following attack against Hitchcock in the *Farmers' Library*. Presumably written by "A Farmer," this letter presents a capsule of Lyon's Republican arguments against lawyers, direct taxes, and the public debt.

> Inconceivable has been my mortification on enquiring the character of this Mr. Hitchcock [for whom the farmer had voted in the previous election] to hear that he was brought up in ideleness, dissipation and extravagance, and at about thirty years of age he undertook to be a Lawyer, that after several years practice in that profession, by the connivance and management of his brother lawyers he was fixed into the office of District Judge with a salary of 800 or 1,000 dollars a year, paid out of the hard earnings of such men as myself, for which he does little or nothing—that he seems now not quite satisfied with that 1,000 dollars a year, but wishes to go to be a Member of Congress so that he may be able to help on the work of making salaries and Pensioners. . . .
>
> I should have sat down in silent shame for my conduct in the last election, in voting for a person without knowing more about him, were not I alarmed by the stating you gave in your last letter.
>
> 84 Millions in Debt
>
> and Vermont got 20,000 dollars direct tax to pay annually!—What is all this for? At the end of the war it was asserted that the public lands would pay all the debts, but now we owe 84,000,000. According to what little I know of history, we have made debt much faster since we began than that extravagant nation from which we have learned the accursed system of funding the public debt, and paying an everlasting interest for it[.]—When Vermont had 30,000 dollars to pay once for all, we thought it hard, and were three or four years about it. Sure there never will be a time when men of economy, and those who know how hard the poor and midling people get their money, will be more wanted than as present. Tis not a time to suffer the voluptuous man, the idler, or gambler, to personate the hardy yeomanry of Vermont in Congress, merely because he is good natured (*FL*, Feb. 1, 1797).

By using such grass-roots appeals as appear in this letter, Lyon captured the votes of the farmers of western Vermont. In the February runoff election, the official count stood:

M. Lyon	2,143
Hitchcock	1,143

I. Smith	346
J. Galusha	151
Saml. Williams	27
Scattering	80[39]

Lyon finally had amassed a majority of 396 votes; his dogged determination over the past six years finally had borne fruit. Fired by his hatred for Nathaniel Chipman and his Federalist associates, Lyon had succeeded in defeating his college-educated, legal opponents. He had electioneered as a representative of the people, but in reality his victory marked not the triumph of the poor versus the rich but the new class of self-made entrepreneurs versus the traditional elite.

7

Herald of Republicanism

Lyon's election resulted from his popularization of the ideology of Republicanism. During the three years preceding his victory at the polls, Lyon laid the foundations for the vigorous Republican movement that elected him. He was the prime mover behind the formation of a Republican press and the organization of local Democratic Societies in western Vermont. As elsewhere throughout the country, these became the chief vehicles through which the growing opposition to Federalist rule expressed itself.

On April 1, 1793, less than a month after his defeat in the election of 1793, Lyon launched a weekly newspaper, which he entitled the *Farmers' Library*. Comparing the influence of this Republican publication to that of Benjamin Franklin Bache's *Aurora*, Lyon later wrote Albert Gallatin that the purpose of his newspaper was "to break down the undue influence of the Aristo-Tory faction" who were deluging New England and New York with an "overpowering flood of anti-Republicanism."[1] Describing this situation in detail to another correspondent, Lyon wrote, "On a sudden I was surrounded by newspapers containing high tone British doctrines flowing in upon us from the hireling presses of New Hampshire in the east, Sedgwick & Co. in the south, New York apostates in the west, and Royalists of Canada in the north. Tory doctrines were flowing freely from the favored presses of Vermont."[2]

Lyon readily acknowledged the electioneering value of his press, claiming it "was the means of saving [the] district I lived in . . . and was in considerable degree instrumental in bringing back the district Williams of New York formerly represented."[3] Nevertheless, he attributed these electoral victories primarily to the role his press played in spreading Republican ideas.

Despite the fact that Lyon made his seventeen-year-old son, James Lyon, the publisher of the *Farmers' Library*, there can be no doubt that he provided the finances. This is substantiated by his statement that "it cost me from $1,000 to $2,000 per annum for about five years to maintain a Republican press."[4] There can also be little doubt that he played a decisive role in determining the contents of the paper, although he hired several different editors during the five years' existence of the *Farmers' Library*. Not only does his personality lead to this conclusion, but he stated, "I hired a printer, the best Republican essays were selected. My pen was not idle . . . by this means the Republican doctrines were scattered through the Northern States."[5]

It is this ideological aspect of Lyon's newspaper that deserves closest examination when analyzing the thrust of his Republicanism. Only during the first three months of the *Farmers' Library*'s publication did the electioneering dialogue between Lyon and Chipman occupy the major space of the paper. On June 10 a letter written by a farmer demanded the cessation of "Electioneering" and the continuation of "Foreign Intelligence," the purpose "for which he subscribed" (*FL*, June 10, 1793). In the following issue, the editor promised to honor the farmer's request, and although there was no dearth of campaigning material in the *Farmers' Library* thereafter, foreign news dominated the paper.

Despite the importance of the ideological conflict over domestic issues that first stimulated the formation of Republican and Federalist factions in Vermont (see chapter 4), the *Farmers' Library* reveals the significant role that the French Revolution played in further polarizing these factions into two divergent parties after 1793. This Republican journal and Lyon's later publication, *The Scourge of Aristocracy*, make it clear that he saw the dominant conflict of the period, both at home and abroad, as that between Monarchism and Republicanism. He saw a close relationship between foreign and domestic policies and branded the American opponents of the French Revolution as Monarchists, who threatened to undermine American Republicanism as well. "This is a day of general insurrection of Man against their tyrants and cruel usurpers of their rights," he declared, "A day when every Despot from the great Moguls and Emperors of the East, down to the Kings and petty princes of Europe and their satellites; and from them even down to the aristocratically made pettifoggers in America, are trembling for fear of the loss of that power they have so cabbalistically acquired over Man" (*FL*, Feb. 17, 1794).

Significantly, it was an address by Thomas Paine to the French National Assembly that introduced the first issue of the *Farmers' Library*. In his speech Paine advocated the trial of Louis XVI, not out of revenge but in the interest of exposing his partnership with "that horde of conspirators . . . among the crowned ruffians of Europe which threatened not only French liberty but likewise that of all nations" (*FL*, Apr. 1, 1793). In ensuing issues of the *Farmers' Library*, Paine continually reappears as the symbol of the common bond between the American and French Revolutions. In 1796, when he was expected to return to America, the *Farmers' Library* commented, "How must every American face blush to see the face of the man who took so conspicuous a part in our emancipation from tyranny, when he shall be told that we have given up that independence for which he CONTENDED, and thrown ourselves into the arms of our former oppressors rather than oppose with manly fortitude their impotent THREATS! ! !" (*FL*, May 30, 1796).

The theme of the shared Republican principles of the two Revolutions appears repeatedly in the pages of the *Farmers' Library*. In its first issue it also reprinted an open letter from the French Republic to the United States, which referred to America's participation in celebrating "this glorious regeneration of Europe, that concern which your principles and past combats reserved to you. Single and alone against the coalition of Kings, we have shewn ourselves worthy of being your brothers."[6]

Lyon himself credited the Declaration of Independence with inspiring the revolutions against tyranny spreading throughout Europe: "As the seeds of those principles began to develop themselves in the minds of mankind, they have enlightened the ignorant, superstitious, king and priest-ridden people; originating in America these principles have penetrated into the entire world and shook the thrones of the most powerful monarchs to their foundations, and excited a spirit of freedom, and inquiry into the rights of Man" (*FL*, July 11, 1796).

The *Farmers' Library* was not completely uncritical of the French Revolution, however. True to the Republican principle enunciated on its masthead, "The Freedom and Impartiality of the Press Shall Remain Inviolate" (*FL*, Apr. 1, 1793), it published conflicting points of view about that great upheaval. On April 8, 1793, for example, it printed an unsympathetic account of the National Convention's "unjust and iniquitous judgement" against Louis Capet (XVI). This article insisted that many members of the convention who voted for Louis's execution were "compelled by the most urgent motives of personal safety. . . . There undoubtedly was great reason for this apprehension; for a most formidable mob was collected, which openly threatened by name, many of the members to murder them on the spot, if they did not vote for the Death of the King" (*FL*, Apr. 8, 1793). In the following issue, April 15, another letter expressed the opposite revolutionary viewpoint: "Let any man only recollect the conduct of Louis Capet, his many heinous crimes, his flight after having taken an oath to be faithful to the nation, the constant impediments he threw in the way of the revolution, the aid he afforded to enemies of France, and lastly his treason and reiterated instances of hypocrisy, I say when a man considers these things, let him reflect if Louis merits our tears of compassion."

Perhaps the most thoughtful remarks to appear in the *Farmers' Library* on the subject of the French Revolution were those of Elias Buell, president of the Rutland Democratic Society. Commenting on the differences between the American and French Revolutions, Buell claimed the "internal placable superiority of the American revolution over that of the French. Theirs, though dictated by the same principles, was too sudden a transition from absolute monarchy to refined democracy." The

American Revolution owed its advantages to the limited democracy experienced under British rule, which "was a sort of limited or restricted Republic deriving from limited Monarchy." He added, in the sardonic metaphor of Samuel Adams, that the British institutions of limited monarchy are "the leeks and onions that many still long after."[7] This speech of Buell's, though thoroughly Republican in its spirit, hardly fits the Jacobin stereotype with which the Federalists branded the Democratic Societies in the 1790s.

Matthew Lyon's clarion call for the formation of Democratic Societies in Vermont in February 1794 (FL, Feb. 17, 1794) reveals the essential reason why these "self-created societies"[8] did comprise a radical threat to the status quo. Lyon urged "that the great body of people themselves undertake to watch over the government." He counseled his fellow citizens "to wake up and shake off those shackles of dilatoriness, want of confidence or bashfulness" that had prevented them in the past from exercising control over their destiny. He urged them to hold regular meetings, study national and state legislation, interview their representatives, examine their conduct, and after proper scrutiny pronounce against those of their servants who "should be found to neglect or operate against the interest of the community" (FL, Feb. 17, 1794).

Inherent in Lyon's statement is Rousseau's political doctrine that the government must constantly reflect the general will of the people. Lyon's words may have been based on a firsthand knowledge of Rousseau's writings,[9] although this concept of government was also a natural outgrowth of the popular democracy practiced in Vermont under its revolutionary constitution, with its unicameral legislature, weak executive, and annual elections. The theory of government that underlay popular thought in Vermont (where Thomas Paine's Age of Reason "was greedily received"[10] in the 1790s) rested on faith in the reason of the common man, and its corollary, faith in government in the hands of the majority. This philosophic conviction, held by most Jeffersonian Republicans in the 1790s, came into direct conflict with the theoretical views held by most Federalists of the era. Alarmed by manifestations of turbulence and threats to property rights inherent in democracy, the Federalists abhorred the concept that government should reflect the popular will. Rather they were strong advocates of separation of powers and balanced government, devices intended to serve as checks upon majority rule. These theoretical differences were at the core of the political conflict that racked the nation in the 1790s. It was not Republicanism versus monarchy, or Jacobinism versus aristocracy, but essentially Jean Jacques Rousseau's concept of the general will versus Edmund Burke's theory of virtual representation. Many of Lyon's Federalist opponents, like Nathaniel Chipman on the local level and John Adams on the national scene, were sincere advocates of the principle of government based on the consent of the governed. According to their understanding of this doctrine, however, once the electorate had selected their representatives, the voters' role in the governing process was completed. Thereafter, the elected representatives would run the government in the people's best interest. Moreover, those to be entrusted with the reins of government should be men of education and responsibility, which almost invariably meant that they should be men of substantial property interests.[11]

Thus Lyon came close to the truth when he criticized the Federalists as "a set of gentry who are interested in keeping the government at a distance from and out of the sight of the people who support it" (*FL*, Feb. 17, 1794). According to John Miller, noted for distilling the essence of the Federalist era,

> The Federalists' objective was to mold the United States in accord with their vision of an established order securely protected against demagogues and democratic majorities. This vision took the form of a highly aristocratic, class-conscious society in which gentlemen knew their privileges and the lower orders knew their place—the price, the Federalists insisted, of order, stability, and progress.[12]

Given these objectives, it is readily understandable that the Federalists viewed with alarm the sudden eruption of local Democratic Societies in the 1790s. Oliver Wolcott wrote his son that the "demoniacal" Democratic Societies were "nurseries of sedition . . . formed for the avowed purpose of general influence and control upon measures of government."[13] Lyon, in his crude frontier language, accurately summarized the elitist philosophy behind the Federalists' opposition to the Democratic Societies:

> These . . . Democratic societies . . . are laughed at and ridiculed by men who consider the science of government to belong naturally only to a few families, and argue, that them families ought to be obeyed & supported in princely grandure; that the common people ought to give half their earnings to these few, for keeping them under, and awing their poor commonalty from destroying one another, which their savage nature would lead to, were it not for the benignity and good sense of the few superiors Heaven has been pleased to plant among them. (*FL*, Feb. 17, 1794)

Within a month after Lyon's call, Democratic Societies began to spring up throughout Vermont. The first was formed in Chittenden County on April 16, 1794, the second in Castletown in Rutland County on April 23, 1794; soon every county west of the Green Mountains had its own Democratic Society.[14] Although Lyon was never an open member of any of these societies, the preceding statements leave no doubt that he spearheaded their formation. Beneath his rhetoric lies the implication that he viewed their development as a source of organizational strength upon which he could rely for political support in his efforts to win the election as western Vermont's representative in Congress. In essence the Democratic Societies were the embryonic beginnings of a distinct Republican party in Vermont, and Lyon used the chief resource at his command, the *Farmers' Library*, to foster them. Week after week he publicized the proceedings and platforms of the Democratic Societies to the readers of his newspaper throughout western Vermont and adjacent areas.

These issues of the *Farmers' Library* document the vitality with which the rationalist ideas of the Enlightenment served as practical guides to action for men far removed from the accustomed centers of cultivation and political power. Another statement by Elias Buell succinctly demonstrates that faith in reason was the fundamental tenet upon which these societies rested. Maintaining that the purpose of association was "to cultivate information and diffuse its usefulness," he argued, "If it be the voice of the people that gives strength, energy and support to law and government . . . then let it be the voice of improved, enlightened, calm reason" (*FL*, Aug. 8, 1796). This faith in knowledge, and its wide dissemination among the populace, was an inherent element of Lyon's Republicanism. It was the avowed purpose of his *Farmers' Library*, whose masthead after May 30, 1794, read:

> The FREEDOM Of the PEOPLE Cannot be SUPPORTED
> without KNOWLEDGE and INDUSTRY.

That Lyon's faith in knowledge was more than a demagogic slogan is evidenced by the fact that he established a thriving publishing house called Voltaire's Head, which also was run by his son James, who published a multiplicity of pamphlets and books ranging from treatises on medicine to Nathaniel Chipman's *Sketches of Government*, as well as *Works of the Late Dr. Benjamin Franklin*.[15]

A respect for books was an essential aspect of Lyon's Enlightenment heritage. Despite his limited formal education, he apparently educated himself by amassing a large personal library, which in turn served as a "reference center" for his neighbors and their children. One of these was young William Miller, who later became an important figure in American Protestantism. In Miller's youth he was first influenced by the "vast array of historical data" he found in Matthew Lyon's library; he consequently became an outspoken advocate of Deism.[16] In addition to disseminating information through his private library, Lyon was instrumental in founding the Fairhaven Library Society in 1794. Two of its co-founders, Nathaniel Dickenson and John Brown, who significantly were also active members of the Rutland County Democratic Society, later sought to incorporate this Library Society.[17] In their petition they borrowed the language of Rousseau, claiming " 'the inestimable advantages to be derived from social compacts when formed in designs to cultivate useful knowledge.' "[18]

Sincere as these sentiments may have been, neither Lyon nor his colleagues in the Democratic Societies were concerned purely with the abstract cultivation of knowledge. The resolutions passed by these societies make it abundantly clear that they viewed knowledge as a prelude to political action. Their aim was to make their views known to Congress, "thereby producing a perfect accord and unanimity between the present Governors and their fellow citizens."[19] This is what Lyon earlier had urged upon his fellow Vermonters; and on the front pages of his newspaper he regularly printed the resolutions of the Democratic Societies, which expressed their position, and his, on the major national and international issues of the day.

A close reading of these resolutions reveals that the central issue that occupied the attention of the members of the Democratic Societies was the threat Great Britain posed to the newly established republics of both the United States and France in 1794. In the preamble to the *Regulations of the Associated Democratic Societies*, they declared that an "enmity" existed between Great Britain and the United States; they next proceeded to list abuse after abuse to prove Britain's hostile designs against the independence and national rights of her former colony. Included among these were:

> her non-payment for the Negros she robbed us of. . . .
> her non-fulfillment . . . of the delivery of our posts. . . .
> her ungenerous prohibitions . . . to our trade, especially to the West Indies. . . .
> her unhuman and disgraceful aid secretly given to the Indians, the better to enable them to scalp, torture and murder the innocent inhabitants of our frontiers (*FL*, Apr. 23, 1794).

After demonstrating Britain's threatening posture toward the United States, the resolutions turn with even more scorn to her involvement in the war against France: "We beg leave to be informed by her [Britain's] adherents in this country, what we have not to fear from such a government . . . which tho' overwhelmed with distress of almost every nature . . . has wantonly plunged herself into a war in direct opposition to the cause of humanity." The underlying reason for Britain's entering the war against France, claims this resolution, was "the strong apprehensions of the downfall of her own corrupt and motley government." This explains "the real source of her unchristian, diabolical and tyranical resentment against that nation, from whose electrical machine of liberty she was fearful some particle of Republican fluid, might glance to her own territories, and create that degree of light which would bring clearly to view the errors and impositions which they have long been the dupes of." In conclusion, the Associated Democratic Societies predict "that a war commenced in dishonor, and continued with injustice, will terminate in disgrace and eternal infamy to the promoters of it" (*FL*, Apr. 23, 1794).

Next the resolutions turn their attention to the United States' relations with France, condemning the "unjustifiable coolness to our faithful allies." This of course referred to the great controversy raging on the national level over honoring the 1778 Treaty of Alliance with France. The Federalists, already wary of the egalitarian direction of the French Revolution, were opposed to our aiding France according to the terms of the Alliance, particularly those provisions in which the United States guaranteed France's possession of its West Indian islands and opened its ports to French privateers. The Republicans, while desirous of remaining neutral in the war between France and Britain, felt their country could do so while also living up to its treaty obligations to France, to whom it was morally and spiritually allied.[20] These Republican sentiments were echoed with vehemence by the Vermont Democratic Societies, which stated that "we detest the conduct of the Vice-President of the United States and twelve Members of the Senate in their attempt to misconstrue and narrow the limits of a treaty made with the French nation, in the time of our distress and their tranquility which upon every honest, or virtuous principle ought to be held sacred when their adversity and our prosperity had changed the scene" (FL, Apr. 23, 1794).

In essence, these Democratic Societies regarded monarchist Britain as the mutual enemy of both France and the United States. Americans who sympathized with Britain were equivalent to traitors. "We are sensible," states one of their resolutions, "that there are some of her former subjects who are amongst the number of our best citizens . . . who differ from the real whigs of this country in political principles." While conceding that these persons and their property ought to be protected from insult and depredation, the resolution insists that "they ought under no pretext whatever to be trusted in any office under government" (FL, Apr. 23, 1794). In a similar vein, the Rutland Democratic Society expressed disapproval "of the evasive conduct of some people in power who have suffered themselves to be cajoled into a state of stupor and inactivity" against British abuses. "It is the opinion of this Society that the attachment shown to the Leeks and Onions of Britain have tended to encourage that haughty nation to proceed" (FL, May 27, 1794).

The British abuse that affected the Vermonters most closely, and the one to which Lyon most frequently alluded in the pages of his Farmers' Library, was the retention of western posts "for the support of a scalping set of savages who destroy our frontiers" (FL, May 27, 1794). This rhetoric fell on responsive ears; Vermonters comprised an important part of General Wayne's Western Army which, according to reports in the Farmers' Library (Apr. 29, 1794), endured battles of "savage fury" with the Indians in the spring of 1794. Since 1790 the Indians had successfully repulsed the Western Army's attempts to subdue them; it was not until August 1794 that Wayne's army finally defeated them at the Battle of Fallen Timbers, but even then war with Britain still loomed as an imminent possibility.[21]

There are many indications that Lyon and his Republican colleagues in the Democratic Societies favored such a war, in which they anticipated realizing their old ambitions of conquering Canada. Lord Dorchester had supplied the Vermonters with the pretext they needed in February 1794, when the war with the Indians was at its height. In an incendiary speech to an assemblage of Indian chiefs in Quebec, he urged them to wreak revenge on the Americans, assuring them that war between England and the United States was almost certain.[22] Shortly afterwards, Lyon published the belligerent reply of the Associated Democratic Societies of Chittenden County, in which they warned his lordship that he was courting a counterattack upon Canada. They reminded him of previous encounters during the American Revolution, when they were the "virtuous sons of Liberty, who in their infant years . . . twice defeated the vain glorious armies of the boasted conquerors of the world." Maintaining that "we are really desirous of peace if it can be on honourable terms," they made it clear that an Indian attack on this country "can be crushed in one campaign by the conquest we shall make in the city of Montreal, and the plains of Abraham" (*FL*, Apr, 29, 1794).

In the event of open hostilities against the British in Canada, the Vermonters fully expected to be supported by the discontented Canadian colonists, who were restive over the authoritarian provisions of the Constitutional Act of 1791, designed to tighten Britain's reins over this remaining segment of her North American empire.[23] The Chittenden Democratic Society made this clear in their reply to Lord Dorchester, in which they stated that they were confident that the "virtuous, truly noble, the generous, the patriotic part" of his nation would not join in an attack on "their many friends and connections in this country" (*FL*, Apr. 29, 1794). The grounds for this optimistic assessment are found in Lyon's paper, which reported with obvious satisfaction on August 19, 1794: "The strongest symptoms of a revolutionary spirit are observable in Lower Canada . . . a rising of the people has already commenced in some parts of the province against the government. We wish them a happy deliverance from tyranic insolence and injustice" (*FL*, Aug, 19, 1794).

Earlier Lyon had linked "the cause of liberty and the French" to the overthrow of British rule in Canada. In November 1793 he wrote an open letter to Citizen Genet, praising the controversial French Minister for his "zeal and activity in the cause of the Republic you represent . . . and the cause of Mankind." Speaking in the name of the *"Old Green Mountain Boys,"* he predicted that "these lovers of rational liberty" would seize all Canada, if war with Britain were the "inevitable consequence of a strict adherence to the treaty with our generous Allies."[24] Two months earlier the British authorities in Canada had been apprised that Genet had sent an emissary by the name of Meziére into lower Canada to disseminate "Democratic Principles" and foment divisions among the populace. From September 1793 on, they were on their guard against insurrectionary activities in Canada, inspired by pro-French Republicans in the United States.[25]

Whether Lyon was cognizant of Meziére's mission in Canada, when he wrote his letter supporting Genet, is open to conjecture. There is, however, strong circumstantial evidence to indicate that in 1794 Lyon was involved in an aborted French plan to provide military support for a revolutionary insurrection against the British in Canada. The person who supplied this testimony was not a man of high credibility, to be sure. He was John A. Graham, who, though secretary of the Rutland Democratic Society in 1794, later became a paid informer for the British.[26] In 1797, while in England, Graham transmitted the following information to the Duke of Portland: "About the latter end of the year 1794 . . . Monsr Genet the French Minister had offered 300 Blank Commissions in French to him [Graham], Genl Clarke and Col^l Lyon, all persons related to and connected with Govr Chittenden and the two last . . . the principal Persons concerned in promoting this plan and gave them the power of filling them up, with the names of any persons they judged proper instruments for Carrying that Plan into effect."[27]

Lyon vehemently denied these charges, when his Federalist opponents made similar allegations against him. "The stuff about my ever being President of a Democratic society, one of Genet's creatures, or having ever opposed the American government, or encouraged the Western Insurrection, are all as groundless as any lie ever conceived by the heart of the author," he insisted.[28] Lyon's protestations and the dubious veracity of John Graham notwithstanding, objective circumstances seem to lend some credence to this British agent's charges. In view of the hostile posture of the Vermont Democratic Societies toward the British in Canada in the spring of 1794, it would seem logical that such key leaders of that organization as Matthew Lyon and Isaac Clark would have given serious consideration to the prospect of leading an expedition into Canada to aid the expected uprising against the British. Indeed in April 1794 the Canadian authorities were informed that the Vermont state government itself had officially "offered to undertake the conquest of Canada, provided the troops were allowed to plunder the inhabitants."[29]

What actually seems to have transpired is that the French offered leaders of the Democratic Societies blank commissions to launch an expedition into Canada, but because of a complicated set of new developments, these leaders eventually rejected the proposal. There is every reason to believe that at this very period both Matthew Lyon and John A. Graham were involved in another scheme, whose purpose was to link Canada and Vermont not by conquest but by collusion with the British. This plot was a revival of many of the elements of the separatist project initiated by Levi Allen in 1789, in which he attempted to bring about a union of Vermont and lower Canada (see chapter 5). An integral part of Levi's original plan had been to secure his ends through gaining the support of the British Anglican Church. In May 1789 Levi had written the Reverend Dr. Morrice, secretary of the Society for the Propagation of the Gospel in Foreign Parts, reminding him of the valuable Vermont lands (650 acres in each township) which his Society was about to lose unless it took immediate action to salvage them. This, Levi proposed, could be accomplished by establishing a bishop at Fort St. John, Canada, and sending a missionary to Vermont "until those Rights of land shall be secured to the Church and your Society." If such action were taken, Levi assured the Reverend Dr. Morrice that Mr. Chittenden and Mr. Allen would "continue to exert themselves" in behalf of saving the Vermont SPG lands.[30]

Actively collaborating with Levi in this scheme had been the exiled New England Tory, the Reverend Samuel Peters, who strove for the appointment as bishop.[31] Levi's draft of a petition to the Archbishop of Canterbury specified a man of Samuel Peters's description for the position of Bishop of "Verdmont," stipulating that he should have "Manners and customs congenial with those of New England."[32] Although this plan was aborted when Vermont joined the United States and adopted the Federal Constitution in 1791, it remained alive in the minds of the members of the Allen-Chittenden faction, including Matthew Lyon. His activities in the Vermont Episcopal Church between 1793 and 1795 leave little room for doubt that he supported the revival of this separatist project.

It will be recalled that Lyon himself had evinced an avid interest in the SPG land from 1786 to 1794, and that on several occasions he petitioned the General Assembly of Vermont to release control of these lands (see chapter 3). Originally his prime motive was to obtain the Society's lands in Orwell for his blast furnace. After his personal petition for this property was defeated, he joined efforts with others to secure the transfer of the SPG lands to the Episcopal Church in Vermont in 1792. In September 1793 he was one of the most active delegates to the Episcopal Church Convention, serving on two of the convention's most significant committees. The first applied to the Society for the Propagation of the Gospel in Foreign Parts "for a conveyance of their lands within this state"; the second nominated a bishop to preside over the church in the state of Vermont.[33] The convention accepted the committee's recommendation and elected the Reverend Dr. Edward Bass of Newburyport to be Bishop of Vermont on September 17, 1793. In the six months that intervened between September 1793 and February 1794, certain political developments took place that apparently caused some of the Vermont Episcopalians to reverse this decision. On February 27, 1794, a special convention of the diocese was held; it elected the Reverend Samuel Peters instead of the Reverend Dr. Bass as the Bishop of Vermont.[34]

The reason for rejecting Dr. Bass was that in his letter of acceptance of January 2, 1794, he made the reservation that he not be required to be in constant residence. Seizing upon this excuse, John A. Graham nominated his "relative and friend," the Reverend Samuel Peters, for bishop. Thus began Graham's double life as an "English American."[35] Significantly, another relative of Samuel Peters, his son-in-law Colonel William Jarvis of Toronto, "was very active and earnest in promoting the interest of his father" at this convention.[36] That Colonel Jarvis's motives were more than filial is suggested by the fact that he was secretary to John Graves Simcoe, Lieutenant Governor of Upper Canada, who had long been an advocate of "nursing" the British interests in Vermont.[37] In January 1794, just one month before the special convention of the diocese was held, Colonel Jarvis had entered into a private agreement with Governor Chittenden, in which Chittenden stated that he opposed war between Britain and the United States, declaring that it would be ruinous to the commerce and welfare of Vermont.[38] Apparently there was a connection between the special convention's sudden decision to elect Peters Bishop of Vermont and the Allen-Chittenden faction's renewal of friendly ties with the British in Canada.

Samuel Peters's subsequent correspondence confirms the suspicion that these Vermonters were reviving the separatist schemes which they had promoted earlier in the Haldimand negotiations and in the 1789 project. In March 1794, one month after the special convention elected him Bishop, Peters wrote a document entitled "Proposals from Vermont." In it he projected the establishment of Vermont as an independent republic, closely allied to Britain by political, commercial, and ecclesiastic ties. Specifically he stated that in case the anticipated war between the United States and Great Britain should materialize, Vermont would become a neutral nation, like a "Swiss Canton," provided Britain would make the following arrangements: 1. grant Vermonters the same commercial privileges as British subjects; 2. appoint a Protestant Episcopal bishop for Vermont and Canada; and 3. support Vermont's annexation of New York as far west as Niagara. Vermont in return would: 1. grant Britain possession of the western posts; 2. protect Canada from invasion by the United States; and 3. prevent other American states from sharing its commercial privileges in the British Empire.[39]

To what extent and at what point Lyon became involved in this separatist project cannot be precisely determined; but it appears almost certain that he did become a party to it, at some point between February 1794 and November 1795. Since no records were kept of the proceedings of the special convention of February 1794, whether Lyon participated in the election of Samuel Peters as bishop cannot be ascertained. It is a matter of record, however, that he did attend the diocese's 1795 convention, to which John A. Graham submitted a report from England on his unsuccessful attempts to secure the consecration of the Reverend Samuel Peters as Bishop of Vermont.[40] The following day, November 14, 1795, Lyon wrote Peters a warm letter expressing the continuing desire of Vermont Episcopalians to have him as their bishop and describing new efforts to have him consecrated in the United States. In this revealing letter Lyon not only thanks Samuel Peters for his "kind attention to my particular friend and favorite," John A. Graham, but also, in an even more incriminating passage, states, "I have lately heard from Col. Jarvis he anxiously expects you to America[;] so we all do and may God have you in his Special Keeping until that time."[41]

The fact that Lyon exchanged correspondence with Colonel Jarvis, secretary to Canada's Lieutenant Governor Simcoe, leaves little room for doubt that he was a participant in the separatist schemes plotted by Levi and Ira Allen, Governor Chittenden, Lieutenant Governor Simcoe, and Colonel William Jarvis. At the time Lyon wrote Samuel Peters, war with England was still a possibility, since the Jay Treaty, which eventually precluded such a war, was then an issue of passionate controversy both in the House of Representatives and in the country at large. In the event of such a war, it appears that Lyon was among those Vermonters who sought to link Vermont to Canada, as an ally of Great Britain rather than a foe.

How, if at all, can Lyon's support of this pro-British alliance be reconciled with his hostility to British monarchism, his support of the French Revolution, and his approval, and possible overt support, of Genet's attempts to instigate a revolutionary uprising against the British in Canada? It is in keeping with Lyon's opportunism that he could have supported both adventures simultaneously, since the practical objectives of both were closely related. If either succeeded, Vermont and Canada would be linked as an economic unit. If Lyon were ideologically consistent, he probably would have preferred a revolutionary uprising in Canada as the means of annexing lower Canada to Vermont. In addition to the economic and political advantages derived from such a conquest, it would have represented a victory of Republicanism over monarchy.

On the other hand, the separatist project also was congenial to Lyon's brand of Republicanism. Had it succeeded, it would have resulted in Vermont's becoming an independent, self-governing republic, allied to Britain only by commercial and political treaties. This would have extricated Vermont from the threat Lyon most dreaded, that of being swallowed up by what he alleged to be the aristocratic centralized government of the United States. As late as May 1794, in a letter complaining of the power of the federal courts, Lyon denounced the loss of self-government in the States under the Constitution, claiming, "the laws of Congress are declared to be the Supreme laws of the land. . . . Should Congress exercise their full power what power would be left to be exercised by the States? The republican government so guaranteed would be a name without a reality. The States would be consolidated into one great State and each corporation may arbitrate some small matters among themselves—Thus the States are saddled by their own act; and must bear patiently the whip of their riders!!" (FL, May 27, 1794).

So weak was Lyon's sense of nationhood, so strong was his sense of local self-government, that in the 1790s he apparently was prepared to give up the one for the other. This represents Republicanism carried to the extreme of folly, an extreme, however, to which many Federalists of the time also were prepared to go, if elements they feared should gain control of the national government. The Reverend Samuel Williams, arch-Federalist and editor of the *Rutland Herald*, expressed these sentiments during the upheaval over the Jay Treaty: "Be assured we will reject the federal Union before we will be governed in the Country by the mobs of Philadelphia, New York or Boston. Moderation in such a case would be an error."[42]

To be charitable, one might concede that Lyon's localism was a reflection of his limited political experience, which thus far had been confined to the affairs of the state of Vermont. Yet Lyon wrote and thought internationally. It is conceivable that, in the worldwide struggle for Republicanism, he viewed the Federalist-controlled government of the United States as an opponent of the self-governing principles for which he strove. Indeed this is the position he soon adopted in Congress, as the Democratic-Republican representative from western Vermont.

8

A Lyon in the House

That the deliberations of the Fifth Congress would provoke unprecedented conflict may well have occurred to Lyon even before he departed from Vermont. President John Adams's urgent call for a special session of Congress should have alerted him to this eventuality; if it did not, the message that the President delivered to the new Congress on May 15, 1797, rang the alarm. In this speech, Adams told of a new emergency in the country's relations with France, which necessitated placing the nation in a state of military preparedness. The immediate cause of this crisis was the French Directory's refusal to receive Charles Cotesworth Pinckney as the United States' new Minister to France.[1]

Underlying France's action was her hostile interpretation of the American foreign policy following the signing of the Jay Treaty, and the subsequent recall of France's friend, James Monroe, as Minister to France. Both of these policies convinced the French that those in charge of the federal government of the United States supported England in the war between Britain and France. Accusing the United States of abrogating the 1778 Treaty of Alliance and Commerce with France, the French not only proceeded to break off diplomatic relations with the United States, but also followed the British example of seizing American vessels at sea.[2]

Lyon maintained that the Jay Treaty "is all the bone of contention," and he therefore attributed France's actions to the hostile foreign policies of the Federalists.[3] To him, and to Republicans generally, John Adams's *Opening Message* to the Fifth Congress added fuel to the war flames already lit by the Federalists. They approved of Adams's stated determination to send another mission to France to attempt further negotiations, but they objected to the self-righteous claims that the United States had been just and impartial in her foreign policies, and they vehemently opposed Adams's recommendations for strengthening the army and navy. In the heated two-week debate over the *Reply to the Presidential Address*, Republican leaders in the House insisted that the French had "legitimate causes of complaint" against the United States and urged an amendment to the *Reply* stating that the new negotiations should lead to placing "France on the footing of other countries."[4]

In the first remarks he ever uttered in Congress, Lyon moved to strike out the words "wisdom, dignity, and moderation" from a passage describing the conduct of the United States toward France, asserting that he "did not come there prepared to approve all the former acts of government, but for other purposes."[5] It was on the issue of delivering the House's *Reply* to the President, however, that Lyon took a stand which marked the beginning of his reputation as a Jacobin. It had become customary, during Washington's administration, to surround the presidential address with elaborate ceremonials. First, both houses composed lengthy addresses replying to the message of the chief executive; he then formally responded, after which all the members of Congress marched in procession through the streets of Philadelphia and deferentially waited upon the President at his residence. It was against this practice, derived from the monarchial ceremonials of the British Parliament, that Lyon took his controversial stand.

On June 3, he moved "that such members as do not chose to attend upon the President to present the Answer to his Speech, shall be excused." Explaining that he had consulted "both sides" on the subject, and that while the Federalists scoffed at him and the Republicans did not wish to offend the new President, he himself

> trusted our magnanimous President would, with the enlightened yeomanry of America despise such a boyish piece of business . . . he had spent a great part of his life amongst a people whose plainness of manners forbids all pageantry. . . . Were he acting in his own personal character, he perhaps might conform to the idle usage, but acting as he was for eighty thousand people, every father of a family in his district would condemn him for such an act.

As for himself, Lyon concluded, he "should have as great an objection to attend this business as a Quaker would to make his obeisance to a magistrate."[6]

To the Federalists, Lyon made a ludicrous spectacle of himself. Nathaniel Chipman, then a member of the Senate, wrote home to Vermont: "You cannot with all your knowledge of the man easily conceive how incredulous a figure he makes. . . . I think, however, he will be of use, as by choosing to take the seat among the Jacobins he will make many more doubtful men of that party ashamed of their association."[7]

Chipman's familiar antipathy to Lyon, the "new man" in politics, paralleled similar responses among his Federalist colleagues. Congressman John Allen, a member of the elitist "Litchfield Junto," who had received his training at Tapping Reeve's Litchfield Law School, famous as a "nursery for young Federalist lawyers,"[8] revealed the underlying social nature of the Federalists' aversion to Lyon. In a speech taking the opposite stand to Lyon's, Allen expressed confidence that "there was American blood enough in the House to approve of this clause, and American accent enough to pronounce it."[9]

Lyon was used to having this type of aspersion cast upon his Irish origins, particularly by the Congregationalist sons of Connecticut. Nathaniel Chipman, who also had trained for the law in Litchfield County, rarely let an occasion pass without reference to it.[10] But Allen's freshly inflicted wound incensed Lyon, and the following day he rose to challenge the very notion of American blood, stating that "before yesterday he never heard of gentlemen boasting of their blood in that House." Asserting that he had no objection "to gentlemen of high blood carrying this address," he declared that he himself "had no pretensions of high blood." However, he could say "that this was his country, because he had no other; and he owned a share of it, which he had bought by means of honest industry; he had fought for his country. In every day of trouble, he had repaired to her standard, and had conquered under it. Conquest had led his country to independence, and being independent, he called no man's blood in question."[11]

This speech captured the imaginations of a number of satirists, including St. John Honeywell, who wrote the following poem:

SPEECH OF A DEMOCRATIC LION

As still as mice the members sat
Expecting royal fun Sir
The speaker gently moved his hat
And Lion thus begun Sir.

I'm rugged Mat, the Democrat,
    Berate me as you please Sir,
True Paddy whack ne'er turn'd his back
    Or bowed his head to Caesar.

Refrain:
Horum, scorum vendum, roarum
Spittam, spattum, squirto,
Tag, rag, derry, merry, raw head and bloody bone,
Sing, Langolee nobody's hurt O!

The Yankee Crew, long since I knew,
    At home I duel them daily,
There's not a man, of all their Clan
    But knows my old Shelalee.

Refrain

The Gentry spout of ancient blood,
    It reddens all their Speeches,

> Zounds sir, my veins, contains as good
>   As theirs who hanged the witches.

Refrain

> We Lyon's bold, abominate
>   To court the great and wealthy
> I did it not in Vermont State
>   I shant in Philadelphia.

Refrain

> Nor was I to this Congress sent
>   To dress like Coxcomb fine, Sir,
> To cringe before the President
>   And taste his Cake and wine, Sir.

Refrain

> Go you who like such royal Cheer
>   And stalk in long procession
> I'll Stay and eat my luncheon here
>   As at the extra session.[12]

No one exceeded the derisive caricatures of William Cobbett, whose *Porcupine's Gazette* abounded with satirical allusions to the "beast" of Vermont. On June 6 it carried a squib describing the capture of the "Lyon" on the bogs of Hibernia, the exchange of this animal for a yoke of bulls, and its consequent domestication in the neighborhood of Governor Chittenden, whose daughter petted him like a monkey. Then, alluding to Lyon's maiden speech, the piece concludes: "It has been mentioned to cage him—as he has discovered much uneasiness at going with the crowd."[13]

While the Federalist press ridiculed Lyon, his own Republican newspaper in Vermont applauded his position. "Much has been said against the French Council of Agents ordering a Quaker to be turned out of their House, for obstinately persisting in keeping on his hat, contrary to the rules of the House," commented the *Farmers' Library.* "The high flying Federalists in this country reprobate their conduct and call it persecution, and yet would oblige citizen Lyon, one of the Members of the House of Representatives, to be dragged in procession before the President, although he has repeatedly declared that it was against his conscience and opinion to join in the ceremonial."[14]

Extreme as Lyon's position may have seemed, and as ludicrous a figure as he undoubtedly appeared to many, he nevertheless pointed up one of the glaring inconsistencies of American public life. These deferential ceremonies obviously were not in keeping with the spirit of a young, democratic republic. Undoubtedly Lyon later felt vindicated when Jefferson insisted upon eliminating royal ceremonies and attire during his administration, and most assuredly he would have been in his element at the inauguration ceremony initiated by Andrew Jackson.

Another issue upon which Lyon took a position in advance of his times arose when the Society of Quakers presented a Memorial to Congress, protesting "the oppressed state of our brethren of the African race." In particular, the Quakers called upon Congress to take action against the reenslavement of 135 North Carolina Negroes, whom members of the Society of Friends had freed. Declaiming against the "existing or retrospective laws" that permitted these freedmen to be "again reduced into cruel bondage," the Memorial also urged Congress to abolish the slave trade, reminding its members that in 1774 the Continental Congress had made a "solemn engagement" to do so.[15]

Immediately the Southern Federalists rose to protest this memorial. John Rutledge, Jr., whose father had fought successfully in the Constitutional Convention for the extension of the slave trade until 1808, condemned the Quakers for inciting insurrections of "similar enormities" to the French Revolution. Robert Goodloe Harper insisted that "this and every other Legislature, ought to set their faces against any remonstrances complaining of what it was utterly impossible to alter."

Lyon, the first of the Republican Congressmen to contest the upholders of slavery, chastised Harper for not attending to the subject matter of the petition. "There was a grievance complained óf," Lyon insisted, "which certainly ought to be remedied, viz: that a number of black persons who had been set at liberty by their masters, were now held in slavery, contrary to right." Lyon maintained that this was indeed an appropriate subject of congressional inquiry; in this he was joined by Albert Gallatin and Edward Livingston. The former asserted that one way Congress could limit the importation of slaves was by imposing a ten dollar duty on each, and the latter maintained that emancipation itself was an appropriate topic for congressional debate, although he doubted that a remedy could be reached.

While this discussion sheds significant light on the intensity of passions over the slavery issue during the era of the Federalist-Republican conflict, it was not one of the main controversies of the Fifth Congress. The principal conflicts took place over implementing the military recommendation proposed by John Adams in his presidential address. Increased revenue was needed for this program, and the Federalists proposed a Stamp Act as one method of raising it. Lyon warned his colleagues that "a stamp tax would go out with a bad name" and took a firmly egalitarian position on taxation in general, maintaining that he would only support such measures as "bear equally on all classes of men."[16] He therefore supported John Nicholas's amendment to strike out the clause exempting bank notes from stamp duties, declaring, "Those who issued these notes got a good profit from them and . . . it was, therefore, reasonable they should pay their proportion towards the support of the government."[17] In a similar vein he tried to prevent the Stamp Act from imposing hardships on those of modest means, proposing that if land deeds be subject to the stamp tax, purchases of small lots should be excluded.[18] When it came to a tax on salt, Lyon opposed it outright as "unjust and unreasonable," bearing hardest on the farmers who used vast amounts of salt, not for consumption but primarily for curing their meats.[19]

A twenty dollar tax on naturalization certificates was another revenue-raising measure proposed by the Federalists. Lyon correctly assailed this Act as a device to discourage immigration and eloquently opposed such a move, declaring, "We had told the world, that there was in this country a good spring of liberty, and invited all to come and drink of it. We had told them that the country was rich and fertile, and invited them to come and taste of our fruits." Now, he continued, we "turn around to them and say, you shall not be admitted as citizens unless you pay twenty dollars." He claimed that this looked like entering into a treaty with the monarch of Britain to prevent his subjects from leaving the country, and he almost suspected that the measure was introduced "on the suggestion of a certain foreign Minister."[20]

This last charge of Lyon's was incorrect, as was borne out later that day by the representative from Massachusetts, Harrison Gray Otis, who made it perfectly clear that it was the Federalists, rather than the British, who initiated the move to close America's gates to foreigners. Otis openly announced that "he did not wish to invite hordes of wild Irishmen nor the turbulent and disorderly of all parts of the world to come here with a view to disturb our tranquility, after having succeeded in the overthrow of their own Governments."[21] His fellow Federalist from South Carolina, Robert Harper, went so far as to advocate that "no man should become a citizen of this country but by birth."[22]

Obviously this wave of nativism carried ill forebodings for the congressman of Irish descent. There were several signs, during the congressional recess that began in July of 1797, that trouble for Lyon was brewing in the Federalist camp. On August 1 *Porcupine's Gazette* attacked him for abusing his franking privilege by sending over two hundred letters a week to his constituents and enclosing in them copies of Benjamin Franklin Bache's *Aurora*. The concluding paragraph furnished the clue to future harassments: "This is the redoubtable hero who, a few years before was sold for his passage from Ireland, and who for his cowardice in the American war, was condemned by General Gates to wear a wooden sword."[23]

Suddenly, twenty-one years after the event, Cobbett was reviving the Jericho incident of the American Revolution in which Lyon's company mutinied and he temporarily was cashiered from the Continental Army (see chapter 2). It seems more than a coincidence that back in Vermont,

Senator Nathaniel Chipman also brought up this incident. Specifically, he asked Lyon "if he did not expect that this ridiculous speech in Congress, relative to the Address, would bring up the wooden sword?" In the course of the ensuing conversation, Lyon made it clear that "if anyone at Philadelphia, or if any member of Congress . . . should insult him with it, or pretend to mention it to him, it should not pass with impunity." Chipman took no pains to prevent any allusion to the insult from occurring. On the contrary, according to his own testimony, he repeated the above conversation "more than once" after they returned to Philadelphia. On one such occasion, the remarks fell upon the very receptive ears of Congressman Roger Griswold of Connecticut, who soon made use of it.[24]

The date was January 30, 1798. There was a lull in the proceedings of the House, while ballots were being counted for the Managers of the Impeachment against William Blount. The Speaker of the House, Jonathan Dayton of New Jersey, took a seat next to the railing and engaged in conversation with Matthew Lyon, who stood outside the bar. In particular Dayton queried Lyon about Vermont's hostile response to the Stamp Act.[25] Apparently news had reached Congress that Liberty Polls were being erected all over the state.[26] Lyon took this occasion to comment upon the conservative character of the representatives from the state of Connecticut, declaring "that they acted in opposition to the interests and opinion of nine-tenths of their constituents" and that "they were pursuing their own private views, without regarding the interests of the people." After charging that the Connecticut representatives blinded and deceived their constituents by only presenting one point of view, Lyon claimed "that if he should go into Connecticut, and manage a press there six months, although the people of that State were not fond of revolutionary principles, he could effect a revolution, and turn out the present Representatives—."[27]

Roger Griswold, who was sitting within earshot of Lyon's pointed declamations, called out from his seat, "If you go into Connecticut, you had better wear your wooden sword."[28] It seems obvious that Griswold intended to provoke Lyon by this slur; he, however, had another explanation of his allusion to the "wooden sword" incident. Referring to Lyon's derogations against Connecticut's representatives, he wrote a friend:

> These observations did not excite in me any indignation—for I knew that the fellow had been considered by every person ever since he came into Congress as a meer beast and the fool of the play, and that nothing which he cou'd say wou'd make any impression on those who heard him, I therefore felt no indignation, but merely contempt . . . to have made a serious reply wou'd have been treating the fellow with more consequence than he deserved—to have resented the expression wou'd have been equally im-

proper—he was too despicable to be entitled to resentment—the idea which occurred was to say something which shou'd excite a laugh in the Company and in that way put an end to such improper observations—the story of the wooden sword naturally presented itself.[29]

When Lyon chose to ignore Griswold's reference to the wooden sword, either Griswold or New York's Congressman David Brooks, who was sitting next to Griswold, commented that Lyon did not hear the remark. At this point Griswold walked up to Lyon, and to make sure he was heard this time, laid his hand on Lyon's arm.[30] Again Griswold asked Lyon if he intended fighting the people of Connecticut with his wooden sword. In reply, Lyon turned to Griswold and spat into his face.

Thus occurred the first public scandal in Congress. Immediately a motion to expel Matthew Lyon for "gross indecency" was made by Samuel Sewall of Massachusetts.[31] The House formed a Committee on Breach of Privilege, which held hearings to investigate the circumstances surrounding this affront to the dignity of this august body.[32] For fourteen days the House debated the pros and cons of expelling Lyon. As Edward Livingston summarized the proceedings, "Gentlemen rose to express their abhorrence of abuse in abusive terms, and their hatred of indecent acts with indecency."[33]

Lyon offered a humble letter of apology to the Speaker of the House, stating that "I feel it incumbent on me to obviate the imputation of intentional disrespect. Permit me, sir, through you, to assure the House of Representatives that I feel as much as any of its members the necessity of preserving the utmost decorum in its proceedings." He went on to explain that he was under the impression that since the House was "not formally constituted and not engaged in actual business" when the incident occurred, it did not "claim any superintendance over its members. . . . If I had been mistaken in my understanding on this subject, I beg the House to believe that my fault had been without intention, and that I am very sorry that I have deserved its censure."[34]

The felicity of this wording suggests that Lyon's Virginia colleagues may have assisted him in composing it. At the time, he resided at a lodging house with other committed Republicans, including Stevens T. Mason, the son of George Mason, who earlier had divulged the guarded secrets of the Jay Treaty to the *Aurora*, as well as Colonel Cabell and two Congressmen from Virginia.[35] One of these may have been the Republican spokesman John Nicholas, whom Albert Gallatin described as "the most modest, the most decent, the most dedicated man" he had ever met. When John Nicholas alone dared "to extenuate the indecency" of Lyon's act, while the Federalists were "tremblingly alive to the least indelicate and vulgar expression of the Vermonter," Gallatin concluded that the entire proceeding was "nothing more than an affected cant of pretended delicacy or the offspring of bitter party spirit."[36]

Indeed party rivalry was at the core of the proceedings to expel Lyon. The Federalists seized upon Lyon's "indecency" as a means of reducing the Republicans' ranks one by one. According to Jefferson, who regarded the entire proceedings as disgusting, "to get rid of his vote was the most material object."[37] Connecticut Congressman Dana's speech, in which he assailed Lyon as a "kennel of filth" to be discarded "as citizens removed impurities and filth from their docks and wharves," was the culmination of two weeks of Federalist vilifications.[38] The degree of humiliation that Lyon experienced would be difficult to calculate. Maligned as a coward, he felt compelled to explain in detail the extenuating circumstances attending the Jericho incident, and presented to Congress a lengthy narrative of his subsequent military and civilian achievements, in justification of his righteous indignation over Griswold's accusation of cowardice.[39]

By and large the Republicans considered Lyon justified in resenting Griswold's deliberate insult, although they hardly could condone the manner or the place he chose to express his injured feelings.[40] Therefore they proposed substitute resolutions to censure his conduct in the House, and even to commit him to the Sergeant at Arms. However, expulsion was the sole object of the Federalists, and against this move the Republicans rallied, to a man. In the fourteen days of acrimonious debate, such Republican luminaries as Nicholas, Macon, Livingston, and Gallatin rose to speak in the Vermonter's defense. Macon opened the debate by declaring that such a punishment was equal to death itself, and Gallatin concluded it by pointing out that Congress was not a fashionable club but a representative body, which had no right to deprive Lyon's district of its representative because its members did not like his manners. In the end the Federalists were unable to muster the two-thirds vote necessary for expulsion. Forty-four Republicans held firm and kept Lyon in the House; they defeated the motion by a vote of 52 for expulsion and 44 against.[41]

Throughout the country, newspapers teemed with caricatures and verses inspired by the fiasco in Congress. Overnight Lyon became a notorious public figure, lampooned as "Spitting Matt," "The Lyon of Vermont," "Matt, the Democrat," "The Spitting Hero," and "The Democratic Lion."[42] In an attempt to counter this adverse publicity, Lyon wrote to his constituents: "Perhaps some will say I did not take the right method with him. We do not always possess the power of judging calmly what is the best mode of resenting an unpardonable insult. Had I borne it patiently I should have been bandied about in all the newspapers on the continent which are supported by British money and federal patronage, as a mean poltroon. The district which sent me would have been scandalized."[43]

Lyon was justified in his concern over his district. The ardent Massachusetts Federalist N. Van Schaack jubilantly wrote Congressman Theodore Sedgwick: "I have conversed with people of all grades in Vermont since I wrote you last and I can assure you that I have not con-

A typical example of caricatures which appeared in newspapers throughout the country following Griswold's verbal attack on Lyon in which he insinuated that Lyon was a coward; Lyon responded by spitting in Griswold's face. The incident occurred in the House of Representatives on January 30, 1798. (Titled "Ve----t Politness," this etching shows a lion with a wooden sword attacking Griswold, who comments: "What a beastly action." Porcupine at left says: "My Quills shall pierce, and my Press shall block you.")

versed with a man so lost to decency to utter a syllable by way of extenuation of Lyon's brutal behavior where the facts relative to it were
known. . . . As I possessed the prominent facts, I found little or no difficulty to put the matter in a clear point of light and I have the pleasure
to tell you that I have not been an unprofitable traveller either as to my
own concerns or as a labourer in the federal vineyard."[44]

On the same day another offended Massachusetts gentleman wrote
Congressman Harrison Gray Otis: "You have the honor of outdoing the
National Convention, and are in a fair way to becoming an assembly of
Gladiators— . . . I feel grieved that the saliva of an Irishman should be
left upon the face of an American and He, a New Englandman." This
correspondent further expressed deep concern about how Griswold
would avenge his honor, stating, "The world say[s] he must beat him
either in or out of the House. One or the other for his own sake."[45]

No Federalist was more anxious than Griswold himself "to avenge my
own wrong." He wrote to a friend, "The House by their decision had
sanctioned violence within those walls where the insult was offered
—that was the proper place of doing it."[46] Having so decided, Griswold
went to McCallister's store on Chestnut Street, and purchased a strong,
yellow, hickory walking stick.[47] Then, on February 15, he took his
revenge. He described the episode:

> As soon as I saw him [Lyon] in his seat I took my cane and walked across the
> floor in front of the speakers chair, which is more than forty feet in
> extent.—He saw me before I struck him, and was endeavoring to draw a
> sword cane when I gave him the first blow—I call'd him a scoundrel &
> struck him with my cane, and pursued him with more than twenty blows on
> his head and back until he got possession of a pair of tongues [tongs], when I
> threw him down and after giving him several blows with my fist, I was
> taken off by his friends—.[48]

Griswold continued, "he was very much bruised— . . . & with blood
running down his face was really more the object of compassion than
anything else—Mr. Sitgreaves however handed me my cane & I might
perhaps have given him a second beating but the House was called to
order and thus ended the disorder—."[49]

And so it was that twice within the space of one month the House of
Representatives was the scene of physical combat between two of its
members. The passions displayed reflected not only the heat of party
conflict but the extreme class animosities harbored by Griswold and his
Federalist colleagues. Griswold, after all, was one of the "Connecticut Illuminati," related to the illustrious Wolcott family.[50] Little wonder that
in further describing Lyon to his friend, he should write: "The other
stories of his being sold for his passage from Ireland, etc. etc. are likewise
true—in short that he is literally one of the most ignorant contemptible
and brutal fellows in Congress—and that is saying a great deal—."[51]

This etching, "Congressional Pugilists," is one of several cartoons depicting the physical confrontation between Griswold and Lyon that subsequently occurred in the House of Representatives.

>(Verse: "He in a trice struck Lyon thrice
>Upon his head, enrag'd Sir,
>Who seiz'd the tongs to ease his wrongs,
>And Griswold thus engag'd Sir."

Below right: "Congress Hall, in Philadᵃ.,Feb. 15, 1798, S.E. Cor. 6ᵗʰ & Chestnut Sᵗ." Names at top and left: "1. Jonᵃ Dayton, Speaker; 2. Jonᵃ W. Condy, Clerk; 3. Rev. Ashbel Green, Chaplain.")

Despite the fact that Griswold's deliberate assault upon Lyon was a much more flagrant abuse of decorum in the House than Lyon's spontaneous act, the Federalists' sensibilities were no longer affronted. The committee that previously had recommended Lyon's expulsion now concluded that neither Griswold nor Lyon should be expelled for converting the House into a "gladiators' " arena. By a vote of 73 to 21, the House upheld the committee's recommendation.[52] One of the few committee members who put principle above party considerations was Congressman Kittera, who wrote Chairman John Rutledge, Jr., that although he was inclined to "support whatever measures my friends may think best to be adopted to promote the public good, I do however still think the honor and the dignity of this government call for the expulsion of both."[53]

With the conclusion of the debates over the expulsion of its contending members, tranquility momentarily appeared to return to the House. The Lyon-Griswold fracas, however, was merely a reflection of the much graver ideological battles being waged in Congress over foreign affairs. Lyon was among those staunch Republicans whose dedication to peace with France approached the proportions of a crusade. In July 1797 he was one of the fifty Congressmen who attended the banquet that enthusiastically welcomed home the discharged Republican Minister to France, James Monroe.[54] Held at Oeller's Hotel in Philadelphia, the celebrated banquet was attended by such notables as General Horatio Gates, Thomas Jefferson, Edward Livingston, and Albert Gallatin. There Lyon joined the assembled gathering in drinking to the freedom of Ireland and toasting "Charles James Fox and the Patriots of England." The hero of the hour, of course, was James Monroe, whom Edward Livingston toasted as "the virtuous citizen who, to keep the peace of the country, refuses to do justice to himself."[55]

Spurred on by the conviction that Monroe would have prevented the existing rupture with France, the Republicans successfully obstructed every major Federalist proposal to place the United States on a war footing against French designs, between November 1797 and February 1798.[56] Apparently nothing but a dire emergency could have enabled the Federalists to put across their program. This the French inadvertently provided.

In March President Adams announced that dispatches from the latest American envoys to France made it clear that hope for peaceful negotiations with France was at an end and that immediate measures of defense must be passed.[57] What the dispatches contained the President did not disclose in his public messages, but the Federalist members of his cabinet and their confidante, Alexander Hamilton, were fully aware of the dynamite contained in them. Realizing that disclosure of the dispatches' contents would win support for war measures, the Federalists demanded their publication.[58] The Republicans, in complete ignorance of their contents, also demanded their production, suspecting that the dispatches contained "resentful expressions of the French respecting our Cabinet."[59]

Of all the Republicans, Matthew Lyon was the most impetuous and naive in his demand for the publication of the dispatches. With the rest of the members of Congress, he sat behind closed doors for three days and heard their guarded, secret contents revealed. In brief, he learned that Talleyrand's agents, designated as X, Y, and Z, had proposed that France would resume negotiations only if the United States would comply with the following conditions: 1. pay a bribe, "a douceur for t[h]e pocket," of fifty thousand sterling to Talleyrand's Directory; 2. advance the French government a large loan; 3. offer adequate apologies for the hostile remarks John Adams made in his presidential address.[60]

While the Federalists gloated over these unscrupulous revelations, the Republicans responded with confusion, incredulity, and disillusion. Although they saw no new grounds for war in the XYZ disclosures, they realized that the public easily could be persuaded that the nation's honor was at stake.[61] Matthew Lyon alone considered the papers "so trifling and unimportant that no printer would risk the printing of them in a pamphlet."[62] When it came to suggesting how many copies of the dispatches Congress should order printed, the Delaware Federalist, Bayard, proposed twelve hundred; his South Carolina colleague, Harper, thought three thousand would be more adequate. The "Vermont Lyon" cavalierly called for the printing of seven thousand.[63]

Lyon soon regretted his mistake as the formerly pro-French population reversed its sentiments and rallied to the war slogan "Millions for defense but not one cent for Tribute."[64] The Federalist press whipped the country into a state of frenzy over the French menace with such claims as "the eyes of the devouring monsters are upon us," and "horrid, outlandish sans-culotte Frenchmen" threaten "your houses and farms with fire, plunder and pillage! and your wives and sweethearts with ravishment and assassination."[65] Porcupine warned. "We do not wish to divide our property with idlers, nor daily to tremble at the guillotine."[66] The country was further aroused by the belligerent war tones in the speeches of President Adams, who proclaimed May 9, 1798, as the day for "Public Humiliation, Fasting and Prayer Throughout the United States." As the people of the country solemnly attended church services and heard sermons against French atheism, rumors spread that the French were about to set fire to Philadelphia.[67] France herself bolstered the arguments to gird for war by her increased depredations on the sea.

Before April 1798, the Republicans in Congress had been able to temporize the Federalists' demands for military expenditures, but the tide had turned decisively in the Federalists' favor after the XYZ disclosures. Public opinion now supported war measures, and the Republicans fought a valiant but losing battle in their attempt to prevent provocative legislation leading toward open warfare with France. Lyon took an active part in these tense proceedings, rising repeatedly to argue against the provisional army, direct taxes, and suspension of both the Franco-American Treaty of Alliance and commercial relations with France.[68]

Essentially Lyon and his Republican colleagues took a strong stand not only against war with France but against any involvement in the wars of Europe. Lyon's isolationism was made abundantly clear in a lengthy letter to his constituents in which he stated: "We felt strong in ourselves, and unconquerable in our internal situation; but external and offensive war, we could not consider to be the occupation, the business, or the interest of Americans, who have neither men nor money to spare, nor a taste for conquest." He then went on to point out to his farmer constituents that the essential purpose of such "an endless and useless contest" concerned "a commerce in which but a small part of the community is interested. We could not but be sensible that the cost of the war must fall on the landed interest. . . . We foresaw that many millions would be sunk." As far as the defense of American commerce was concerned, Lyon maintained that although he wished for markets for all the country's spare products, "and I am willing . . . that Americans should be our carriers, if they choose; but I am not so attached to that commerce . . . as to consent to involve my country in an everlasting war, for the mere name of defending it without the power. I had much rather leave the carriage of the produce of this country to foreigners" (SA, Oct. 1, 1798).

Lyon's viewpoint, of course, was completely antithetical to that of the Federalists, most of whom represented the commercial interests. Despite the fact that the Jay Treaty had not resolved the problem of British depredations on American commerce, the Federalists' sympathies and commercial ties were with the British. Conversely, they were determined to oppose by force French attacks on American commerce. During the spring and summer of 1798 they succeeded in passing legislation that provided appropriations for a navy, a provisional army totaling fifty thousand men, and new, direct taxes to pay for the war expenditures.[69]

The war cloud that hung over the country provided the Federalists with the opportunity they needed to undermine their political enemies at home as well. In this same session they passed four repressive laws, popularly known as the Alien and Sedition Acts. Of these, the most effective, in terms of striking at the political opposition, was the Sedition Act. Using the pretext of a pending war with France, the Federalists took the occasion to attempt to repress the Jeffersonian-Republican Party, whose growth throughout the 1790s threatened their power and elitist philosophy. The arch-Federalist from Massachusetts, Theodore Sedgwick, expressed the thinking of his political colleagues when he wrote that the XYZ disclosures "will afford a glorious opportunity to destroy faction. Improve it."[70]

Sedgwick's prophecy was fulfilled the following summer when the Senate made the Fourth of July a date of double historic significance by passing the Sedition Act. None had been more vocal in the clamor for the act than John Allen, who had previously expressed his contempt for Matthew Lyon's social origins. His arguments for passage of the act foreshadowed the grounds upon which Lyon and leading Republican publishers would be prosecuted. "I believe," he declared, "there are men in this country, in this House, whose hatred and abhorrence of our Government leads them to prefer another, profligate and ferocious as it is." He added that it was through the Republican press that a "flood of calumny is constantly poured forth against those whom the people have chosen as the government of the nation."[71]

The final law, revised considerably by the House, made it a criminal offense, punishable by imprisonment and heavy fines, to write, publish, or utter anything of a "false, scandalous or malicious" nature against the government, Congress, or the President of the United States with intent to defame them, bring them into contempt or disrepute, or excite against them the hatred of the people.[72] Several features of the Act departed from those of British common law regarding seditious libel: the Sedition Act allowed a defendant to prove the truth of his statements as a defense against the charge of libel, and it gave the jury, instead of the judge, the power to decide whether statements constituted seditious libel.

Because of these provisions the Federalist defenders of the Act maintained that it was remarkably lenient and humane. Nevertheless they proclaimed their belief in the basic British common law doctrine of seditious libel inherent in the Act's major provisions. Representative Otis succinctly expressed their philosophy when he stated, "liberty of the press is merely an exemption from all previous restraints." Although the Constitution guaranteed "the liberty of writing, publishing and speaking one's thoughts," he argued, it did so "under the condition of being answerable to the injured party, whether it be the Government or an individual, for false, malicious and seditious expressions."[73] This was the thrust of the arguments made by other leading Federalist speakers, Robert Goodloe Harper, John Allen, and Samuel Dana.[74]

It was in the press, rather than on the floor of the House, that Lyon chose to express his views on this crucial legislation. Because the Reverend Dr. Samuel Williams, editor of the *Rutland Herald*, refused to publish Lyon's letter to his constituents, Lyon launched a new Republican magazine, which he entitled *The Scourge of Aristocracy*.[75] In this as well as other publications, he opposed the Sedition Act with arguments that closely resembled the contents, though hardly the style, of the civil liberties position taken by prominent Republicans in Congress.

"A sedition bill is talked of in Congress," he wrote on June 20. "Its advocates say it is calculated to suppress the villainous falsehoods which men of base principles are circulating against the constituted authorities. However, it might tend to check the fulminations of such wretches as attack me, I do not propose to vote for it, as it will tend to prevent due investigation; nor shall I fear after it is passed, to expose the truth in my usual way to my constituents."[76] While not alluding to the First Amendment, as Gallatin did in his speech of July 10, Lyon here defends the concept of freedom of speech and insists on the right to criticize the government and its officials, no matter what the latter's political persuasions may be. This was quite the opposite of the position taken by John Allen and other Federalist spokesmen, who clearly indicated that they considered the political views of their Republican opponents as seditious libel.[77] While Gallatin pointed out in the House that the real purpose of the bill was "to enable one party to oppress the other,"[78] Lyon stated in his magazine (SA, Oct. 1, 1798): "Everyone who is not in favor of this mad war is branded with the epithet of Opposers of Government, disorganizers, Jacobins, etc."

Elsewhere Lyon warned that under the Sedition Act people "had better hold their tongues and make toothpicks of their pens."[79] In less colorful language, John Nicholas of Virginia developed this point, while demolishing the argument that truth was a defense under the Act, and therefore publishers of true statements would not be convicted for seditious libel. Anything offensive to the government, he insisted, invariably would be interpreted as false. Printers would refrain from publishing anything questionable, for fear of their inability to prove "truth to the satisfaction of a court of justice."[80]

Lyon too ridiculed "those poor creatures" who believe "the law must be mild" because of the "section which allows the person prosecuted to give the truth of a matter." He added that other "Aristos," a little more knowing, claim that the purpose of this law is "only to punish such persons as are found guilty of abusing and vilifying their rulers—If this proposition were true, which is by no means the case," Lyon continued,"what confidence ought to be placed in men who legislate on matters, which the Constitution they have sworn to support, forbids them meddling with on the firm hypothesis that the laws of the several states are ample and sufficient on the subject"(SA, Oct. 1, 1798).

Here Lyon raised one of the constitutional arguments brought up by Edward Livingston during the heated House debate. The New York Republican maintained, "There is a remedy for offences of this kind in the laws of every State in the Union. Every man's character is protected by law, and every man who shall publish a libel on any part of the Government, is liable to punishment."[81]

This constitutional argument used by Lyon and Livingston was also made by the leading Republican spokesmen of the period including Jefferson, Gallatin, Nicholas, and Macon.[82] Because they interpreted the Sedition Act as unconstitutional, partly on the grounds that the power to pass laws restraining personal and political libels was reserved to the states, it has been asserted by Leonard W. Levy that the Republicans "did not repudiate the concept of seditious libel and did not deny the power of the states to control speech and press." Although Levy concedes that this argument may have been used as a tactic to deny federal jurisdiction, he maintains that use of it was incompatible with an intention to exempt speech and press "from subsequent punishment for abuse."

Certain it is that the position of the Republicans was ambiguous. They accepted the doctrine of seditious libel, while at the same time insisting that the First Amendment protected freedom of speech and press. When the bill was first introduced, Jefferson wrote Madison: "They have brought into the lower house a sedition bill which among other enormities, undertakes to make printing certain matters criminal tho' one of the amendments of the Constitution has so expressly taken religion, printing press, etc. out of their coercion."[83] Albert Gallatin, in his closely reasoned arguments against the Federalists' "previous restraints" position, asserted that he had always understood that the First Amendment "provided against the passing of any law abridging either the liberty of the press or the freedom of speech." In an earlier passage he maintained that this restriction applied to "any real or supposed abuse of the press."[84]

Lyon's subsequent prosecution under the Sedition Act forced the Republicans in Congress to refine and enlarge their concept of the First Amendment. In chapter 10 we shall see how they analyzed in detail the contradictions between the doctrine of seditious libel and the principles of freedom of expression of dissenting opinion. In a later period Lyon declared unequivocally that the Sedition Act was unconstitutional on the sole grounds that it violated the First Amendment's protection of freedom of speech and press.[85] At the time the Act was passed, he instinctively acted on this assumption by refusing to submit to its restraints.

He left Philadelphia determined to continue his opposition to Federalist measures by candidly presenting his views to his constituents. That this was his right and duty, as a congressman standing for reelection, he had no doubt. That he would exercise this right at great personal risk immediately became apparent on his journey home. In New York a band of boisterous youths roamed the streets between 10:00 P.M. and midnight, demonstrating in front of the lodgings of Lyon, Gallatin, and Livingston. Singing "God Save the King," and hurling such epithets at the congressmen as "Jacobin," "Frenchman," and "Democrat,"[86] this crowd gave Lyon advance warning of the charged atmosphere in which he could expect to campaign.

9

On Trial for Sedition

The tensions engendered in the election campaign of 1798 reached their climax in a courtroom in western Vermont. There Congressman Matthew Lyon was the first to stand trial under the Sedition Act.[1]

Long before his return to Vermont in July, Lyon had begun to campaign for reelection from Congress. As early as January, a prominent Massachusetts Federalist reported to Congressman Theodore Sedgwick, "In Vermont there is the devil to pay—Lyon's letters,' covering Bache's papers, have wrought a wonderful stock of Jacobinical principles—The poison is increasing and spreading even over the mountain—To judge of the present disposition Lyon will most assuredly be reelected and Governor Tichnor dropped." The letter went on to urge more vigorous action by Vermont Federalists in Congress, who should "condescend to write influential characters and explain the measures of Government." To expedite this urgent matter, the author volunteered to carry up any letter Nathaniel Chipman might wish to write.[2]

Several months later a scathing letter attacking Lyon as a corrupt Jacobin appeared in *Spooner's Vermont Journal* (May 28, 1798). The author, whose biting style bore Nathaniel Chipman's characteristic stamp, concluded his diatribe with the charge that Lyon was criminally guilty of acting in opposition to the Executive.

In a white heat, Lyon replied to Chipman's accusations in a letter to the editor, dated June 20. One of the passages contained the following acerbic remarks concerning his attitude toward the President:

> As to the Executive, when I shall see the efforts of that power bent on the promotion of the comfort, the happiness, and accommodation of the people, that Executive shall have my zealous and uniform support. But when I see every consideration of the public welfare swallowed up in a continual grasp for power, in an unbounded thirst for ridiculous pomp, foolish adulation, or selfish avarice; when I shall behold men of real merit daily turned out of office for no other cause but independence of sentiment; when I shall see men of firmness, merit, years, abilities, and experience, discarded on their application for office, for fear they possess that independence; and men of

meanness preferred for the ease with which they take up and advocate opinions, the consequence of which they know but little of; when I shall see the sacred name of religion employed as a State engine to make mankind hate and persecute one another, I shall not be their humble advocate.[3]

This passage was soon to become Count One in Lyon's indictment under the Sedition Act. Ironically, Lyon concluded this letter with his warning that Congress was considering a Sedition Bill and that he intended to ignore it because it prevented "due investigation" and exposure of the truth to the electorate.

Upon his return to Vermont, Lyon lived up to these words by ignoring the threat of the Sedition Act, and exposing "the truth" to his constituents. One of the major emphases of his campaign was to clarify the Republicans' position concerning France. After the XYZ disclosures, many of Lyon's former supporters were swept up in the general frenzy over the alleged threat of a French invasion. Lyon commented that the "noise" about the XYZ Papers "had answered the purposes of the aristocrats over the mountain completely to exasperate the unthinking people against every republican" (Lyon to Mason).

Avoidance of war was Lyon's keynote; reawakening the former feelings of attachment to France's Republicanism and opposition to British monarchism were among his main objects. While he was in Congress, he heard a letter read that ideally suited his purposes. It was written by the popular American poet Joel Barlow, the bard of the American and French Revolutions, who was then in France on both private and public business. The letter, addressed to Barlow's brother-in-law, Abraham Baldwin, a Republican congressman from Georgia, was a denunciation of President Adams's message to congress advocating preparedness for war with France. The letter struck Lyon as an informative "statement of the causes of the differences between this country and France" (SA, Dec. 15, 1798); he obtained permission to copy it on the proviso that he not publish it. The key paragraph of the letter, which later was to constitute Counts Two and Three of Lyon's indictment under the Sedition Act, read as follows:

> The misunderstanding between the two Governments has become extremely alarming, confidence is completely destroyed, mistrusts, jealousy, and a disposition to a wrong attribution of motives, are so apparent as to require the utmost caution in every word and action that are to come before your Executive—I mean if your object is to avoid hostilities. Had this truth been understood with you before the recall of Monroe, before the coming and second coming of Pinckney; had it guided the pens that wrote the bullying Speech of your President, and stupid answer of your Senate, at the opening of Congress in November last, I should probably have had no occasion to address you this letter. But when we found him borrowing the language of Edmund Burke, and telling the world that, although he should succeed in treating with the French, there was no dependence to be placed on any of

their engagements; that their religion and morality were at an end; that they had turned pirates and plunderers; and it would be necessary to be perpetually armed against them, though they are at peace; We wondered that the answer of both Houses had not been an order to send him to a madhouse. Instead of this, the Senate have echoed the Speech with more servility than ever George III experienced from either House of Parliament.[4]

Lyon read his copy of the Barlow letter to listeners in town after town as he campaigned throughout western Vermont. A glimpse into the tension surrounding Lyon's campaign can be gleaned from the trial testimony of two young Federalists who claimed that Lyon's reading of the Barlow letter had caused a tumult at Middletown. Lyon accused them "of following me on purpose to cause a disturbance" (Lyon to Mason). Apparently the incendiary issues of the day were argued in the town squares, and partisan feelings flared high.

In this atmosphere Lyon carried on his crusade for Republicanism, knowing full well its potential dangers. Expecting the worst from his enemies, it probably came as no surprise to him when a friend appeared at his home on October 5 to warn him that steps were being taken to indict him for violating the Sedition Act. When the bill was before Congress, Lyon had told his colleague Senator Stevens T. Mason "that it was doubtlessly intended for the members of Congress, and very likely would be brought to bear on me the very first" (Lyon to Mason).

His Vermont friend urged Lyon "to be out of the way of being taken" because the jurymen had been selected from towns unfriendly to Lyon. Twelve out of the fourteen selected had opposed Lyon in the last election, he warned, and there were "several zealous partisans for Presidential infallibility among them." Lyon thought better of this advice, and assured the deputy marshal "he need bring no posse . . . there should be no resistance." The following night the marshal appeared with the warrant for his arrest. Lyon appeared at the Rutland Court House at 9:00 the following morning. There he was called to the bar to hear the indictment of the Grand Jury (Lyon to Mason).

Describing Lyon as "a malicious and seditious person, and of a depraved mind and a wicked and diabolical disposition," [5] it charged him with violating the Sedition Act on three counts: (1) writing and procuring publication of the letter in *Spooner's Vermont Journal*; (2) the publication of Barlow's letter on September 1; and (3) the assisting, aiding, and abetting of the publication of Barlow's letter.

The indictment cited in full the passages quoted earlier in this chapter, charging that each contained "scandalous and seditious writing, or libel," and that Lyon "did with force and violence, wickedly, knowingly, and maliciously write, print, utter and publish" them. He did so with "intent and design to excite against the said Government and President the hatred of the good people of the United States, and to stir up sedition in the United States" by "deceitfully, wickedly and maliciously contriving . . . with intent and design to defame the said Government of the United States."[6]

The key words of the indictment, as far as the applicability of the Sedition Act is concerned, are "intent and design." Did Lyon, in uttering or writing the passages cited, *intend* to defame the President and government and stir up sedition? This issue was the nub of the trial.

Lyon emphatically pleaded not guilty to the charges of the indictment, but informed the court he was without counsel to defend his plea. The court offered to postpone the trial until the May session of the court in Windsor, but Lyon declined, feeling that in eastern Vermont the jury was bound to be completely hostile to him (Lyon to Mason). He therefore posted bonds of $1,000 for his appearance in court the following Monday. The two men who acted as surety for Lyon during the trial were Stephen Williams and Elias Buell, former president of the Rutland Democratic Society. Each put up $1,000 bail to assure the defendant's appearance before the court from day to day.[7] Their presence is one of the few indications in the trial record that anyone befriended Lyon during this time of crisis.

Over the weekend Lyon sent a messenger to Bennington to obtain the legal services of two prominent Republican lawyers, Messrs. Fay and Robinson. The messenger, delayed by the storms of the weekend, had not arrived when the court opened on Monday. When he finally did appear, he bore the tidings that neither lawyer could serve as counsel. Mr. Fay's wife was very ill, and Mr. Robinson was preparing to attend the session of the state legislature.

As a last resort, Lyon selected as his counsel his old rival, Israel Smith. Now a judge, Smith also was running against Lyon in the present election; but he was a Republican, and Lyon's friends prevailed upon him to assist Lyon (Lyon to Mason). According to *The Spectator*'s account of the trial, Smith "declined being particularly assigned as counsel, but at Mr. Lyon's desire he sat by him during the trial and advised." [8] Later in the campaign, Lyon accused Smith of opportunism in Congress and desertion of Republicanism (SA, Nov. 1, 1798). This leads to speculation on how cooperative the courtroom relationship between the two longstanding rivals really was. In any case, Lyon acted as his own attorney throughout the trial, cross-examining witnesses and pleading his own defense.

The trial opened on Monday, October 9. On the bench were the presiding judges: Associate Justice of the Supreme Court William Paterson, and District Judge Samuel Hitchcock, Lyon's principal opponent in the runoff election for congressman in 1796. The prosecuting attorney was Federal District Attorney Charles Marsh, who derived his "old school ideal of paternalistic government" from his training at Tapping Reeve's Litchfield Law School.[9]

Marsh's Litchfield background is not without significance. There was a curious link between the Litchfield environment and the Federalists whose animus toward Lyon was most pronounced. Nathaniel Chipman, for example, was also raised and trained for the law in Litchfield County. In Vermont, Charles Marsh was his close friend and political associate, leading one writer to suggest the possibility that Chipman instigated Marsh to bring Lyon to trial under the Sedition Act.[10] Congressman John Allen also illustrates the Litchfield connection. This graduate of the Litchfield Law School was actually present in the courtroom throughout Lyon's trial.[11] Allen's derisive opposition to Lyon in Congress, his strong advocacy of the Sedition Act, combined with his presence at the trial, suggests the possibility that he too may have played a role in securing Lyon's indictment. As a member of the Litchfield Junto,[12] Allen had close connections with a number of prominent personages who harbored a deep hatred of Lyon and deplored all that this former Litchfield indentured servant symbolized. Frederick Wolcott, brother-in-law of Roger Griswold and a leading figure in this junto, later that year involved himself in the concerted campaign against Lyon by incarcerating the Reverend Dr. John C. Ogden, who had petitioned the President to pardon the Vermont congressman (see chapter 10).

The question of the composition of the jury was the first matter to come before the court. In an open letter to his congressional ally Stevens T. Mason, Lyon maintained that the marshal, Jabez Fitch, had intentionally summoned the jurors "from towns that were particularly distinguished by their enmity to me," and that the jury was composed predominantly of "men who had been accustomed to speak ill of me." However, "of the fourteen jurymen before me I thought I saw one or two persons who knew me and would never consent to say that I was guilty of an intention of stirring up sedition." His plan was to "object off the inveterate part of the jury." When he challenged two of the jurors, Judge Paterson inquired, "For what reason?" Lyon replied that he thought he had a right to challenge a number of jurors without giving a reason. Astonishingly, the judge informed him that he had no such right and that he would have no such right in a similar case in the state court, commenting that Lyon did not know the laws of his own state. At the time, Lyon accepted the judge's ruling and comment, but while in jail he looked up the state laws and discovered that in state cases punishing individuals for defaming any court of justice or magistrate judge, the defendant could preemptively challenge six of the jurors without cause and any additional ones by showing good cause. Inferring that this was the state practice to which Judge Paterson referred, Lyon lamented, "Thus it may be seen how I have been dealt with about a jury" (Lyon to Mason).

Disadvantaged by his lack of professional legal representation, Lyon succeeded in eliminating only one juror, "who was shown to have been the author of an article in a newspaper, inveighing politically and personally against the defendant." Judge Paterson ruled: "The cause shown is sufficient, as a difference of this nature is a disqualification."[13]

District Attorney Marsh also challenged a juror, a Mr. Board. Marsh "produced one of the Deputy Sheriffs who had summoned the jury, who testified that he heard the juror say he thought Mr. Lyon would not, or should not, be condemned."[14] The judge disqualified him. Commented Lyon, "Thus was the only man sworn away that knew me enough to judge of my intentions" (Lyon to Mason).

As soon as the jury was sworn, Lyon interposed a plea challenging the jurisdiction of the court on the grounds that the Sedition Act was unconstitutional. Judge Paterson overruled the plea, but said Lyon could make use of the argument in another stage of the trial.

District Attorney Marsh opened the case by presenting Lyon's letter that had been published July 31 in *Spooner's Vermont Journal*. The letter was dated June 20, and bore the Philadelphia postmark July 7. Both these dates preceded the passage of the Sedition Act on July 14. The District Attorney interrogated two witnesses in an effort to prove that the letter did not reach the newspaper in Windsor until after July 14. Lyon reported, "The printer's boy thought it did not arrive until the 20th, and Mr. Buck saw the setting from it about the 23rd or later; I acknowledged the letter" (Lyon to Mason).

The technical problem facing the district attorney was to prove Lyon guilty of having violated the Sedition Act on the basis of the "libelous" contents of a letter that had been written before the Sedition Act was passed.

The purpose of the District Attorney's questions was to prove that the letter was published after the Sedition Act and that Lyon was responsible for procuring its publication. The Republicans subsequently insisted that this ex post facto application of the Sedition Act to Lyon's letter was a violation of Article 1 of the Constitution. As a member of the Constitutional Convention, Judge Paterson was particularly sensitive to this accusation, which he attempted to refute in an extensive correspondence with Congressman Joseph H. Nicholson. Acknowledging that "nothing can be more evident to a legal mind than that an indictment cannot be sustained under a statute for an offense perpetrated before the statute was made," he nevertheless insisted that the jury acted within the law. He gave as grounds for this assertion the fact that Lyon's letter was published on July 31, seventeen days after the Sedition Act was enacted, maintaining "that he, who procures another to publish a libel, becomes the publisher himself."[15]

In reply, Nicholson cogently argued, "I presume the only manner in which it is pretended that he procured the Printer to publish it, was by his letter dated in June in Philadelphia; at which time his Right to publish was not impaired—If then at that time he had a Right to print or publish, he certainly had a Right to Request another to print or publish, for the Right to do it himself would not exist without the Right to request another to do it likewise." In conclusion, Nicholson queried:

> What kind of presumption is that, which makes Mr. Lyon acquainted with a Law that had no existence at the time of his Request, punished him for knowingly and willingly violating its Provisions when it is impossible from the nature of things that he could be acquainted with them or that they could be known to anyone?[16]

Had Nicholson thus defended Lyon at the trial itself, it is doubtful that he would have dissuaded Justice Paterson from circumventing the ex post facto protections of the Constitution. According to Lyon's later account of the trial, "the party judge," after acknowledging that Lyon had written the letter before passage of the Sedition Act, admonished the jury to note that he was a member of Congress who knew the Sedition Act was about to be passed and probably hurried his letter to evade the law.[17]

When District Attorney Marsh turned to the Barlow letter, he extensively developed the government's case. The witnesses he called upon testified they had heard Lyon read the letter often during his political campaign and that its effect upon a gathering in Middletown was to promote revolution and provoke disorder.[18] Lyon countered by attempting to prove, in his cross-examination, that it was the boisterous heckling of these very witnesses that provoked the disturbance (Lyon to Mason). As far as the publication of the letter was concerned, a printer testified that Lyon's wife brought him a copy to publish; but, upon Lyon's cross-examination, he acknowledged that Lyon "had endeavored to prevent it from being printed."[19] Years later, in a speech to Congress, Lyon clarifed this seemingly contradictory testimony. "The fact was," he explained, "that my wife was persuaded by a gentleman who is now a member of this House that the Republican cause and my election (which was pending) would be injured if the letter was not published."[20] Consequently she gave the letter to the printer in Lyon's absence; but when he learned of its publication, he immediately "suppressed the remainder of the edition," because of his promise to Abraham Baldwin. As far as Justice Paterson was concerned, whether or not Lyon secured the printing of the Barlow letter, he in all events was guilty of its publication, for "reading a libel . . . to a number of people . . . amounts to a publication."[21]

In his summation, Marsh dwelt at length upon the libelous nature of the passages in the indictment. He called the jury's special attention to the intent of Lyon's words, charging that Lyon's libels were expressly intended to do the things the Sedition Act prohibited: defame the President and government, excite the hatred of the American people, and stir up sedition.[22]

After the prosecution rested its cast, Judge Paterson rose to give his charge to the jury. Lyon interrupted to ask why he should not address the jury, since his counsel had declined on the grounds that he had not had time to prepare his case. Receiving permission, Lyon addressed the jury for over two and a half hours. Unfortunately, what he said is only briefly recorded. According to Wharton's record of the trial:

> The defendent stated his defense to consist in three points:
> first, that the court had no jurisdiction of the offence, the act of Congress being unconstitutional and void, if not so generally, at least as to writings composed before its passage; second, that the publication was innocent; and third, that the contents were true. . . . The defendent addressed the jury at great length, insisting on the unconstitutionality of the law, and the insufficiency of the evidence to show anything more than legitimate opposition.[23]

Of primary interest is the question: Upon what grounds did Lyon argue the unconstitutionality of the Sedition Act? It has been noted previously that in his magazine Lyon took the general Republican position that the seditious libel laws were the exclusive province of state legislation. Apparently he used this as one of his arguments during his address to the jury, for in Justice Paterson's notes on the trial, we find this counterargument: "Govt. must defend itself—must not appeal to another state or tribunal . . . the offense is agt. the United States."[24]

Equally significant is an earlier entry in Judge Paterson's notes, marked "free discussion." This notation is the only one the Justice chose to underline, and indicates that Lyon strongly challenged the constitutionality of the Sedition Act on the grounds that it violated the First Amendment's protection of freedom of speech. This impression is corroborated by the following notes that Justice Paterson also made on Lyon's summation: "Thought there was a majority in Congress not well disposed to the liberties of the country. Did not vote for the bill and saying so is seditious. . . . Such an arbitrary act. Consider his situation as a representative."[25]

Piecing together the fragmentary material from Justice Paterson's notes and Francis Wharton's record of the trial, one is led to the conclusion that Lyon based his defense primarily on his concept of "legitimate opposition," which in essence meant freedom to criticize and oppose policies of the government.[26] He wrote a clear statement of this position in *The Scourge of Aristocracy* just before his indictment; it is not unlikely that he repeated many of these ideas in his address to the jury:

> I do not understand what people can mean by opposition to Government, applied to the Representatives of the People, in that capacity. We have been accustomed to suppose that Representatives are sent to vote, and support by their arguments their own opinions, and that of their constituents, and to act for the interest of their country. It is quite a new kind of jargon to call a Representative of the People an Opposer of the Government, because he does not, as a Legislator, advocate and acquiesce in every proposition that comes before the Executive. I have no particular interest of my own in cross-

ing the view of the Executive. When a proposition comes from that quarter, which I think, if gained, will be injurious to my constituents and the Constitution, I am bound by oath, as well as by every consideration of duty to oppose it; if outvoted it is my duty to acquiesce—I do so; but measures which I opposed from duty, as injurious to the liberty and interest of this country in Congress, you cannot expect me to advocate at home. (SA, Oct. 1, 1798)

Following this line of argument, Lyon attempted to disprove what he called the prosecution's charge of "evil intentions" (Lyon to Mason). According to the *Spectator*, Mr. Lyon proceeded to read several parts of the publications complained of, and to make several observations.[27] When Lyon says he addressed the jury on the "innocence of the passage in my letter, and the innocence of the manner in which I read the letter," his line of argument becomes more clear (Lyon to Mason). He probably read sections of the passages in question to show that the intent of the material was innocent; that is, the intent was not to defame or stir up sedition against the Executive and the Government, but to oppose legitimately policies with which he was in disagreement.

Since the Sedition Act allowed the truth of statement to be presented as a defense, Lyon attempted to prove the validity of his statements concerning President Adams. This section of his summation lent the one humorous note to his trial. In a completely unorthodox move, he called upon Justice Paterson to testify. Was it not true, Lyon asked the Justice, that he had frequently dined with the President and observed his "ridiculous pomp and parade"? Judge Paterson in turn replied that he had dined with the President on rare occasions, but had observed only "plainness and simplicity." Lyon pressed the point further. Was it not true, he asked, that the Judge had seen more pomp and servants at the President's than at the tavern in Rutland? To this the Justice made no reply.[28]

Ludicrous as this cross-examination may have been, it illustrates the weakness of the Sedition Act's provision that statements which could be proven true would not be punishable under the Act. Whether President Adams surrounded his office with "pomp and parade" or "plainness and simplicity" was a matter of opinion dependent upon the vantage point of the observer. Neither opinion could be proven true or false. What was true for Matthew Lyon, the self-made frontiersman, differed markedly from the truth as seen by William Paterson, the eminent Supreme Court Justice.

In his charge to the jury, Judge Paterson spelled out clearly the issues upon which the jurors were to decide Lyon's guilt or innocence: "You have nothing whatever to do with the constitutionality or unconstitutionality of the sedition law. . . . The only question you are to determine is . . . Did Mr. Lyon publish the writing given in the indictment? Did he do so seditiously? On the first point the evidence is undisputed, and in fact, he himself concedes the fact of publication as to a large portion of libellous matter."[29]

According to Lyon, Judge Paterson also implied the Barlow letter was a forgery, saying, "Let men of letters read that letter and compare it with Barlow's writings, and they would pronounce it none of his" (Lyon to Mason).

The essential emphasis of the charge was on the question of intent; here too Judge Paterson made his position clear:

> As to the second point you will have to consider whether language such as that here complained of could have been uttered with any other intent than that of making odious or contemptible the President and government, and bringing them both into disrepute. If you find such is the case, the offence is made out, and you must render a verdict of guilty. Nor should the political rank of the defendent, his past services, or the dependant position of his family, deter you from this duty.

At the end of his charge, he added: "In order to render a verdict of guilty, you must be satisfied beyond all reasonable doubt that the hypothesis of innocence is unsustainable."[30]

The jury deliberated an hour.[31] It returned with a verdict of guilty. The judge gave Lyon the opportunity to show cause why judgment should not be pronounced. Lyon declined to comment. He was then told to describe his ability or inabilty to pay a fine. Lyon explained that his property had been valued around $20,000 several years ago, but since then he had been forced to sell a great share of it, and what remained would barely bring in $200 in the present circumstances of scarcity of cash and reduced values of land (Lyon to Mason).

Before passing sentence, Judge Paterson first addressed Lyon on the gravity of his crime:

> Matthew Lyon, as a member of the federal legislature, you must be well acquainted with the mischiefs which flow from an unlicensed abuse of government, and of the motives which led to the passage of the act under which this indictment is framed. No one, also, can be better acquainted than yourself with the existence and nature of the act. Your position, so far from making the case one which might slip with a nominal fine through the hands of the court, would make impunity conspicuous should such a fine be imposed. What, however, has tended to mitigate the sentence which would otherwise have been imposed is, what I am sorry to hear of, the reduced condition of your estate.

He then delivered the sentence: "The judgement of the court is, that you stand imprisoned four months, pay the costs of prosecution, and a fine of one thousand dollars, and stand committed until this sentence be complied with."[32]

The sentence came as a thunderbolt to the defendant. "No one expected imprisonment," he asserted (Lyon to Mason). Accustomed as he was to political acrimony, particularly during election campaigns, he was unprepared for outright political persecution.

The situation whereby a Congressman could be imprisoned for criticizing the policies of the government focused sharply the question of opposing political parties. The impact of the Sedition Act was to deny the legitimacy of party politics. According to the Federalists' view of the political process sanctioned by the Constitution, once the elected government decided upon a policy, the populace was obliged to support it. There was no room in Federalist thought for opposition to the government. At the least, such opposition was factious. At the most, an organized opposition party that appealed to the populace to change government policy was seditious.

Matthew Lyon and the other victims of the Sedition Act, who were mainly editors of Republican newspapers, forced the country to face the issues of free speech and legitimate party opposition, and eventually to forge a broader concept of the democratic process.[33]

10

Free Speech Vindicated

Instead of silencing Lyon, prison made a martyr of him. Instead of removing him from the congressional race, prison resulted in his election to Congress. From his jail cell, he waged an election battle that not only brought him victory in Vermont but brought new adherents to the Republican Party throughout the country. The instrument he used was his pen; the medium, his new Republican magazine, *The Scourge of Aristocracy*.

It was under the most ignominious conditions that Lyon waged this battle from jail. From the moment he was sentenced, he was subjected to a continuing series of indignities. Instead of being imprisoned in his home county of Rutland, where the trial had taken place, he was taken on a two-day journey, under guard, to a jail in Vergennes, forty-four miles away. Jabez Fitch, the marshal in charge of his imprisonment, was a longstanding enemy of Lyon's and went to considerable lengths to maximize his prisoner's mortification and distress. After forcing him to take a circuitous route to the jail, in order to display him triumphantly before the inhabitants of Vergennes, Fitch assigned him to a cell that Lyon described as "the common receptacle for horse-thieves, money makers, runaway negroes, or any kind of felons" (Lyon to Mason). This was not the only cell available; Lyon later bitterly pointed out that one of his judges was imprisoned for debt during Lyon's internment and was given a room of his own in the same jail.[1]

In the corner of this "loathsome dungeon," which Lyon sporadically shared with a variety of vagrant prisoners, was a "necessary" that, in Lyon's pungent words, afforded "a stench about equal to the Philadelphia docks in the month of August" (Lyon to Mason). Equally unbearable was the bitter cold, which blew through the bars of the cell's glassless window. Lyon's friends protested these conditions to the Town Council, which finally promised to install window panes and a stove. It took the Council three weeks to make good on its promise about the window; when the stove was not forthcoming, Lyon's supporters eventually provided him with one. However, wrote Lyon, "I was near four weeks without sight of fire, except my candle; in which time I suffered more with the cold than I had in twenty years before."[2]

Lyon came to the conclusion that his harsh treatment was designed "to drive the people of this country (who have been highly agitated) to extremities, and to irritate them to break the gaol, and release me." He estimated that one thousand persons were on the verge of insurrection and predicted that if they weren't curbed, their actions would be used as justification for even more sweeping repression. For this reason, and because of his "repugnance against insurrection and mobbery," he firmly resolved "to suffer any kind of death here, rather than be taken out by violence" (SA, Dec. 15, 1798). Fortunately Lyon dissuaded his indignant followers, who thereafter restricted their efforts in his behalf to legitimate forms of political action.

In the meantime Republicans from other sections of the country rallied to Lyon's support. His leading champion was the ardent Republican Senator from Virginia, Stevens T. Mason, who had been his lodging mate during the tense conflicts of the Fifth Congress. Mason informed Lyon of the shock which his imprisonment had produced and reported: "Several with whom I have conversed agree that the personal suffering to which you are exposed, is much more than the proportion you ought to bear in the common cause of Republicanism; and as the fine is the only part of the sentence which can be participated by others, they have suggested that it should be paid by subscription among the enemies of political persecution."[3] Lyon later stated that "much money was collected" by this subscription, but that he never asked for, nor would he have accepted a cent of this gratuity if he could have avoided it without insulting the benevolent efforts of General Mason.[4]

In order to pay the fine himself, Lyon decided to raise the money by raffling some of his own property. At first his leading Federalist opponent in the election campaign, the Reverend Dr. Samuel Williams, attempted to block this move. At the time he was Chief Judge of the County Court. In this capacity he issued a proclamation declaring the lottery to be illegal, since a bond of $500 had not been deposited with the court. Once again Elias Buell of the Rutland Democratic Society rushed to Lyon's aid. He arranged to comply with the technicality, thus forcing Judge Williams to retract his prohibition of the lottery.[5] Lyon then published a list of the valuable prizes he was offering to holders of the winning tickets. The first prize amounted to $1,500, "to be paid in a farm in West Haven, containing 500 acres"; the second prize was valued at $1,000, "to be paid in a house and farm of good land and conveniences, on the main road in Fair Haven"; fifty additional prizes worth six and ten dollars were to be paid "one-half in cash and one-half in books, at cash prices, at the book store in Fair Haven."[6]

Obviously Lyon was forced to sacrifice a considerable portion of his

Fairhaven property to raise the then staggering sum of $1,000 in cash. His efforts met with success, and the proceeds from the lottery eventually exceeded the amount needed to pay the fine.[7] Presumably, from this surplus Lyon paid back most though not all of the contributors to Mason's fund. He later stated that Mason gave him the list of contributors "while the thing was fresh in everyone's mind," and Lyon paid back everyone who was within reach.[8]

While receiving support from all sides during his imprisonment, Lyon devoted his own energies to continuing his election campaign through the pages of his new journal. He and his son James had begun publication of *The Scourge of Aristocracy* prior to his incarceration; in the first issue they stated its underlying purpose and philosophy: "to oppose truth to falsehood . . . to elucidate the real situation of this country . . . at this agitated and awful crisis, when everything is industriously circulated, which can corrupt or mislead the public sentiment, and prepare the American mind for a state of abject slavery, and degrading subjection to a set of assuming High Mightinesses in our own country, and a close connection with a corrupt, tottering monarchy in Europe" (*SA*, Oct. 1, 1798).

As in the *Farmers' Library*, Lyon made this conflict between Republicanism and aristocracy the predominant theme of his publication. In addition, he expounded upon the current issues that had caused many of his former supporters to become disaffected. Foremost among these was the question of war with France. As an astute politician, Lyon addressed himself directly to the questions he knew were disturbing his constituents. He employed the homespun journalistic technique of a dialogue with a neighbor and answered questions one by one. The following extracts illustrate his teaching technique.

"Neighbor.—Your enemies say, you have joined the interests of the French, and wish to see this country subjugated by them. What have you to say to that?" Lyon replied that he felt only indignation over France's depredations upon American commerce, and that if he had thought war would put an end to them, he would not have hesitated one moment in giving his assent to a resort to arms; but "when I could see but little injury we could do them, and the vast calamity it would cause to this country, I could not concur in any measure which in my opinion led to it."

"Neighbor.—Have not the French given sufficient provocation to this country to justify us in going to war with them?" By European standards, Lyon acknowledged, "the French have given us tenfold provocation for a declaration of war against them." However, he insisted, the United States was in a position to avoid the European "habits of war." There, overcrowded nations were reduced to "perpetually conquering and plundering one another . . . but a country situated like this, secured, as it were, from them by an immense ocean, with a country in our possession craving a population of at least twenty or thirty fold, should never think of a war as a trade." The only justification for war would be an invasion, in which case the country should rise in mass, drive out the invaders, and return to their homes and farms immediately.

"Neighbor.—You seem not to regard the commerce of this country; don't you know that the agricultural interest of this country cannot flourish without commerce?" Lyon took this occasion to point out that the back-country agrarian interests were separate from those of the commercial interests: "It is but very little interesting to the back country people whether our produce is carried away by Americans or by foreigners," he explained to his neighbor. Moreover, "the people who make their own necessaries in back countries are not involved in foreign commerce" (*SA*, Oct. 1, 1798).

Thus he disposed of the farmers' economic concerns and indicated that those who favored war with France were the commercial interests. Next he addressed himself to his constituents' patriotic outrage over the XYZ affair.

"Neighbor.—Did not the usage of the French Government toward our Envoys rouse your indignation to a willingness to go to war with France? Nothing vexed me like that." Lyon replied that the dispatches had been distorted and exaggerated, and that the real motive for publicizing them "was for the purpose of exasperating the people to a willingness to pay the taxes which the enormous expenses projected would naturally produce." In this way Lyon tied the war to the unpopular issue of taxes. He spelled out in detail the costs incurred for vessels of war, for the subsistence of officers and men in the standing army, for fortifications and allied military matters. After hearing this itemized list of expenditures, Lyon's astounded neighbor exclaimed: "This is a large sum indeed! It amounts, I think, to $14,600,000—it is more than three dollars a head for every man, woman and child in the United States" (*SA*, Oct. 15, 1798). Before the stunned neighbor could catch his breath, Lyon pointed to his own voting record to show his opposition to such measures as the land and salt taxes, which fell most heavily upon the landholders of the country. The farmers of western Vermont were hard hit by the barrage of new federal taxes, and Lyon undoubtedly touched a responsive chord in many of them with his disarming dialogue.

However, it was the Sedition Act itself that proved to be Lyon's most provocative campaign issue. In a series of open letters to Stevens T. Mason, in several issues of *The Scourge of Aristocracy*, Lyon vividly portrayed the Act's effects by describing in detail his trial and imprisonment. Subsequently Republican newspapers throughout the country reprinted these letters, and Senator Mason commented that Lyon's prosecution under the Sedition Act served "more to open the eyes of our fellow citizens than all the speeches of all the republican orators in the last two sessions of Congress."[9]

In this same letter Stevens Mason made it clear that he considered the Sedition Act unconstitutional not on the grounds for which Professor

Levy criticizes the Republicans, that is, that the states had exclusive right to pass seditious libel laws, but because both the federal and state constitutions guaranteed freedom of speech and press. He was the son of George Mason and, as such, was familiar with the intentions of those who insisted upon a Bill of Rights in the federal Constitution. For this reason, and because his statement sheds further light on the civil liberties issues raised by Levy by revealing at least one more Republican who considered the Sedition Act unconstitutional on First Amendment grounds, his words warrant repeating at length:

> In the minds of the Virginians, particularly, it sinks deep because we well remember that when the constitution was proposed for our adoption, and the want of a bill of rights complained of, we were told that personal liberty never could be endangered under the Constitution; . . . that those barriers which were provided by the state constitutions to protect civil and religious liberty, were unnecessary in that instrument, because it contained no delegation of power which could possibly affect these rights. . . . It was found necessary to reconcile the Constitution, even to those majorities who had adopted it, by incorporating provisions equivalent to a bill of rights on the subjects of religious freedom, trial by jury, the liberty of speech, and of the press; rights heretofore held sacred in America, but which will soon pass away and be forgotten, like the dreams of the night, unless the people shall be aroused by such flagrant violations of our social compact as are now passing in review before them.[10]

Lyon's constituents proved in word and deed the extent to which they were aroused by these "flagrant violations." His imprisonment even inspired some to express their indignation in verse, such as the following:

Sentiments of Matthew Lyon, 1798
At Vergens Jail
by Z. Porter

When the Morning first blushed a Long in the East
I haste to my daily employment
I drudge all the day while the high Born can Feast
tis they that can afford the enjoyment
Our Rulers can feast on six dollars pr day
the poor Must be taxt their extorsion to pay
And if I Should unto them any Thing say
they would trump up a Bill of Sedition.

Being fired with courage I flew to the Field
and Joined with My Musket the army
determined to perish before I would yield
The Wrongs of my country alarmed me
at the walls of quebec I bled in the War
both Yorktown and Monmouth they left me a scar
For in jail I must Lie for Sedition.

I Oft Time have Thought with sigh in my heart
What a fool is a poor man for fighting
if the tyrants will quarrel shall we take their part
in war Blood and carnage delighting
We soon may disown before it be long
that while we were fighting we fought for a wrong
if knaves will Oppress us and make themselves strong
By the help of a Bill of Sedition.

Coventry, Vt. Nov. 10, 1798[11]

It was at the polls that the people of western Vermont most concretely expressed their antipathy to the Sedition Act. When election day rolled around in December 1798, almost two thousand more persons participated in this runoff election than had taken part in the September balloting.[12] Both sides had conducted intensive campaigns, and the adherents of each were adamant. It is part of the folklore of Poultney, Vermont, for example, that a crippled voter was brought to the polls in his bed. When one of the opposition expressed surprise at his being strong enough to be out of doors, the staunch Republican waved his ballot and replied that he was strong enough to carry a "Lyon" in his hand.[13]

Although the Reverend Dr. Samuel Williams increased his vote from 1,544 in September to 2,444 in December, Lyon far outstripped him, increasing his vote from 3,482 to 4,576. When all the ballots were tallied, Lyon's total exceeded the combined votes of all his opponents by 199 votes.[14] He had won the election!

Lyon's victory was a cause for rejoicing among Republicans. Jefferson jubilantly wrote Madison, "Lyon is elected. His majority is great. Reports vary from 600 to 900."[15] From the Federalist press came outcries of disgust, such as the following: "The lowest class of citizens will now be as well *represented* as the Sanscullottes were ever by the patriotic Marat. . . . In the western District of Vermont, a very large part of its ill manners, seditious dispositions, low intrigues and Irish league of insurrection will be very truly *represented to the life*."[16]

By their votes the citizens of western Vermont registered their mandate that Matthew Lyon represent them in Congress. Since he was forced to remain in jail until his prison term expired, the citizens of Rutland County petitioned Congress to repeal the Sedition Act, declaring, "We boast the privilege of electing our own representatives; but what consolation results to Freemen from this nominal (mockery of) right, while the degrading operations of the Sedition Act is to restrain the man of our choice from his seat in Congress."[17]

In another memorial, several thousand citizens of western Vermont petitioned President Adams to pardon Lyon and remit his fine. Avowing their complete loyalty to America, they beseeched the President to restore their rights of representation, assuring him that if he pardoned

Lyon he would earn "the praises of millions."[18] The Reverend Dr. John Cosens Ogden, an itinerant Episcopal minister from New Hampshire, who had worked closely with Lyon in Episcopal conventions,[19] insisted upon delivering the petition to President Adams in person, feeling certain that he could persuade the President to grant clemency.[20] However, when he finally received an audience with the President, after his four-hundred-mile journey to Philadelphia, John Adams denied the petition. First he inquired whether Lyon himself had requested a pardon. When Ogden replied that he had not, Adams declared, "penitence must pre-cede pardon."[21]

Lyon had warned his friend to expect his journey to end in disappoint-ment and vindictiveness, but neither man could have anticipated the final outcome of the minister's mission on Lyon's behalf.[22] On his return trip to Vermont, Dr. Ogden was sentenced to jail in Litchfield, Connect-icut. Secretary of the Treasury Oliver Wolcott secured his arrest for non-payment of a $200 debt.[23] Dr. Ogden attributed his arrest to the fact that "the Secretary does not feel good tempered to me because Col¹. Lyon has ever said there were an hundred young men in the country who would do the duty of Secretary of the Treasury as well as the present possessor, for one half the sum."[24] Beyond this, Ogden saw a connection between religion and politics in his persecution. Writing to Ephraim Kirby, a Litchfield attorney, who was both a staunch Republican and an active Episcopalian, Ogden acerbically commented on the undue influence that the Wolcotts and their fellow Congregationalists exerted in New England politics.[25] He pledged that he and Colonel Lyon would expose their role in the coming year and requested Kirby to furnish some of the documents.[26]

True to his word, he wrote a pamphlet entitled *A Short History of the Late Ecclesiastical Oppressions in New England and Vermont*, which Matthew Lyon's son James published late in 1799. It presented a scathing attack upon Illuminatism, or Edwardianism, which Ogden defined as "That union of church and state, of religion and politics, of rich lay men and ecclesiastics who wish to destroy every religion and government which do not accord with their ambition or wishes, or pursue their delu-sions." After attributing Oliver Wolcott's former position as governor of Connecticut to "the influence of the clergy over the election," the pam-phlet proceeded to describe the efforts of the Edwardians "to extend their tyrannies into Vermont," where Episcopalians, Methodists, Roman Catholics, and Baptists had sought refuge from the persecutions of the established Congregational Church. The major thrust of the pamphlet was to show how the Congregational Church and its missionary ministers in Vermont gradually had acquired control of the lands originally belonging to the Episcopal Church. The climax of these oppressions was reached in 1794, when the Vermont legislature turned over the con-fiscated Glebe Lands to the local townships, for the use of common schools. According to Ogden, those most responsible for this legislation were the Harvard-trained Reverend Dr. Samuel Williams, the "father of these measures"; Ira Allen, who had acquired prominence by conversion to Edwardianism; and two leading gentlemen of Vermont, Mr. Chipman and Mr. Jacobs, who were reared in Connecticut and Massachusetts— "those theatres of controversy, bigotry and spiritual tyranny."[27]

This pamphlet, as well as the close association of Matthew Lyon and Dr. Ogden, emphasizes the significant role that religious minorities played in the New England conflict between Republicans and Federalists. Opposition to the religious and political domination of the established Congregationalists was one of the important strains in Lyon's Republicanism, and Episcopalians like Dr. Ogden and Ephraim Kirby represented a significant social component of the Republican movement in Vermont and Connecticut. Similarly, Lyon's leading adversaries were to be found among the New England "Illuminati," ranging from Nathaniel Chipman and the Reverend Samuel Williams in Vermont to John Allen, Roger Griswold, and Oliver Wolcott in Connecticut.

It is not surprising, therefore, that on the day of his release from jail, Lyon directed one of his first conversations to the subject of the unrepresentative character of Connecticut's public officials. Calling upon Governor Tichenor of Vermont for his credentials, Lyon reasserted the claim he had made to Roger Griswold in Congress that "nothing would be more easy than for him to change the Sentiments of the Connecticut people . . . he would want but one hour in Each Town, in the hearing of all the people."[28]

Undoubtedly Lyon's exuberant confidence reflected the overwhelming acclaim that the citizens of Vermont had showered upon him that auspicious day. From his vantage point in the state's capital, Governor Tichenor viewed Bennington's enthusiastic reception of Lyon with incredulous disdain. Particularly obnoxious to the Federalist governor was the role of Bennington's Republican journalist, Anthony Haswell, who welcomed Lyon in behalf of the large gathering and rejoiced in his triumph over repression. "At the close," Governor Tichenor contemptuously observed, "two songs, penned by Haswell, were chanted in the open air by about 30 Choristers—all to the tune of 'ding, dong Bell Oh.' "[29] Entitled "Patriotic Exultation on Lyon's Release from the Federal Bastille in Vergennes," Haswell's verses sang the praises of Lyon and the Bill of Rights. The last stanza rang out:

> Come take the glass and drink his health,
> Who is a friend of Lyon,
> First martyr under federal law
> The junto dared to try on.[30]

Nine months later, Anthony Haswell suffered the same fate as the man whose freedom he celebrated that day. In fact, one of the counts in his indictment was the publication of seditious statements in the advertisement of Lyon's lottery.[31]

As in Bennington, so all along the route from jail to Congress throngs of admirers gathered to hail Lyon as a hero. The crowd that greeted him outside the jail in Vergennes followed him in procession for twelve miles, and in town after town, young and old joined in celebrations extolling in verses, songs, and toasts the virtues of Lyon and liberty.[32]

In Congress a less salutary reception awaited Lyon. Immediately after he resumed his seat, Congressman Bayard of Delaware stepped forward with a resolution to expel Lyon from the House because of his conviction and imprisonment as "a notorious and Seditious person."[33] The Republican spokesman from Virginia, John Nicholas, then rose to Lyon's defense, asserting that he "should have thought that after a member of this House had suffered so severely . . . it would [not] have been thought necessary to go into a consideration of the nature of the offence of which he is said to have been guilty."

In the ensuing debate both Nicholas and Gallatin conducted an intensive investigation into Lyon's trial, subjecting the doctrine of seditious libel to close scrutiny. From these debates it becomes apparent how the Sedition Act forced the Republicans to refine and enlarge their concept of free speech. In their arguments Gallatin and Nicholas presented a clarification of what could and what could not be considered libel. Only the statement of false facts could be judged as libelous, they maintained, but the truth or falseness of an opinion could not be ascertained. Therefore expressions of opinion were outside the scope of the doctrine of seditious libel.

Lyon had been convicted of uttering false and malicious statements against the government; but, insisted Nicholas, Lyon's words were statements of opinion, not fact. "Do gentlemen say opinions can be false. . . ? Men's opinions are as various as their faces, and the truth or falseness of these opinions are not fit subjects for the decision of a jury." Gallatin pursued this issue further, attacking as deceitful the purportedly liberal provision of the Sedition Act that allowed the truth of a statement to be offered as a defense. This provision had been offered by Bayard himself, the man who now insisted that opinions as well as facts could be judged false. Gallatin then proceeded to analyze paragraph by paragraph the statements for which Lyon was convicted, proving in each instance that jury members could not determine the truth or falseness of the statement, but only whether they agreed with it or not. For example, Gallatin argued,

> supposing that the member from Vermont had declared it his opinion "that the efforts of the Executive power was not bent on the promotion of the comfort, the happiness, and the accommodation of the people" [,] he wished to know whether this could be considered as a declaration of fact or opinion? There is perhaps no measure passed by Congress, which one or another may not think will be contrary to the happiness, comfort and accommoda-

tion of the people of the United States. We had . . . the question of a navy before us, the establishment of which many believe is necessary for the promotion of the comfort, happiness, and accommodation of the people; whereas, in my opinion and in the opinion of many others, it will produce the very reverse. How is this question to be decided? . . . doubtless this is a mere matter of opinion and not susceptible of proof by evidence. In order to prove the truth of either assertion, you must bring forward a dissertation pro and con.

In his concluding remarks, Nicholas asserted that he "most religiously believed" the Sedition Act to be unconstitutional; therefore "he could not, without a breach of his oath, do any act to punish a breach of that law." In a similar vein Gallatin charged that Lyon had been tried "for a political offence"; to expel him would be to commit an additional act of political persecution. Lyon escaped this second humiliation by a hair's breadth. The vote for his expulsion was 49 to 45; but since a two-thirds vote was necessary to expel a member of the House, Lyon retained his seat.

Thus Lyon remained on the scene to participate in the dramatic proceedings of the House of Representatives, when the conflict between the Federalists and Republicans reached its climax in the election of 1800. Since he had become a figure of national repute, he played an active role in the campaign activities that preceded the election. During the summer of 1800, he made a tour of the South, stumping principally in Virginia, where he spent more than a month campaigning in behalf of Republicanism and "a general ticket for President." He later commented that "being just out of prison, I was looked to as a martyr, and every word had weight."[34] It was through the written as well as the spoken word that Lyon helped the Republican cause in Virginia during this heated election campaign. At the request of Jefferson, he helped subsidize a Republican press, run by his son and nephew in Staunton, Virginia.[35] Their first publication bore the title of its Vermont predecessor, *The Scourge of Aristocracy*.

Lyon returned to Congress convinced that the Republicans would win the election. In December, as the last electoral returns were coming in, he wrote Mathew Carey, "I give you joy on Mr. Jefferson's election which is so certain."[36] Six days later, an ironic turn of events forced him to retract his premature congratulations. Although the Republicans had won, the presidency hung in the balance. Jefferson and Burr had tied with seventy-three votes each in the electoral college. It now devolved upon the House to select one of these two Republican candidates as President. Writing Carey of the state of affairs in the House, Lyon declared, "We are threatened with Anarchy, Confusion and disorganization, by the devout friends of Order."[37] The Federalists, he thought, were in a position to create an impasse in the election.

In February, when the balloting in the House began, Lyon's prediction proved accurate. The Federalists had decided to throw their votes to Aaron Burr, rather than allow Jefferson to become president. They, however, controlled the votes of only six states, while the Republicans, standing firmly behind Jefferson, controlled the votes of eight states. Two states were divided; one of these was Vermont, with Lyon voting for Jefferson and Lewis Morris voting for Burr. Since the vote of nine states was necessary for either candidate to win the election, the House had reached a stalemate. The voting remained unchanged through thirty-five roll calls, extending from February 10 through February 17.

Behind the scenes, all kinds of overtures were being made to break the deadlock. According to Lyon, John Brown of Rhode Island "urged me to set a price on my Vote for Burr and said I should have whatever I requested in office or in money."[38] Moreover, friends from Vermont barraged him with letters urging support of Burr. Lyon suspected that Burr himself initiated these pressures, despite the fact that he had removed himself from the Washington scene and given assurances of his support for Jefferson.[39]

In the Federalist camp, more complex maneuvers were taking place. Hamilton tried in vain to persuade his party colleagues to change their votes to Jefferson as the lesser of the two evils. Finally, after the thirty-fifth ballot, Bayard of Delaware turned the tide in this direction by announcing that he would no longer support Burr. "After a week's struggle the firmness of the Republicans have been crowned with success," jubilantly reported Stevens T. Mason in a letter describing the final turn of events. "Today at 1 o'clock the Feds broke ground and on the 36th ballot Vermont and Maryland voted for Mr. Jefferson. Morris of Vermont was out of the way and Lyon gave the vote of that State. S. Cara. & Delaware put in blank tickets so that the vote stands for Mr. Jefferson 10 States for Mr. Burr 4. Accept my congratulations on this pleasing event."[40]

As the representative from Vermont, the last state on the roll call, Lyon cast the final vote in Jefferson's favor. While he reveled in the glory of this fact, the Federalists found further grist for their mill. "It must be a very gratifying reflection to the native inhabitants of the United States that the important point—who should be President—was settled by the power of Matthew Lyon," commented one Federalist scribe, who proceeded to elaborate on this theme in verse:

SYMPTOMS OF THE MILLENIUM IN 1801

Scarce had the world with tearful eye
Bade the Old Century 'good bye'
When lo! there rose a mighty stir
Twixt Jefferson and Col. Burr
A direful contest then ensued
Which some suppos'd would end in blood

At length a Lyon grim and bold
The desperate massave fam'd of old
Declar'd himself Behemoth's friend
And brought the combat to an end
Bade dire hostility to cease
And hush'd 'Republicans' to peace
Then join'd the Presidential flocks
And at the herbage like an ox
And Still around the pasture strays
Among the Master's Beasts to graze[.][41]

That Lyon cast the deciding vote for Jefferson hardly entitled him to this dubious credit for Jefferson's victory. He did, however, earn more valid credit for making a major contribution to the Republican victory of 1800. His imprisonment under the Sedition Act brought to national attention the extent to which the Federalists were stifling the right to dissent. Civil liberties became one of the major campaign issues of the election, and Lyon's resistance to suppression was vindicated when the electorate cast their votes in favor of the founding principles of Republicanism.

11

Lyon's Kentucky Career

In a bitter note of triumph to "Citizen John Adams," written a minute after both their terms expired, Matthew Lyon stated: "I am going to retire of my own accord, to the extreme western parts of the United States, where I had fixed myself an asylum from the persecutions of a party, the most base, cruel, assuming and faithless, that ever disgraced the councils of any nation."[1]

At first glance, it seems an irrational decision of Lyon's to uproot himself and his family at the age of fifty and abandon the work of a lifetime—the enterprises, the home, the position, the town he founded —in order to seek a haven from his political enemies, whom he had already gloriously overcome.

Indeed the decision may well have been an emotional one. The hostility Lyon felt toward the Vermont Federalists, who had succeeded in jailing him, may have been so enormous that it overshadowed his final victory over them. But Lyon's move to Kentucky was probably motivated by positive emotions as well. It was while he was in an affirmative, almost euphoric mood during the election campaign for Jefferson in 1799, when he was hailed as a martyred hero throughout the South, that Lyon first conceived of the idea of moving to the southwestern frontier. According to his own words, it was a visit to the Tennessee home of his Republican colleague Andrew Jackson that first inspired him: "Your country," he wrote the young Tennessean in 1800, "is far superior to any I have ever seen and it has never been long out of my thought since I saw it. To enjoy the blessings of such a country, such a soil, and such a climate in a good neighborhood is what is most wished for by your Devoted friend."[2]

Thus in 1800 Lyon was repeating an old pattern: following the dream promised by a new land of opportunity. His was the eternal quest for perfection—ever restless, ever ambitious, ever driven. It was in this mood that Lyon undertook to start life anew in Kentucky.

Shortly after he wrote Andrew Jackson of his aspirations, Lyon took steps to realize them. He wrote his son-in-law from Congress: "I made a lucky bargain about two weeks ago and put away my slitting mill and some other property at Fairhaven for 5800 acres of land in the Western country."[3] The land was not in Andrew Jackson's Tennessee, but it was close enough, in the neighboring frontier state of Kentucky.

From the moment Lyon acquired his Kentucky land, he plunged into a frenzy of activity to wind up his affairs in Fairhaven. He sold most of his remaining property including his paper and sawmills to a Squire Norton; and "for the consideration of the friendship he bore the town of Fairhaven" he deeded to the town five pieces of land to be used, in part, for a public library and a burying ground.[4]

Most important, from the point of view of his future ventures, he convinced a number of his employees and other Vermont associates to join him in the move "to the Westward."[5] His daughter later described the arrangements he made with his mechanics as follows: "That he would take as many mechanics as would go with him, with their families, defray their expenses on the journey, and deed them a home on their arrival, and they should work for him at a reasonable compensation, until they paid him for the same."[6] Ten families agreed to these arrangements, thus guaranteeing Lyon a nucleus of reliable mechanics to begin his new undertakings.

He placed his greatest dependence upon John Messenger, the husband of his oldest daughter, Ann. Messenger was a man whose many talents ideally suited Lyon's needs. He combined organizational ability with the mechanical skills of a millwright and a surveyor. Almost immediately after Lyon purchased his Kentucky land, he wrote John asking: "I want to know if there is like to be any change in your affairs favorable to your moveing next fall or winter to the Westward."[7]

John Messenger replied in the affirmative. So did another son-in-law, Dr. George Catlett, who had married Lyon's second daughter, Pamelia. These two families, along with Loraine, Lyon's youngest daughter by his first marriage, made up an advance party, which proceeded to Kentucky to lay the groundwork for the future settlement. There, on a bluff overlooking the Cumberland River, they first erected crude log cabins. Then, with the help of local workmen, they constructed a sawmill and began erecting permanent homes for the Lyon family and their friends from Vermont.[8]

Meanwhile, in Fairhaven, Lyon made elaborate plans to transport the second contingent of his family and the ten other families who were joining the embarkation. Before returning to Congress in November, Lyon left instructions for three teams to be brought to New Geneva on the Monongahela River, the home, coincidentally, of his political associate Albert Gallatin.[9] In Vermont the departing pioneers made an indelible impression on the minds of those they left behind. Years later, Reverend Beamann wrote, "I well remember watching the emigrant wagons, as they passed thru Hampton, making a fine display of their imposing white canvass, proclaiming their departure to the great unknown Southwest. It was a thing to be remembered and talked about."[10]

That fateful winter of 1800, while Lyon participated in the heated House contest over the election of Jefferson or Burr, the members of his migrant train spent the winter in Pittsburgh, preparing for the final lap of their voyage down the Ohio River. "The mechanics were employed during the winter in constructing flatboats," wrote Matthew Lyon's daughter, who gave the following description of these vessels to her readers: They are "clumsy looking water craft . . . flat on bottom, the sides are boarded up five or six feet, and the top is covered over tight. . . . They are generally from 50 to 60 feet in length and are designed only to float down stream."[11]

Finally, after triumphantly attending Jefferson's inauguration in March 1801, Lyon joined his family and friends, who boarded the flatboats and proceeded on their journey down the Ohio that spring. According to Lyon's daughter, they often lashed the several boats in their flotilla together, in order to exchange social visits and pass the time away imagining the future life that awaited them. Her description of their long-awaited arrival, captures the mixture of joy and tragedy that accompanied their move westward.[12]

When they sighted the bluffs of his Eddyville property, Lyon ordered the crew to "give them a few guns to let them know we are coming." The party that had remained behind in Kentucky had been out of communication with their family for over a year, there being no mail routes from this undeveloped section of the country. The sound of the guns must have filled them with both exhilaration and distress; for in that year of silence, Lyon's daughter Loraine had died of "billious fever." Dr. Catlett broke the news to the Lyons as he accompanied them to the top of the bluff, where Loraine's "silent grave" awaited them.[13]

After he recovered from the initial shock of this ominous beginning to his new life, Lyon devoted himself to building his Kentucky enterprises. His new property consisted of 5,800 acres of uncultivated land in the frontier settlement of Eddyville, located on the Cumberland and Tennessee rivers. So situated, it was natural for Lyon to enter commerce and assume the new role of merchant.

By operating barges that traversed the Mississippi River, Lyon and his stepson, Elijah Galusha, carried on a thriving business trading the produce of the Cumberland region. As early as 1802 Elijah reported that they were carrying "Pork, Bacon Lard and Venison hams for the Orleans market and cotton for Philadelphia, New York or Boston." As a resourceful merchant, Lyon used his political connections to expand his mercantile activities beyond the private market and sought a contract for "victualizing the troops at Kaskasais and Massac."[14] His subsequent appointment as commissary general of the Western Army did not go unnoticed by his political adversaries. Commented a Federalist newspaper, "No appointment of Mr. Jefferson, since he has been President of the United States, courted observation and abhorrence more than that of Matthew Lyon, as commissary for furnishing supplies for the western army."[15] Just how handsome the returns from this patronage appointment were, Lyon revealed in a letter to his northern business agent, Mathew Carey, whom he instructed to collect $8,000 from the secretary of war.[16]

Another phase of Lyon's mercantile activity was bookselling, which formed the basis of his business relationship with Mathew Carey, prominent Republican bookdealer, publicist, and economist. Describing his barge as a "moving bookstore," Lyon apprised Carey of the lucrative book market he had tapped in the West, claiming, "I have sold a Vast many more books I am sure than all the merchants below the Kentucky river." So extensive were his book sales that they enabled him to "purchase some of the best land in the country."[17] Besides the pecuniary rewards, the book business enabled Lyon to continue his roles as promulgator of Republican ideas. His correspondence with Carey over the years indicates that he was particularly interested in obtaining books of ideological content such as Rousseau's *Social Compact*, More's *Utopia*, and current interpretations of the French Revolution.[18]

With barges so essential a component of his mercantile activity, it was logical that Lyon next branch out into the shipbuilding industry. In the beginning, his son James undertook the management of this phase of Lyon's enterprises. In addition to barges, his shipyard produced a variety of sloops and gunboats, which he sold to the federal government.[19] Just how ambitious a shipping enterprise James operated is indicated by a letter from him to Andrew Jackson, in which he solicits the Tennessean's trade in a new ship built for transatlantic voyages, specifying that he planned to transport cotton to Liverpool.[20]

As Lyon's gunboat contracts and army commissary agreements indicate, he viewed the government as a business client and sought federal contracts whenever possible, even after he returned to Congress in 1803. "Dear Children, Among other contracts I have obtained for Elijah the Contract for Carrying the Mail from St. Vincent to Cahokia," he jubilantly informed his family in 1805.[21] This was one of seven other mail routes along the inland waterways that he had obtained from the office of the postmaster general, Gideon Granger.[22] When these agreements were later called into question by John Randolph, during the heat of the Yazoo land controversy, Lyon defended his business dealings with the government in a statement which frankly expressed his view of the unfettered rights of the entrepreneur: "I act like other merchants, look out for customers with whom I can make advantageous bargains to both parties. It is all the same to me whether I contract with an individual or the public; I see no constitutional impediment to a member of this House serving the public for the same reward the public gives another."[23]

Obviously Matthew Lyon was as avid a defender of free enterprise as he was of free speech. He tolerated no restraint upon his freedom to pursue his private business interests, even while serving as a public official supposedly dedicated to the public interest. Apparently he was unaware of the conflict of interest doctrine, or insensitive to it.

Lyon imprinted the stamp of his aggressive enterprising spirit on the town of Eddyville by launching a variety of other operations. In addition to a sawmill, gristmill, and paper mill, reminiscent of those he had built in Fairhaven, he adapted to the economy of the South by investing in a cotton gin and a wool and cotton carding machine.[24] As early as 1802 he informed Mathew Carey that he "shall be able to send by my stepson this fall $2,000 worth of cotton."[25]

Inevitably Lyon faced the problem of engaging slave labor in his new household. His daughter's reminiscences convey the impression that he despised the South's institution of involuntary servitude but was forced to purchase slaves as domestic workers because white labor was not available for household work in Kentucky. Responding to his wife's commiseration with the lot of local Blacks, he made it a policy to purchase the servants of harsh masters, and then contracted with them to work until they paid off their purchase price. In essence, he treated these slaves like indentured servants, who eventually would become free workers.[26]

Implicit in his daughter's account is the assumption that Lyon opposed slavery as a matter of principle. Other evidence, however, seems to indicate that Lyon's daughter attributed her own abolitionist sentiments to her father. On the floor of Congress, in 1803, he indicated that he had already adapted himself to the prevailing labor practices of the South, saying: "The opportunity I have had of feeling the operation of both the freedom and the slavery of the black people, convinces me that the blacks who are slaves are much more useful and beneficial to the community and to the nation, according to their number, than those that are free."[27] This, from the man who five years earlier went to jail as the defender of the equal rights of man.

On slavery, as on so many other matters, Lyon's position was ambivalent. His daughter's reminiscences of the Lyon family's experience with slavery on the Kentucky frontier, while no doubt colored by her later commitment to the colonization and abolition movements, describe the conflict Lyon and his wife experienced, and the compromises they made with the South's "Peculiar Institution," after leaving the anti-slavery environment of Vermont.

According to his daughter's account, before Lyon arrived in Kentucky, he told his wife, "We are not going to Kentucky to be slaveholders. We are going to show them how happy, neat and comfortable we can live without them." However sincere these sentiments might have been, Lyon found it difficult if not impossible to disregard the pressures that the mere presence of slave labor exerted upon an employer. Even though the settlers in the communities surrounding Eddyville were poor farmers who owned only ten acres of land and lived in log cabins, most of their households boasted at least two slaves. In some instances a slave was a parting gift from a father, to lighten the burden of the emigrating family in their difficult new surroundings. In others, slaves were to be the source of lucrative incomes for shrewd frontiersmen who brought numbers of them to this unsettled region, in order to rent them out to people who had no other source of labor.

This was the position in which Matthew Lyon found himself. He needed workers for both his home and his enterprises. Inevitably he was confronted with the problem of whether to purchase slaves to meet his needs. His daughter recounts the circumstances under which he made this choice, and how he modified the prevailing practices of slave ownership to accommodate them to his Republican principles.

The Lyons made their first concession to slavery when they were unable to engage the services of a white cook. Upon a visit to their poorer neighbors in the settlement of Eddy Grove, they learned about Chloe, a former Carolina household slave, now owned by an impecunious farmer who was happy to benefit from her exceptional culinary ability by renting her out to the Lyons for $60 a year.

While the Lyons actively sought the services of Chloe, quite a different set of circumstances accounted for the purchase of their next slave, Anna. She had been a household slave in Carolina, but when her new master brought her to Kentucky, he insisted that she do the work of a field hand. He was infuriated by her ineptitude at these new tasks, beat her, and set his dogs upon her. In desperation, she finally ran away and sought refuge in Lyon's "Yankee Settlement." Chloe found Anna hiding in a cave and, upon Anna's request, brought her to Lyon, to beseech him to purchase her. Although Mrs. Lyon demurred, fearing they would become confirmed slaveholders, Lyon convinced her that it was better to buy Anna than to rent her services, because he would allow her to work off her purchase price and then would free her.

Here the plot thickened, for Anna wanted to marry another of her master's slaves, George, and pleaded with Lyon to buy him also. Again, over Mrs. Lyon's protestations, Lyon bought George for $1,000. He had George trained as a carpenter and joiner and agreed to allow him to work off his purchase price by allowing $18 a month for his services over a period of five years. In the meantime, Lyon officiated over the wedding ceremony of George and Anna, declaring the couple married in the sight of God and the community. Then he opened his home to a festive wedding party attended by the slaves, their friends from Eddy Grove, and the Lyon family. In this way Lyon gave to the marriage of his slaves the recognition and dignity denied them by Southern law.

Lyon's purchase of the slave Richard was significant for other reasons. This young black man had been raised in Carolina by a pious farmer who had taught him to read the Bible. While still a youth, Richard experienced conversion and afterwards preached the word of the Lord to his fellow slaves. He told Lyon that his master said, "I spiles his niggers," and indeed it was because he was so annoyed with Richard's preaching that his master offered to sell him to Lyon.

Again Lyon agreed to grant Richard his freedom after he worked off his purchase price. In the meantime Lyon gave him every weekend off so that on Saturdays he could visit his family, who were still held by his former master in Eddy Grove, and on Sundays he could preach at Aunt Chloe's meeting house.

When the time came to grant Richard his freedom, Lyon gave him $40, a horse, and a letter of recommendation to "influential men" who could help him raise a subscription of $1,400 with which to purchase his wife and children. Eventually Richard raised the necessary money and settled in Silver Creek, Missouri, where he lived out his remaining life as a gospel minister.

The last slave that Lyon's daughter portrayed in her reminiscences was Aunt Leanna, the heroine of her antislavery narrative. Lyon purchased her at a slave auction while on a business trip and made the same arrangements to grant her freedom as he did with his other slaves. Aunt Leanna became the Earth Mother of Lyon's household; she nursed his youngest children, was a companion to his wife, and in his last years served as Lyon's housekeeper in an Indian trading post in Arkansas, where he was severed from all the graces of civilization. On his deathbed, Lyon's last act was to provide for the freedom papers of Aunt Leanna.

If Lyon's daughter's memoirs are to be trusted, they indicate that in principle he remained opposed to slavery throughout his years in the South. Yet he did not refuse to become a slaveholder; he did not insist upon living by his principles. Perhaps it would be too much to expect that Lyon, as an individual, should refuse to participate in a social and economic institution that pervaded the South. He alone could not abolish slavery by refusing to own slaves; on the other hand, such an act of moral consistency would have crippled him economically. If this was the direction of his thinking, as it seems to have been in the case of other Southern Republicans, such as Jefferson, one might have expected Lyon to advocate the abolition of slavery through legal acts that would have struck at the root of the hated institution. This, apparently, Lyon did not do. On the contrary, as we have seen, he expressed himself in Congress as an advocate of slavery. In view of his liberal conduct toward his own slaves, this statement may possibly be interpreted as an act of political opportunism, designed to ingratiate himself with his southern constituents and his fellow southerners in Congress.

Lyon's position on slavery can be summarized as both accommodating and principled. To his credit, it should be acknowledged that he regarded his slaves as human beings, rather than mere property, that in a number of respects—such as training them as artisans, recognizing their marriage relationships, and giving them freedom to worship—he deviated from conventional practices of Southern slaveholders. Most important, he enabled a number of his slaves to earn their freedom, an indication that, in principle, he still subscribed to the doctrine of natural rights.

Despite numerous domestic and business responsibilities, Lyon found the lure of political life irresistible. He won the Congressional race for Caldwell County's seat in 1803 and continued to represent his district in the House of Representatives until 1811. In this interval he again took an aggressive position on many key issues, but he no longer played the role of ideologue of Republicanism. In fact, he split with Republicans, both North and South, on various occasions, indicating the lack of cohesion within the party's ranks once it assumed power. Lyon was no longer a spokesman for a crusading political movement; during his second congressional career, his position in Congress reflected his new concerns both as a merchant and as a representative of the southwestern frontier.

The sensational Yazoo land controversy brought Lyon to the fore of public attention in 1804, when he locked horns with the formidable House majority leader, John Randolph of Virginia. The dispute originated in 1795, when the state legislature of Georgia sold to four speculative land companies 35,000,000 acres of land lying between its western boundary and the Mississippi River, for the trivial sum of $500,000. An aroused public soon exposed flagrant corruption behind the Yazoo Act of 1795, revealing that every legislator but one was personally interested in these lands, either through investment or bribery. Responding to the public indignation in 1796, the Georgia legislature repealed the infamous act of the previous year, tearing its pages from the legislative journal, burning them, and pronouncing the contract null and void.

The matter was not allowed to rest with this action, however. Thousands of speculators in the East, who had bought property from the original, culpable land companies, considered themselves innocent victims of Georgia's abrogation of the contract. Insisting that they had bought the land in good faith from the original purchasers, they formed the New England and Mississippi Company to defend their claims, selecting Postmaster General Gideon Granger as their agent.

In the meantime Georgia had ceded its western lands to the federal government, including the land involved in the Yazoo Act of 1795. A federal commission proposed a compromise whereby 5,000,000 of the original 35,000,000 acres of the Yazoo lands be set aside to settle any claims that might arise. The matter was then submitted to Congress for approval.[28]

At this juncture, John Randolph rose in righteous indignation to conduct a furious attack on any compromise that would make concessions to
the practices of bribery and corruption. In the name of Republican vir-
tue, he introduced a series of resolutions upholding "the inalienable
right of a people" to abrogate an act "endeavoring to betray them,"[29] insisting that no claims under the Yazoo Act of 1795 be recognized. Because the majority of claimants were Northerners, the dispute assumed a
sectional character, with the Southern Republicans supporting Randolph
and the Northerners, both Republicans and Federalists, opposing him.[30]

Matthew Lyon disassociated himself from his Southern colleagues by
vigorously opposing Randolph's resolutions. He added amendments of his
own that paved the way to compromise. When he was accused of betraying the Republican cause, he countered that Randolph's resolutions contained "political heresy."[31] Lyon aimed the main thrust of his argument
at Randolph's contention that the Georgia legislature had the right to
abrogate the treaty of 1795. He insisted that Georgia's actions violated
the sanctity of contract obligations, arguing that "one of the most
valuable traits in our Government is that property is secured by known
and established rules in the acquirement and transfer of it; the Legislature that gave it has no more right to snatch it back again than individuals have when they give away or sell their property."[32]

Six years later, Chief Justice Marshall used similar arguments in the
case of *Fletcher v. Peck*, ruling that Georgia's 1796 Repeal Act was unconstitutional because the state violated its contract obligations.[33]
Significantly, Matthew Lyon, the former standard-bearer of Republicanism, and Chief Justice John Marshall, the high priest of Federalism,
shared the same views concerning the priority of property rights over
moral considerations. Lyon's political positions after 1800 increasingly
reflect his viewpoint as an entrepreneur, placing him, on more than one
occasion, in agreement with the Federalists.

Continuing his argument, Lyon insisted that "Public faith, once
pledged by the Constitutional authority had ever been with me sacred as
the sanctum sanctorum itself."[34] As an illustration, he made an analogy
between the Yazoo land scandal and the speculation accompanying
Hamilton's program for funding the debt in 1791. He pointed out that he
had considered the funding system brought about by corruption, and the
most insidious means by which men rose from indigence to opulence, yet,
much as he hated the transaction, once public faith was pledged he could
not consent to a breach of it. Any other remedy "would encourage a
revolutionary spirit . . . a spirit which would tend to disorganization, to
anarchy and confusion." Once again, Lyon's position resembled that of
his former political opponents. In language borrowed from the high
Federalists of the 1790s he upheld the cause of order, while Randolph
continued the Republican tradition of crusading against speculation and
corruption.

As far as bribery was concerned, Lyon cavalierly commented that "very few titles in the United States would bear investigation" if they were to be invalidated because of bribery. He went back into history to show the favoritism that accompanied the land grants made by the Crown and gave further examples of questionable land grants made to members of the Vermont legislature. The cure for corruption, he insisted, was not to invalidate the titles, which would injure innocent parties, but for the electorate to oust the offending legislators.

Another of Lyon's arguments was that the courts rather than the legislature should have sole power of adjudicating property disputes. He charged the "wise men of the South" with "assuming to themselves in a Legislative capacity the power of the Judiciary of the Nation and denouncing in more cases than one the claims of people who could not even have a hearing before them." Alluding to his experience in Vermont, he stated that he had learned "that a Legislative body is of all others the most incompetent to the adjudication of disputes about property."[35]

Finally, Lyon explained why the issue of the Yazoo lands was a matter of personal concern to him. It was his "high interest" in the settlement of the western country. At present, he explained, the country lying between his residence and the seats of commerce on the Mississippi is a "harbor for the most desperate robbers and murderers," who harass his neighbors on their way to and from the market. The remedy to this lawless condition is settlement of the country by "owners of the soil," but such settlement, he maintained "must be retarded by the doubt of the title which is offered while two claims exist."[36]

This argument was probably Lyon's most fundamental reason for opposing Randolph's intransigent position. It served the best interests of frontier settlers like himself to resolve the Yazoo controversy so that the land adjoining them would soon be settled and cultivated. His position paralleled that of the federal commissioners appointed by Jefferson, who justified their compromise proposal on the grounds that it would ensure tranquility and security of land titles for future settlers.[37]

Randolph, enraged by Lyon's opposition, attributed a more dubious set of motives to his stand. He linked him to Postmaster General Gideon Granger, who had petitioned Congress in behalf of the New England and Mississippi Company. Randolph charged that Granger used the "tremendous patronage" at his disposal to bribe Lyon and other Congressmen with contracts for carrying the mail. In a scathing reference to Lyon, Randolph asserted that Granger "maintains a jackal, fed, not as you would suppose, upon the offal of contract, but with the fairest pieces in the shambles; and at night, when honest men are in bed, does this obscene animal prowl through the streets of this vast and desolate city, seeking whom he may tamper with."[38] He specifically charged that Lyon had offered a postal contract to a member of the House in an attempt to influence his vote. Shortly after this "independent man" declared he would take the contract but would vote against the Yazoo claims compromise, he was told that the contract "was previously bespoken."[39]

Lyon rose the following day to prove that he was Randolph's equal in spewing invective. Asserting that Randolph's allegations were "the braying of a jackal and fulminations of a madman," he declaimed, "these charges have been brought against me by a person nursed in the bosom of opulence, inheriting the life services of a numerous train of the human species, and extensive fields, the original proprietors of which property, in all probability, came no honester by it than the purchasers of the Georgia lands did by what they claim." Lyon further charged that Randolph's animosity toward him was induced by his false sense of class superiority: "It is long since I have observed that the very sight of my plebian face has had an unpleasant effect on the gentleman's nose."[40] The theme of Lyon's rhetoric remained the same as in the 1790s; he continued to malign his enemies as "aristocrats."

So far as his postal contracts were concerned, Lyon freely acknowledged and listed them, stating that he obtained his earliest agreements before he enjoyed the "pleasure of a personal acquaintance with the present Postmaster General." He insisted that, as a merchant, he had a legitimate right to obtain them, and emphatically denied that he received or offered such contracts as a bribe. Far from assuming a defensive position, he charged that he and Gideon Granger had been "eggregiously belied" by Randolph, and he challenged Randolph "to bring forward his boasted proof." This John Randolph failed to do.

Despite the aspersions that the House Speaker cast upon Matthew Lyon's postal contracts, it is doubtful, though not inconceivable, that Lyon adopted his position on the Yazoo lands because of his patronage ties to Gideon Granger. It is more likely that his stand coincided with that of the postmaster general because of Lyon's desire to bring about settlement in the western territory. This was the cornerstone of his position, and both within Congress and without, he attacked the Southerners for being satisfied with leaving the land uncultivated. In his opinion it was the Southerners' fear of competition from the west that accounted for their refusal to compromise the Yazoo land question. "I fancy that the Southern gentry begin to be alarmed for their markets," he wrote Ninian Edwards in the midst of the debate in Congress. "They begin to see that in proportion as the Western Country grows in population and industry their markets for tobacco, flour and cotton will be overstocked."[41]

Whether or not Lyon was correct in assessing their underlying motives, John Randolph and his Southern followers succeeded in blocking any settlement of the Yazoo land issue until Randolph was no longer in Congress. It was not until 1814 that the issue was finally resolved along the lines of compromise that Lyon advocated in 1805.

Lyon had a penchant for making alliances of a questionable nature. Among his close acquaintances he numbered General James Wilkinson,

military governor of the Louisiana Territory, who was to achieve national notoriety for his suspicious connections with Aaron Burr. It was
General Wilkinson who in 1806 disclosed Burr's allegedly treasonable
plot to sever the western part of the Union and possibly also to conquer
Mexico. The full participation of Wilkinson's troops was indispensable to
Burr's projected military exploits. That the general was "implicated up to
his armpits in the conspiracy"[42] has been proven by later research, but at
the time of his disclosures, his role was ambiguous and unclear. Apparently, Wilkinson was aware that rumors were rampant in New
Orleans about Burr's plans, and so he disclosed them to President Jefferson in order to disassociate himself from Burr and his conspiracy. He
pretended that his involvement was merely to entrap Burr.

Matthew Lyon first made James Wilkinson's acquaintance during the
Revolution, when Lyon served as his scout during the Battle of Bennington. At that time Lyon thought him "the likeliest young man I ever
saw." These sentiments he expressed to President Jefferson in 1801, in a
letter reporting his impressions of the western country. The occasion for
these comments was his renewed acquaintance with the general, whom
he described to the President as "industrious and zealous for the public
welfare."[43]

At the time Lyon wrote of the general in these glowing terms, he could
have had no premonitions of his later course. In 1805, however, James
Wilkinson gave Lyon grounds for suspicion by bringing him perilously
close to his intrigues with Aaron Burr. Lyon was in Congress at the time.
As the session was about to adjourn, General Wilkinson approached him
to recommend some office for Aaron Burr, whose term of office as vice
president would soon expire. Matthew Lyon previously had spurned
Burr's acquaintance because of his attempt to buy Lyon's vote during the
heated contest for the presidency in the House election of 1800. Nevertheless, in 1805, when Burr's political prospects in the East were destroyed because of the fatal outcome of his duel with Alexander Hamilton,
Lyon considered him "persecuted for what I considered no more than
fair play among duelists."[44] He therefore willingly mapped out a plan for
reviving Aaron Burr's political fortunes in the West, suggesting that he
settle in Nashville and set up a law practice there. By the following summer, Lyon predicted, "his pre-eminent talents and suavity of manners"
should have won him sufficient friends to secure his election to the House
of Representatives, where he would probably become Speaker.

James Wilkinson responded enthusiastically to Lyon's plan of action
and immediately arranged an appointment between Lyon and the "little
counsellor." Lyon commented, however, that Aaron Burr "did not seem
so much enamored of the project as General Wilkinson." He told Lyon
he had "indispensable" business to attend to, involving a trip to Philadelphia and an excursion down the Ohio into the western country. Lyon

warned him that "all chances of obtaining the election in Tennessee would be jeopardized if not lost, by such a delay."

According to Lyon's testimony, he inadvertently maintained contact with James Wilkinson and Aaron Burr during the pair's fateful journey down the Ohio. He was on his way to Eddyville, traveling as usual by boat. Although he refused Burr's request to delay his departure from Pittsburgh so that they could all travel together, Burr and General Wilkinson later caught up with him, and they lashed their boats together until they reached Marietta, Ohio. There the two parties separated. Burr and Wilkinson stopped at an island on the Ohio River owned by an Irish refugee, Harman Blennerhassett, who later was charged with being a co-conspirator. His island was to serve as a base from which recruits would join up with General Wilkinson's troops.[45] There is every reason to suspect that the scheming triumvirate hatched this part of their plot on this occasion.

Soon after their departure from Blennerhassett's island, Burr and Wilkinson rejoined Lyon at the Ohio falls. One is forced to question whether they kept their schemes a secret from him. Certainly they were in closest communication throughout this significant voyage; Aaron Burr, in fact, stopped at Matthew Lyon's home in Eddyville before departing for Nashville. In Lyon's account of their conversations, he disclosed only discussions of Burr's electoral prospects in Tennessee, reporting that he advised the aspiring candidate that his chances for obtaining the nomination had diminished because of the delay that his trip had caused. Whether they also discussed Aaron Burr's more devious schemes, Lyon, of course, did not disclose, and one can only conjecture whether the conspirators confided their plot to him. Although there is a distinct possibility that he had knowledge of the conspiracy, Lyon reported only that he suspected Burr of having "other objects in view to which I could not penetrate. . . . There seemed too much mystery in his conduct."

After this memorable trip, Lyon showed ambivalence in his attitude toward General Wilkinson. On the one hand, he wrote his son-in-law in March 1806, "I have reason to believe General Wilkinson is my friend and will befriend you . . . if you treat him and his opinions as a Man in his station and his great Merit and experience deserves, I don't mean I am a friend to his Errors, Every Man has his faults."[46]

While expressing continued respect and friendship for James Wilkinson in this letter, a month later Lyon conveyed distrust of his old friend in an urgent letter to President Jefferson. By this time rumors of a secession movement were rampant in New Orleans,[47] and Lyon sent President Jefferson a circular containing a scathing attack on the general. He warned that the circular expressed the sentiments of the president's best friends and advised: "I am inclined to think an order to the General to remove to some place nearer to the Spanish Frontier where he could conveniently direct the operations and watch the movement of the Spanish forces, would give great satisfaction to the friends of the administration and his place might then be filled more unexceptionably and the murmur pass away."[48]

Lyon prefaced this suggestion with the comment, "I am not in the habit of deserting those I profess friendship to" and indicated that only exceptional circumstances would prompt him to make such a proposal. From his extreme recommendation that the president transfer and replace General Wilkinson as military governor of Louisiana, a fair inference can be made that Lyon strongly suspected or actually knew of the general's separatist plot and sought to forestall it in this manner.

It was Wilkinson who finally quashed the Burr conspiracy and at the same time saved his own neck, by relaying to President Jefferson the contents of a message from Burr, which he supposedly intercepted. President Jefferson received the message on November 25, 1806, and immediately ordered a trial, which became one of the most controversial criminal prosecutions in the nation's history. Although Aaron Burr escaped conviction of treason on technical grounds, reams of evidence testified to the far-ranging lengths of his plot. While it was never made clear just what Burr was up to, the testimony indicated that among his alternatives were plans to lead a secession of the western states and to launch an attack upon Mexico. By providing much of the testimony, General Wilkinson aroused the suspicions of John Randolph who, as foreman of the grand jury, found serious grounds for thinking him guilty of treason. Upon his return to Congress, the enraged Randolph demanded a House investigation of charges that Wilkinson had received money from Spain while a United States Army officer. The sensationalism of Burr's trial became transferred to the House, as John Randolph branded the controversial general with such epithets as "rogue, peculator and would be murderer."[49]

As a member of the House, Matthew Lyon at first opposed a Congressional investigation of General Wilkinson on constitutional grounds. He insisted that "to determine a man guilty of crimes of great enormity without a hearing, without examination of testimony, and without a possible defense was hostile to every principle of justice and common humanity." Lyon took pains to explain that he was not attempting to protect the General, for he admitted "he had long had a suspicion of this man." Although he thought a "thorough investigation" was necessary, it should not be conducted by a legislative body; the proper mode to be pursued, Lyon maintained, was a military trial.[50]

Although he correctly understood the jeopardy to civil liberties that a nonjudicial investigation entailed, Lyon was unable to withstand the pressure of public opinion. Ever the opportunist, he abandoned his principled position several days later and advocated that the members of the

House "should show the world that they were not ashamed to go on with an inquiry which every part of the nation called for."[51]

Before the investigation took place, Lyon again went on record as an opponent of his former friend. In February 1808 he advised President Jefferson to fill the vacancy immediately for the governorship of Louisiana. Otherwise, he warned, "your enemies will say you mean to keep the emoluments of that Office for General Wilkinson . . . as to reward him for his atrocities."[52]

James Wilkinson apparently still believed he could count on Matthew Lyon's support. During the House inquiry that took place in 1811, he called upon him to testify to the general's innocence of Aaron Burr's plans in the spring of 1805. The purport of the written questions he addressed to Lyon was to show that the object of Aaron Burr's trip down the Ohio to Tennessee was "for the professed intention to canvas for the proposed election to Congress."[53]

In his deposition Matthew Lyon acknowledged that the Tennessee election was discussed, but added that, at the time, he suspected that Aaron Burr had "other objects" in mind. "These objects," he continued, "I then believed were known to General Wilkinson; but I had no idea at that time, of his having any treasonable project in his head."[54] Thus, far from clearing James Wilkinson, Matthew Lyon absolved himself while implicating the general. During this period neither Matthew Lyon's testimony nor the massive data presented to the House Committee and two successive courts-martial were sufficient to convict the evasive general. Only years later did the opening of the Spanish archives reveal that James Wilkinson acted as a paid agent of the Spanish government.[55]

It is doubtful that Matthew Lyon knew the full extent of James Wilkinson's treasonous designs, particularly his collaboration with the Spanish government. Nevertheless the evidence suggests that he may have gleaned intimations of the secessionist plot in its initial stage, when he was on friendly terms with the general. Apparently this relationship proved a source of embarrassment to Matthew Lyon after 1805, when he disassociated himself from the general by renouncing him in public circles. Whether he did so out of patriotism or from self-interest is a matter of conjecture.

While the furor over the Burr conspiracy preoccupied the nation domestically during most of the years that Matthew Lyon served as Congressman from Kentucky, foreboding events also loomed on the international scene. England and France, who were locked in combat on land and sea, attacked the neutral rights of American ships, making it hazardous to trade with either country. In an effort to retaliate and yet avoid war, President Jefferson urged Congress to pass an embargo that would deprive both powers of American goods by forbidding American ships to leave United States ports.

As a merchant engaged in commerce, Matthew Lyon took violent exception to the embargo because of its drastic curtailment of American trade. He rose repeatedly in Congress to oppose this "political hydrophobia," arguing that "it was a curious mode of retaliation . . . to thrash ourselves."[56] In his view the embargo represented "the very essence of submission," through which we sacrificed not only our ocean trade but also, what was of direct concern to Matthew Lyon, "our innocent coasting trade." He advanced instead a typical laissez faire position, "in which every man is allowed to embargo himself or to exercise his energies and employ his capital or his credit to his own emolument, and the benefit of the nation."[57] In essence, Matthew Lyon adopted the same position as the New England Federalists; like them, he viewed national policy from the vantage point of a merchant.

It is interesting to note, however, that Matthew Lyon also reflected the influence of the frontier, by advocating an aggressive policy towards Canada. In February 1808 he wrote President Jefferson that "the time for preparing to take Montreal this year . . . is fast slipping away," explaining that Montreal could be captured easily if approached by ice before the spring thaw set in. In great detail he mapped out a strategy for seizing Montreal, based on his knowledge of the region gained from his Vermont experience, and reminiscent of his expansionist aspirations of those years. However, Matthew Lyon's strategy this time was not to annex Canada, but to use Montreal as a pawn with which to bring the British to terms. He made certain to caution the president against asking Congress to sanction this move by a declaration of war, stating, "I am so much a Quaker politician I shall hardly ever be brought to vote for a declaration of war."[58]

It was on these ostensibly pacifist grounds that he opposed the Non-Intercourse Act, maintaining that if France dropped her orders against American shipping, the United States would become her ally and be plunged into war with Great Britain. As this possibility loomed more imminent, Matthew Lyon became more vociferous. "War, war seems to be the cry," he protested, warning that "the power and the strength of this nation . . . is totally inadequate to waging war."[59]

The thrust of Matthew Lyon's position was accommodation. He insisted that the United States recognize the realities of her military position and demanded, "Will you fight on the ocean with a power vastly superior to yourselves for the command of that ocean, or will you content yourselves with that use of the ocean which your relative power, strength and importance as a nation entitle you to expect . . . ?"[60] From his commercial point of view, the solution to the problems with Great Britain lay not in war but in the negotiation of a "most favored nation" trade agreement.[61]

While attempting to circumvent an aggressive war at any cost, Lyon conceded the necessity of making preparations for a defensive war. Although he opposed strengthening the Navy to fight Great Britain on the ocean as a "Quixotic expedition," he was critical of the "partial" defensive preparation made by Congress and advocated a "whole system" of military preparedness at home.[62]

In opposing the embargo, the Non-Intercourse legislation, and finally the war itself, Lyon split with the leadership of the Republican Party. He referred derisively to Thomas Jefferson and James Madison as "our great men" and accused them of betraying the "Old Republican Party of 1798." That party, he lamented, no longer exists: it is "broken down and its leaders, in desperation, have formed themselves into a caucus to save the remnants."[63]

As a dissident within the party, Lyon bitterly assailed the minority control exercised by the caucus members. "It seems as if we are to look for all national measures to be first canvassed in these midnight meetings by this self-created caucus gentry," he complained in 1809. He not only objected to "a caucus army . . . a caucus non-intercourse . . . a caucus loan" but to the ultimate consequence of this system, "the election of a caucus President."[64] His position on this issue foreshadowed that of Andrew Jackson; several years before Jackson made the caucus a national campaign issue, Matthew Lyon wrote President Monroe of his detestation of the "caucus mode of nomination," which he viewed as an "Unconstitutional usurpation" of power subject to "corruption."[65]

So strong was Lyon's opposition to the dominant group in the party that in 1812 he offered himself as candidate for the Electoral College, committing himself to oppose the nomination of James Madison. He blamed the president for urging Congress to declare war when the nation was insufficiently fortified and pledged himself to cast his vote for "a Republican candidate . . . who is most likely to bring this war to a conclusion by an honorable peace."[66]

In this same circular Lyon defended himself against charges of "antirepublican federalism." His war hawk opponents in Kentucky had branded him a "tory" and a "British partisan" and ultimately succeeded in linking Lyon with his former Federalist foes. There is little doubt that his positions in Congress paralleled those of the New England Federalists and supported the "commercial interests" they represented. Moreover, Lyon became a close personal friend of Massachusetts Federalist Josiah Quincy during the Embargo controversy, a further corroboration to his critics of his shift in political bedfellows.[67]

While siding with the New England Federalists before 1812, Lyon did, however, take extreme exception to their separatist schemes after the war broke out. He wrote Josiah Quincy, "The step I most dreaded seems ready to be taken; I mean the separation of the States, and that through the folly of the National Government. . . . Permit me, my dear sir, once more to remind you of the importance of preserving the Union to the last extremity."[68] Lyon later described the Federalist activities during the Hartford Convention as the "designs of the malcontent disseverating gentry," an indication that his identification with the New England Federalists was less than complete.[69]

From 1811 on, however, the electorate of Kentucky identified him with the Federalist opponents of the War of 1812 and refused to reelect him, although he repeatedly ran for his former seat. With accurate prophecy, one of his critics commented, "His palpable apostasy, when in Congress, from Democratic principles—his long devotion to the cause of the opposition—his intemperance, his ungentlemanly manners etc. have sunk his popularity so far below par that he will never regain it."[70]

It should not be assumed that because Matthew Lyon opposed the War of 1812 he was either an isolationist or a pacifist. On the contrary, within the next few years he emerged as an ardent expansionist, an early proponent of "Manifest Destiny" who welcomed war with Spain. "Believing as I do that the more America comes under the control of the Anglo-Americans the better for the world, I care not how soon a rupture takes place," he wrote President-elect James Monroe in 1816.[71] By later publishing this letter, Lyon circulated views that soon became the common currency of the aggressive frontiersmen of the southwest. He decried Northern jealousy of the growing power and population of the South and West, and he talked of America becoming "a larger empire than ever yet created."[72] This was to be accomplished by eliminating Spain as a colonial power in both North and South America. Anticipating future developments, Lyon advocated supporting the revolutionists in Cuba and predicted that Florida "will fade into our hands without a struggle." He correctly predicted that Britain would support our opposition to Spain in Latin America, for "whatever of this continent becomes ours, the trade of it is open to them." Therefore England "will look with complacency" on American acquisition of Spanish territory, "however it may hasten the time when our power as a nation will exceed hers."[73]

When Lyon wrote this letter in 1816, his personal as well as political fortunes were at their lowest ebb. Recently he had suffered an economic blow from which he never recovered. A ship that he had just built, loaded with $50,000 worth of beef and pork, hit a sand bar on the way to New Orleans and could not be dislodged before the cargo rotted in the sun. Lyon had counted on discharging his New York debts, amounting to over $25,000, from the sale of the damaged merchandise. Since he knew he was ruined and hoped to save his valuable home and slaves from attachment by his creditors, he shrewdly turned his entire business holdings over to his son Chittenden, who in turn put the business property at the disposal of the creditors.[74]

While Chittenden Lyon continued to manage his father's tottering enterprises, Matthew Lyon severed all connections with these ventures and found himself with no means of gaining a livelihood. In his desperate attempt to seek alternate means of deriving an income, Lyon left no stone unturned. He petitioned Congress to remit the "illegal" fine imposed under the Sedition Act; he was more successful in seeking and obtaining a pension for his services during the Revolutionary War.[75] To friends in public and private life he wrote lengthy letters describing his past services and pleading for some form of employment. Finally he appealed directly to President Monroe, suggesting the possibility of a post as secretary of the Missouri Territory.[76]

In 1820 the President, with the approval of Congress, finally appointed him to the much more humble position of U.S. Factor to the Cherokee Indians, located at Spadre Bluffs in the wilds of Arkansas. Here Lyon spent the remaining two years of his life, undertaking the new assignment with characteristic vigor and enthusiasm. One of the purposes of the Indian factory system, which was organized in 1795, was to control the Indian trade and retain it for the United States rather than Britain or Spain. Lyon's function as factor was to supervise a trading post by buying such Indian products as fur, deer tallow, corn, and buffalo horns and selling the Indians commodities they needed. The government was not to make a profit in its trading operations but render the Indians a service, on the assumption that they in turn would be friendly to the United States government and refrain from engaging in war.[77]

Among Lyon's responsibilities were the transporting, packing, and purchasing of the traded items, which involved long and strenuous trips on flatboats, also constructed under his supervision.[78] The crudeness of his living conditions he described to his family on a visit to Eddyville:

> Mr. Jones and myself have lived there alone on venison and bear meat broiled on the coals, and hoe cake baked in the ashes, with coffee when we wished and we have slept upon bear skins upon the floor; I have not laid my old worn-out frame upon a feather bed since I left this house.[79]

Quite understandably Lyon's family tried to prevail upon him to remain at home, insisting that at the age of seventy-one the life of an Indian trader was too arduous. Rather than stagnate at home, Lyon countered, he preferred the stimulation of useful work among the Indians.[80]

Prior to his experience at Spadre Bluffs, Lyon had harbored the hostile frontier stereotype of the Indians as "savages." He shared his attitude with Andrew Jackson in 1816, when he described a discussion of the Indian problem he had had with President Madison several years earlier. "Colonel Lyon," the President asked, "don't you think the Indians originally the right and proper owners of the Soil of this country?" Lyon sarcastically replied, "Yes Sir, in conjunction with the Bears and the

Wolves." He boasted that after the lengthy conversation that ensued, he convinced the President to change a report he planned "on the injurious manner the Indians had been treated respecting their lands."[81]

Not only did Lyon repudiate the humane concern for the Indians that was typical of such Republicans as Jefferson and Madison, he actively supported the repressive policies of Andrew Jackson. In jubilation over Jackson's victory in the Seminole War, Lyon wrote the General in August 1818, "I cannot avoid expressing to you something of the pride I feel in haveing freely anticipated the Glory with which you covered yourself, and the honour and service you have done your Country."[82]

His experience as factor to the Indians altered Lyon's attitude markedly. This metamorphosis is apparent from the comments made by the superintendent of Indian trade, Colonel Thomas L. McKinney, in reply to Lyon's correspondence. On one occasion he praised Lyon for attending a Cherokee dance and said "that 'God of one blood' made them as well as you."[83]

On a more practical matter, Lyon urged the superintendent to supply the Cherokees with a cotton gin so they could learn to cultivate the soil. In his reply, McKinney promised to fulfill Lyon's request and applauded his goal. "Our object," he agreed, "is not to keep these Indians hunters eternally. We want to make citizens out of them, and they must first be anchored in the soil."[84] When the government dallied in delivering the cotton gin, Lyon became impatient and talked of taking steps to transport his own cotton gin by keel boat from Eddyville to Spadre Bluffs.[85]

Whether Lyon's constructive plans for the Indians ever materialized is doubtful; unexpected circumstances intervened to frustrate what might have been his last creative enterprise. In 1822 Thomas McKinney wrote him that the government's cotton gin had to be deferred until Congress decided on the continuance or abandonment of the factory system.[86] The following May, under pressure from private fur trading companies, Congress voted to terminate this early experiment in government enterprise.[87]

Before this denouement, Lyon made one last foray into the political arena, and entered the Congressional race for the House of Representatives from the Arkansas Territory. The election was close; his family fully expected him to win, but on October 31, 1821, Chittenden Lyon informed his relatives that "Father has lost the election in Arkansas by 61 votes."[88]

The following year Lyon died a lonely death, away from his family in an Arkansas trading post. He was laid to rest at first in the Mission at Spadre Bluffs, but his family later honored his dying wish by transporting his remains to Eddyville, where they buried him with Masonic rites. According to his daughter, over 4,000 persons attended the ceremonies, to pay a more fitting farewell to a man who had spent the prime of his life as a representative of the people.[89]

Matthew Lyon departed from this world as he had lived in it—with a flourish. Since the Indians claimed they had preserved his body when they buried him more than ten years earlier, his admirers raised the lid of the coffin to take one parting look at him. When the air touched his skin, the clear features of his face disintegrated before their astonished eyes, and blew away to the four corners of the earth.

Conclusion: An Ambivalent Legacy

An intriguing dimension of the life of Matthew Lyon is the confluence of his emotional drives with the mainstream of the movement of his times. This overlapping and interacting of the external currents of society and the internal currents of individual lives is what creates motion in history. The foregoing biography of Matthew Lyon offers us an opportunity to make a case analysis of this process by scrutinizing the relationship of his personality to the role he played in the "Democratic Revolution" of his era.

I use the term analysis in its broadest, nontechnical sense. Since there is so little material available concerning his childhood, an attempt at a psychoanalytic interpretation of his personality is untenable. For the purposes of this interpretation, the available information that begins with his adolescence must suffice to account for the relationship between his emotional complexities and his political behavior. From this material, certain patterns of behavior emerge with sufficient consistency to enable us to attempt a diagnosis of their wellsprings.

Certainly there is evidence that he was wounded deeply by his position of social inferiority as an indentured servant, that he was extremely sensitive about any allusion to it, and that he spent his entire life attempting to elevate his status and overcome this sense of inferiority.

Certainly also there is evidence that he harbored deep anger against those who claimed superiority over him. One need only recall that he threw a mallet at his master, Hugh Hannah, in colonial Connecticut; that he beat up Nathaniel Chipman, his Yale-educated political rival on the Vermont frontier; and that he spat in the face of another luminous opponent, Roger Griswold, in the halls of Congress, to illustrate the physical manifestations of his rage.

Had Matthew Lyon lived in an earlier period of American history, his anger against the entrenched elite might have been directed into antisocial channels. As it was, the Revolution and the ensuing Democratic-Republican movement gave Lyon the opportunity to express both his aggression and his ambition constructively. His anger and his need to overcome his sense of inferiority served as the dynamic impetus behind his political activity in behalf of the "democratic revolution" of his time.

Throughout his career, the target of his hostility was the aristocracy. His favorite label of contempt was "aristocrat," an epithet he applied to his political enemies of every period, whether they be Yorkers in the 1770s, the British during the Revolution, the Federalists in the 1790s, or Southern slaveholders in the Yazoo land controversy of the early 1800s. His goal was nothing less than to be the "scourge of aristocracy," as he boldly declared in the title of his Republican magazine.

These observations are not meant to suggest that Lyon's political activity was based on neurotic fantasies and irrational projections of his hostility. His scars were real. The elite *had* wounded him: in Ireland, in Connecticut, in Vermont. He battled for social equality because his own emotional experience of inequality and oppression enabled him to identify with the oppressed. His anger toward his own oppressors energized him; this accounts for the vigor with which he fought his political battles against aristocracy.

Ironically, the same sense of inferiority that enabled him to identify with the weak also caused him to identify with the strong. To outdo the elite, he had to become one of them. Thus he not only aspired to positions of economic and political power, but he consistently achieved them. His behavior as Fairhaven's founder, who attempted to control the votes of his townsmen and lower the wages of his workingmen, indicates that even the most vehement champions of the oppressed can become oppressive themselves, if their underlying motives are status and power.

He demanded of the townspeople of Fairhaven a deference similar to that of the "aristocrats" he so vociferously denounced. Of course, the basis of the deference demanded by Lyon was different from that expected by the colonial elite. It was not because of his family's status or inherited wealth or superior culture that Matthew Lyon felt entitled to political office, but because of his own achievements, which were responsible for the enterprises that gave his employees their livelihood. In essence, he substituted the self-made man for the aristocrat as the object of deference, in a spirit similar to Jefferson's substitution of natural aristocracy for inherited aristocracy.

Lyon's personality was one of contradictions. He was a complex person, at once warm and hostile, idealistic and opportunistic, informed and untutored, sensitive and crude. His political personality too was one of ambivalence. On the one hand, he was opportunistic and self-serving. Throughout his career he was guilty of using political office to feather his own nest. As secretary of the Board of Confiscation, he used his inside position to obtain valuable confiscated and Crown lands, which, he boasted, made him rich after the Revolution. As a representative in the Vermont legislature, he attempted to obtain subsidies that would protect his infant iron manufactures, and as a representative from Kentucky he managed to obtain contracts from the government that redounded to his benefit as a frontier merchant. This was the side of Matthew Lyon that looked after his private interests.

On the other hand, he spent the major part of his political life serving the public interest. From the Revolution on, he gave unstintingly of himself to build a new Republican society. When Burgoyne's invasion made Vermont the first battleground of the Revolution, he suffered bitter hardships and served as soldier, scout, and public official to bring the Revolution to a victorious conclusion. When, in the 1790s, he believed the prevailing Federalists were threatening to undermine the egalitarian and libertarian ideals of the Revolution, he financed a Republican newspaper and used his pungent pen to alert his fellow citizens to defend their rights. In the course of his publishing activities, he invented a process for manufacturing paper out of wood pulp and bade mankind welcome to his invention without patenting it for his own benefit. He spearheaded the formation of Vermont Democratic-Republican Societies, planting the ideological seeds that eventually flowered into the Jeffersonian Republican Party.

Later, in Congress during the 1790s, he brashly challenged every practice and policy that smacked of aristocracy and boldly defended the French Revolution as the sister of America's own. His allegiance to the rights of man was instinctive and passionate, making him even more of an anathema to the Federalists than the well-born and well-bred Republican Congressmen who also opposed preparing for war against the French Republic.

Little wonder that this "raw new man" was the first victim of the Sedition Act of 1798. His behavior in the Vergennes jail was more than that of a martyr; it was that of a crusader mustering all of his resources to do battle for a sacred cause. Thus he eventually "converted" his constituents, who freed him from jail and sent him back to Congress to continue to defend Republicanism and its cardinal principle of dissent. If it is true that the decade of the 1790s was the era in which the party system emerged as the democratic method of transferring power,[1] then surely Matthew Lyon deserves a page in history as one whose sacrifices helped to forge that political pattern.

Although his energies after 1800 were mainly channeled into rebuilding his economic and political fortunes, it is significant that in his final years he turned again to service to sustain his vitality. Although others of his status may have found the position of an Indian Factor beneath their dignity, Lyon derived satisfaction not only from being active again, but particularly from being "useful." This was part of his Republican creed and represents the side of him that was dedicated to his fellow man rather than merely to his own private interests.

Is there any resolution to this apparent contradiction between Matthew Lyon's self-serving egotism and his dedicated humanism? Or is this ambiguity merely a reflection of the complexity of the human condition, an example of the ambivalent currents that stir in all of us? Perhaps. But perhaps also there are other avenues to explore, avenues affected by the external currents of his time. Surely Lyon was influenced by the Enlightenment ideas of the eighteenth century, the "harmonizing sentiments of the day,"[2] which Jefferson summarized in the Declaration of Independence.

Could it be, finally, that the ambiguity we find in Matthew Lyon is a reflection of the ambivalence of the heritage of the American Revolution itself?

It has been argued recently by Garry Wills that there is a conflict between the right to property and the right to the pursuit of happiness, both of which are part of the Enlightenment heritage of the American Revolution. According to Wills's argument, while John Locke of the English Enlightenment stressed the egocentric, private nature of property rights, Francis Hutcheson of the Scotch Enlightenment stressed the benevolent, social nature of man's right to pursue happiness.

Jefferson was embracing Hutcheson's doctrine when he listed the pursuit of happiness as an unalienable right, in the Declaration of Independence. This right, he believed, derived from man's innate "moral sense," his need to contribute to the well-being of his fellow man in order to find personal happiness, which in turn depended upon the well-being of the social community.

To Hutcheson and Jefferson, continues Wills's argument, property was a social rather than a natural right. Its purpose was not to satisfy individual selfish propensities but "to promote human intercourse and solidarity." The difference between the two doctrines is that the right to property centers around the advancement of the individual, while the right to pursuit of happiness ties individual advancement to the well-being of the community.[3]

Scholars are likely to debate the merits of this argument ad infinitum,[4] but if they wish to find an example of a figure who embraced both of these divergent strands of the democratic revolution, they would be well-advised to turn to the life of Matthew Lyon.

Notes

Most citations in the notes are in short form; complete references appear in the Bibliography. Items cited frequently are abbreviated as follows:

ALR, Deeds   Arlington Land Records, Record of Deeds
Annals   *Debates and Proceedings in the Congress of the United States*
EA Narr.   *Narrative of Ethan Allen*
FL   *Farmers' Library* (Fairhaven, Vt.)
HC   Haldimand Correspondence (in VRGC, 2)
Lyon to Mason   Letter, Matthew Lyon to General Stevens T. Mason, in jail at Vergennes, Oct. 14, 1798, in *The Scourge of Aristocracy*, October 15, 1798.
MSS SPV   Manuscript State Papers of Vermont
SA   *The Scourge of Aristocracy* (Fairhaven, Vt.)
SPV   *State Papers of Vermont*
VRGC   *Vermont Records of Governor and Council*

Historical Societies, Libraries, and Manuscript Collections

Conn. SL   Connecticut State Library
Ill. SHL Messenger Illinois State Historical Library, Messenger Papers
JMMF   James Monroe Memorial Foundation
LHS Ransom   Litchfield Historical Society, Ransom Collection
Mass. HS   Massachusetts Historical Society
N.C. SHC   University of North Carolina, Southern Historical Collection
N.Y. HS   New York Historical Society
N.Y. PL   New York Public Library
N.Y. SL   New York State Library
Pa. HS   Pennsylvania Historical Society
Vt. HS   Vermont Historical Society
Vt. WL   University of Vermont, Wilbur Library
Wis. HS   State Historical Society of Wisconsin
YUL   Yale University Library

Introduction   (pages 1–5)

1. Hofstadter, *American Political Tradition*, p. 56.
2. Quoted in Young, *Democratic Republicans*, p. 33.
3. Quoted in Wood, *Creation of the American Republic*, p. 477.

4. "Changing Interpretations of Early American Politics," in Billington, ed., *Reinterpretations of Early American History*, p. 173.

5. Wood, *Creation of the American Republic*, p. 480.

6. *FL*, Feb. 17, 1794.

7. The concept of the "democratic revolution" as an international movement is fully developed in Palmer, *Age of the Democratic Revolution*.

8. Main, *Upper House*; Martin, *Men in Rebellion*.

9. Goodman, *Democratic-Republicans*, pp. 77, 108–15.

10. Young, *Democratic Republicans*, pp. 34–39, 48–49, 54.

11. Baumann, "John Swanwick," p. 139.

12. *Political Censor*, May 1796, p. 192.

13. *Biographical Directory of the American Congress*, p. 1285; Brunhouse, *Counter-Revolution in Pennsylvania*, pp. 214, 217, 263; Link, *Democratic-Republican Societies*, p. 89.

Chapter 1   (pages 7–13)

1. Matthew S. Lyon to Pliny White, Sept. 12, 1858, Vt. HS, Pliny White Papers.

2. This deduction is based on the following information. On June 28, 1820, Lyon swore an affidavit stating he was seventy years, eleven months, and sixteen days old. This affidavit is recorded in the proceedings of the Circuit Court of Caldwell County, Ky., July 12, 1820, and is contained in the *Revolutionary War Pension File of Matthew Lyon S36 689*. Most biographical sketches of Lyon have accepted as his birthdate July 14, 1750, given by J.F. McLaughlin in 1900 in the only full-length biography of Matthew Lyon to date. McLaughlin based his acceptance of this date on a handwritten family record, which he speculated was entered by Lyon's widow after her husband's death (see pp. 29–33). The date, July 14, 1749, based on Lyon's own sworn testimony, should supersede the secondhand testimony upon which McLaughlin based his estimate of Lyon's birthdate.

3. Lyon to Worsley, Dec. 1, 1819, Wis. HS, Draper Manuscripts, Kentucky Papers.

4. Mittelberger, *Journey to Pennsylvania*, pp. 12–16.

5. Roe to J. Fairfax McLaughlin, May 24, 1881, reproduced in J.F. McLaughlin, *Matthew Lyon*, pp. 39–41.

6. Matthew S. Lyon to Pliny White, Sept. 12, 1858, Vt. HS, Pliny White Papers.

7. Cothren, *Ancient Woodbury*, p. 320; Kilbourne, *Biographical History of Litchfield*, p. 358; Woodruff, *History of the Town of Litchfield* (1845), quoted in McLaughlin, *Matthew Lyon*, p. 62.

8. Cothren, *Ancient Woodbury*, pp. 352–53.

9. Litchfield County Court Records, Books III–V (1762–75), Conn. SL. Lyon's name does not appear in any of the above records, as it might have if either he or his master had asserted their legal privilege of suing for breach of contract.

10. Morris, *Government and Labor*, pp. 400, 402, 417, 437, 438, 510.

11. Matthew S. Lyon to Pliny White, Vt. HS, Pliny White Papers.

12. Cothren, *Ancient Woodbury*, p. 320; Woodruff, *History of Litchfield*, quoted in McLaughlin, *Matthew Lyon*, p. 62. Woodruff, writing in 1845, refers only to Lyon's assignment to Hugh Hannah. Cothren, writing in 1854, specifies that Lyon was assigned to Hugh Hannah by Jabez Bacon.

13. Quoted in McLaughlin, *Matthew Lyon*, p. 36. In 1796 Fessenden had studied law under Nathaniel Chipman, a leading Vermont Federalist and Lyon's most venomous political opponent. At this time Fessenden also began his career as a poet and political satirist, writing verses for the *Farmers' Weekly Museum*, many of which resembled the above in their lampooning slurs upon the background and "Jacobin" views of Lyon and his Republican colleagues. Perrin, *Thomas Green Fessenden*, pp. 39, 41, 43, 87, 98.

14. McLaughlin, *Matthew Lyon*, p. 35.

15. Kilbourne, article submitted to the editor of the *New York Evening Post*, June 26, 1858, NYPL, Manuscript's Division, Matthew Lyon Miscellaneous Papers.

16. Roe to McLaughlin, May 24, 1881, in McLaughlin, *Matthew Lyon*, p. 41.

17. Starr, *A History of Cornwall*, p. 329.

18. Connecticut Probate Records, No. 2951, Conn. SL.

19. In the Conn. SL's Church Records Catalog, we find the following entry:

> "*Horsford*, Mary
> wid., dism. Mar. 26, 1764, of Cornwall, 'dissenting collector'
>
> Rev. T. Davies Rec.
>
> 1761–1766
> Private Records
> Litchfield Co. P.50"

E.D. Starr cites another record made by Reverend Thomas Davies, which reveals that he discharged seventeen members, including widow Mary Horsford and widow Allen and two sons, "to the dissenting collector for (Episcopalians) on March 26, 1764." *History of Cornwall*, pp. 49, 85.

20. Heimert, *Religion and the American Mind*, p. 2; Koch, *Republican Religion*, p. 286.

21. Pell, *Ethan Allen*, p. 3.

22. *Annals*, 5, 1 (June 3, 1797): 234–35.

23. Bigger, "Captain Lyon." According to this author, Bishop Lyon was formerly one of Queen Elizabeth's "Sea Hawks," and his appointment as bishop was a reward for his services.

24. *Index to the Books of the Diocese of Dublin*, pp. 57, 105.

25. Perkins, *Narrative of a Tour through Vermont*, p. 26; Anna H. Weeks to Holland Weeks, Oct. 20, 1796, Sheldon Museum; Roe, *Recollections of Frontier Life*, pp. 20–21.

26. *Ye Horsforde Book*, p. 43.

27. Starr, *History of Cornwall*, p. 329.

28. Land Records of Wallingford, Vermont, 1, no. 176, Vermont Public Records Division.

Chapter 2   (pages 14–29)

1. The following sources have been consulted for this discussion of the Hampshire Grants Controversy: *VRGC*, 1; Wilbur, *Ira Allen*; Williams, *Vermont During the War for Independence*; Williamson, *Vermont in Quandary*; Jellison, *Ethan Allen*; Pell, *Ethan Allen*.

2. Pell, *Ethan Allen*, p. 50.

3. Lyon to Hon. Armisted C. Mason, Jan. 16, 1817, JMMF.

4. *EA Narr.*, p. 5. I have consulted the following sources for the ensuing military history of the northern campaign from 1775 to 1777: Alden, *American Revolution 1775–83*; French, *Taking of Ticonderoga*; French, *First Year of the American Revolution*, Appendix 14.

5. *EA Narr.*, p. 9.

6. Lyon to Armisted C. Mason, Jan. 16, 1817, JMMF.

7. Ibid.

8. After the defeat and death of Montgomery in Montreal, however, General Wooster urgently wrote to Colonel Warner: "You, sir, and the valiant Green Mountain corps, are in our neighborhood. . . . Therefore let me beg you to raise as many men as you can, and somehow get into the country and stay with us till we can have relief from the colonies." To this plea, Warner and the Green Mountain Boys responded with "promptness and alacrity." *VRGC*, 1:18.

9. Lyon to Armisted C. Mason, Jan. 16, 1817, JMMF.

10. Fox, "Col. Matthew Lyon," p. 179.

11. *Revolutionary War Pension File of Matthew Lyon S36 689*, National Archives, Veterans Records.

12. *Annals*, 5, 2 (Feb. 12, 1798): 1025–29. Quotations in this and the following two paragraphs are from this source.

13. Schuyler to Warner, July 15, 1777, Vermont Secretary of State's Office, Stevens Papers.

14. *Revolutionary War Pension File of Matthew Lyon S36 689*, National Archives, Veterans Records.

15. Starr, *History of Cornwall*, p. 329; *Annals* 5, 2 (Feb. 12, 1798): 1028.

16. Wilkinson, *Memoirs of My Own Times*, 1: 123. Wilkinson is referring to Lyon's rank as a lieutenant in the militia in this passage. The events he describes occurred seven days before General Schuyler promoted Lyon to the rank of captain in the Continental Army.

17. Lyon to Armisted C. Mason, Jan. 16, 1817, JMMF.

18. *VRGC*, 1: 20.

19. Ibid., p. 18.

20. Williamson, *Vermont in Quandary*, pp. 18–20.

21. Ibid., pp. 61–62.

22. *VRGC*, 1: 109. Lyon is listed here as a "probable" member of this body. Since the original list of Council members is among the missing records of the Windsor Convention, Lyon's membership is not a certainty. However, the editor lists a number of "strong points in favor of the probability that he, rather than . . . any other man who can be suggested was the twelfth member of the Council" (*VRGC*, 1: 72–73). The most convincing among these is the fact that in 1777, after the Windsor Convention, Lyon moved into the Tory stronghold of Arlington with two known members of the Council, Thomas Chittenden and Ira Allen. Moreover, the fact that Lyon was elected Deputy Secretary of the Governor and Council the following April (1778), when all the other known members of the First Council of Safety were retained in that body, suggests that Lyon was in fact a member of the First Council of Safety in 1777.

23. "[Letter of Dr. Young] To the INHABITANTS OF VERMONT . . .," Philadelphia, April 11, 1777, *VRGC* 1: 395–96.

24. Ibid., p. 83. Ira Allen conferred with the Council about the Constitution on November 2, 1777. Although Lyon was still a captain in Colonel Warner's regiment, as paymaster he apparently spent much of his time "rideing express." Thus he probably could have arranged to be present at this significant meeting.

25. *VRGC*, 1: 83–95.

26. Hemenway, *Vt. Hist. Gaz.*, 2: 906–29.

27. Pell, *Ethan Allen*, p. 16; Jellison, *Ethan Allen*, p. 5.

28. MSS SPV, 17: 188.

29. *SPV*, 6: 7. The discussion in this and the following paragraph is based on pp. 7–17.

30. MSS SPV, 37: 81, 84.

31. *SPV*, 6: 32.

32. MSS SPV, 37: 38.

33. Ibid., pp. 64, 162. Later, the Commissioner of Sales reported, "I find difficulty with regard to giving him possession. I have agreed to take back one of said farms, particularly the Parrish farm and consequently there is owing the said Lyon £150." Ibid., p. 171.

34. Ibid., p. 64.

35. *SPV*, 6: 392.

36. *VRGC*, 2: 23.

37. Ibid., pp. 23–24.

38. Audit of State Treasurer's Accounts March 1777 to October 1787, cited in *VRGC*, 2: 64.

39. *VRGC*, 2: 63.

40. James Madison to General George Washington, May 1, 1782, cited in *VRGC*, 2: 394–95.

41. *VRGC*, 2: 63.

42. *SPV*, 5: 200, 258.

43. MSS SPV, 21: 19, 105, 114.

44. Adams, *History of Fairhaven*, pp. 35–36.

45. Lyon to Armisted C. Mason, Jan. 16, 1817, JMMF.

46. Jameson, *American Revolution as a Social Movement*, p. 26.

47. ALR, Deeds, 1: 54–66.

48. See note 50 for Matthew Lyon's purchase of the deed to Samuel Addams's property "for payment of public land tax." Another example is a deed from Abraham Ives, Sheriff, Collector of the Land Tax in Neshoba, to Nathaniel Chipman, dated Jan. 1, 1785. In this transaction, Chipman acquired 1 Proprietor's Share in the town of Neshoba for £ 1/9. Vt. HS, Nathaniel Chipman Collection.

49. ALR, Deeds, 1: 105, 141, 146, 153, 157, 158, 159, 160, 162, 170, 187, 201, 249, 345, 346; 2: 79, 101.

50. ALR, Deeds, 1: 146.

51. This concession stemmed from Vermont's efforts to appease the British during the Haldimand negotiations; see concluding section of this chapter.

52. Lyon to Col. Andrew Addams, Oct. 9, 1782, Vt. HS, Ellis Collection.

53. Lyon to Andrew Addams, Jan. 2, 1783, Vt. WL.

54. ALR, Deeds, 1: 146.

55. Letter, Haldimand to Lord George Germain, Jan. 11, 1779, *VRGC*, 2: 397. In Appendix 1 of this volume, the editor has reproduced those documents of the Haldimand correspondence pertaining to Vermont from the Stevens Papers, Haldimand, vols. 1 and 2. This collection, housed in the office of the Secretary of State of Vermont, consists of selections made from the British archives by Jared Sparks, which were transmitted to the Vermont historian Henry Stevens. Henceforth, materials from this source will be cited as HC.

56. HC, 397.

57. *VRGC*, 2: 47.

58. "Memoranda of Dispatch from Gen'l Haldimand to Lord Germaine concerning Ira Allen's Conversations as Commissioner from Vermont, May 8–25, 1781," HC, 414.

59. HC, 428.

60. Ibid.

61. Ibid., pp. 472–79.

62. SA, Oct. 1, 1798.

Chapter 3   (pages 30–44)

1. Adams, *History of Fairhaven*, pp. 36–37.

2. From 1779 to 1785, Lyon served on a state "Committee to Burn Money." (MSS SPV, 8: 256; 9: 146, 199, 225, 231; 10: 105.) The mere existence of this committee is an obvious indication that the state had issued an excessive amount of currency, which it recognized as causing a severe depreciation problem.

3. Adams, *History of Fairhaven*, pp. 36–37.

4. Clark, *History of Manufacturers*, p. 177.

5. Adams, *History of Fairhaven*, p. 190.

6. Fox, "Col. Matthew Lyon," p. 165.

7. Lyon to General Stevens Thompson Mason, SA, Oct. 15, 1798.

8. Lyon to Armisted C. Mason, Jan. 16, 1817, JMMF.

9. W.C. Kittredge to Pliny White, Sept. 7, 1858, Vt. HS, Pliny White Papers. Judge Kittredge was given this description of Beulah Lyon by eighty-one-year-old Curtis Kelsey, who was a boy of four when Fairhaven was first founded by Lyon.

10. William Bigelow to Pliny H. White, Sept. 10, 1858, Vt. HS, Pliny White Papers. Mr. Bigelow states that he derived his information about Lyon "From 'Major Tilly Gibert' who had know him intimately and lived in his family."

11. Adams, *History of Fairhaven*, p. 63.

12. *FL*, May 13, 1793.

13. Adams, *History of Fairhaven*, pp. 126–32.

14. Ibid., p. 126.

15. *Annals*, 8, 2 (Feb. 1, 1805): 1125–26.

16. Lyon to Mr. Levi Allen, Merchant, Oct. 30, 1786, Vt. WL. For other examples of the prevalent currency shortage, see chapter 4, note 26.

17. Adams, *History of Fairhaven*, p. 145.

18. *FL*, June 3, 1793.

19. *FL*, Oct. 28, 1794.

20. Hunter, *Papermaking*, pp. 327, 333–40.

21. Further verification of Lyon's manufacture of wood paper in the 1790s is found in the following observations made by Dr. John A. Graham in 1797: "It is a curious fact that Colonel Lyon has executed a good deal of printing at his office, on paper manufactured by himself of the bark of the basswood tree, and which is found to answer every purpose for common printing." *Descriptive Sketch*, pp. 180–81.

22. Hunter, *Papermaking*, p. 514. Joel Munsell was a nineteenth-century American printer who wrote several well-informed books on the history of printing. The one to which Hunter makes reference here was *Chronology of the Origin and Progress of Paper and Paper Making*, 1876 ed., p. 52.

23. Hunter, *Papermaking*, p. 340; Fisher, "Paper Manufacture," p. 727.

24. Hunter, *Papermaking*, p. 513.

25. *FL*, Oct. 28, 1794.

26. The instructions read as follows: "Directions for peeling and rotting Basswood bark to make paper: —The bark should be peeled off early in the Spring as it will cleave from the tree; it should be put immediately into a pond of standing water, as it is destructive to the bark to dry after it is peeled and before it is rotted. It should lie about three weeks in the water, then be taken out, and the rots [two words illegible] bark stripped off entirely; the bark to be prepared must then be dried in the sun." *Lyon's Vermont Calendar*, p. 62.

27. Hamilton, "Report on Manufactures," in Cole, *Correspondence of Alexander Hamilton*, p. 316.

28. Adams, *History of Fairhaven*, p. 141.

29. Bishop, *History of Manufactures*, 1: 625.

30. *SPV*, 3: 148–49.

31. Bishop, *History of Manufactures*, 1: 631.

32. Loomis was on the committee with Chipman and Tichenor to revise the Betterment Acts sponsored by Lyon and his faction (*VRGC*, 3: 349). For a full discussion of this and related factional conflicts, see chapter 4.

33. Hamilton, "Report on Manufactures," pp. 301–02.

34. Clark, *History of Manufacturers*, p. 172.

35. John Spargo, "Iron Business in Bennington," *Banner*, Dec. 2, 1937.

36. Fox, "Col. Matthew Lyon," p. 168.

37. Hamilton, "Report on Manufactures," p. 301.

38. Fox, "Col. Matthew Lyon," p. 168.

39. *FL*, May 13, 1793.

40. Ibid.

41. Ira Allen to Levi Allen, July 5, 1787, N.Y. SL, Stevens Papers, Levi Allen Papers, Box 1.

42. Matthew Lyon, Iron Master to ——, Dec. 20, 1786, LHS Ransom, SS 8: 2.

43. Bishop, *History of Manufactures*, 1: 524.

44. *VRGC*, 1: 12.

45. Hartley, *Ironworks on the Saugus*, p. 179.

46. Litchfield County Centennial Celebration, pp. 47–48, cited in Herrick, "Matthew Lyon."

47. Adams, *History of Fairhaven*, pp. 65–66; Roe, *Recollections of Frontier Life*, pp. 13–14.

48. White, *Life and Services of Matthew Lyon*, p. 12.

49. Spargo, "Iron Business in Bennington," *Banner*, Dec. 2, 1937.

50. "Copy of a letter from Col. M. Lyon to me Oliver Platt. Dated Fairhaven, June 25, 1785," N.Y. SL, Zephaniah Platt Papers.

51. "Copy of an answer to a letter from C^O Lyon to me Oliver Platt to C^O Lyon, Plattsburgh, July 1, 1785," N.Y. SL, Zephaniah Platt Papers.

52. Bishop, *History of Manufactures*, 6: 523–24.

53. George C. Foote, as vice president of the Witherbee Sherman Corporation in Fort Henry, New York, deduced that Lyon obtained his iron ore from the Cheever mine about two miles north of Port Henry. Mr. Zenas H. Ellis, an avid admirer of Lyon, who collected considerable manuscript material on his Vermont activities, asserts that Lyon transported the ore across the ice of Lake Champlain. Fox, "Col. Matthew Lyon," pp. 163–80.

54. *SPV*, 3: 169.

55. *Vermont Gazette*, Oct. 6, 1788.

56. Matthew Lyon, Iron Master, to ——, Dec. 20, 1786, LHS Ransom, 28: 2.

57. Lyon to Ira Allen, May 2, 1789, Vt. HS.

58. Hartley, *Ironworks on the Saugus*, pp. 10–11, 171.

59. Quoted in Bishop, *History of Manufactures*, 1: 490.

60. Ibid.

61. *Vermont Gazette*, Oct. 6, 1788.

62. Hamilton, "Report on Manufactures," p. 302.

63. Graham, *Sketch of Vermont*. This book was published in 1797, which indicates that the blast furnace certainly had been in operation by that date. A committee of the Vermont Assembly in 1791 recommended that Lyon's blast furnace in Orwell be repaired and set in blast, which indicates that the blast furnace had been erected by that date, but was out of operation because of either fire damage or other mechanical difficulties. *SPV*, 3: 261–62.

64. William Bigelow to Pliny H. White, Sept. 10, 1858, Vt. HS, Pliny White Papers.

65. *SPV*, 9: 116.

66. Ibid., pp. 116–17.

67. Ibid, 5: 374.

68. Ibid, 3, part 4: 202.

69. Ibid, 4: 94, 105.

70. Ibid, 3, part 4: 261–62.

71. Clark, *History of Manufacturers*, 1: 42.

72. Ibid, p. 43.

73. Davis, *History of Corporations*, 1: 265.

74. *SPV*, 5: 70.

75. Ibid, 3, part 4: 112.

76. Ibid., pp. 133–34.

77. Ibid., p. 138.

78. Davis, *History of Corporations*, 1: 283. Several state-chartered corporations cited by Davis not only have a marked resemblance to the one sought by Lyon, but also received generous encouragement from the state legislatures, for example: New York Manufacturing Society (Textile), incorporated 1790, state subscribed one hundred shares (p. 275); New Jersey Society for Establishing Useful Manufactures (Textiles), chartered 1793 (pp. 275–76); an Albany Glass Corporation, to which the state loaned £3,000 for three years without interest and for the next five years at 5%; and the Salem Iron Factory, incorporated May 1800.

79. Lyon to Phelps, Oct. 11, 1795, N.Y. SL, Phelps Gorham Collection, Box 21.

80. Graham, *Sketch of Vermont*, p. 181.

Chapter 4   (pages 45–54)

1. Lyon to Armisted Mason, Jan. 17, 1817, JMMF.

2. Fischer, *American Conservatism*, pp. 243, 290; Jones, "America's First Law School," pp. 3–4. That Chipman may have been a pupil of Tapping Reeve is deduced from the fact that Reeve tutored law students privately before founding his famous Litchfield Law School in 1784, although he "failed to maintain adequate records, such as roster of students" before that date. Among the future Federalists whom he trained were John Allen, Charles Marsh, Oliver Wolcott, and Uriah Tracy, all of whom were close associates of Nathaniel Chipman and vigorous opponents of Matthew Lyon in the Federalist-Republican conflicts of the 1790s.

3. Unless otherwise noted, the material in the above biographical sketch was obtained from E.P. Walton, "Address on the Dedication of the Chipman Monument at Tinmouth 1873," in: Hemenway, *Vermont Historical Gazetteer*, 3: 1154–59.

4. Quoted in Kilbourne, *Biographical History of Litchfield*, p. 72.

5. "A letter of Mr. Chipman of Vermont to the Chairman of the Committee on Breach of Privileges," *Annals*, 5, 2 (Feb. 9, 1798): 999–1000.

6. Ibid.

7. *VRGC*, 3: 343.

8. Chipman, *Nathaniel Chipman*, p. 62.

9. *VRGC*, 3: 341–56.

10. Ibid., pp. 348–49.

11. *Vermont Gazette*, Dec. 6, 1784.

12. *Nathaniel Chipman*, p. 65.

13. *VRGC*, 3: 347.

14. Ibid., p. 349.

15. Ibid, p. 351.

16. *SPV*, 3, part 3: 86. The delegates from western Vermont cast 23 votes in favor of the bill and 18 opposed to it. Those from eastern Vermont cast 16 in favor and 36 opposed.

17. Ludlum, *Social Ferment in Vermont*, pp. 11–12.

18. B. Hall, *History of Eastern Vermont*, pp. 427–55; H. Hall, *History of Vermont*, pp. 390–97, 430–32. These recalcitrant residents of Windham County only succumbed to Vermont authority after Ethan Allen, acting in behalf of the state government, exerted military authority and brought leading Yorker sympathizers to trial.

19. Anna H. Weeks to Holland Weeks, Oct. 20, 1796, Sheldon Museum.

20. This exception was William Ward, Judge of Rutland County Court, who had participated in the conventions asserting Vermont's independence and generally shared the prevalent background and attitude of western Vermonters. His biographer stresses that he was a self-educated frontiersman who rejected "the blandishments . . . of refined society." Hemenway, *Vermont Historical Gazetteer*, 3: 982–83.

21. The graduates of these institutions were Nathaniel Niles, Nathaniel Chipman, and Isaac Tichenor. Hemenway, *Vermont Historical Gazetteer*, 2: 907; 3: 1154–59; 1: 174–75.

22. *Nathaniel Chipman*, p. 62.

23. *FL*, Aug. 19, 1794.

24. *VRGC*, 3: 359–61.

25. MSS SPV, 17: 209.

26. *VRGC*, 3: 358, editor's note: "Specie was rarely seen, and the paper currency was for the most part of doubtful value." Lyon corroborates this statement in a letter to Levi Allen: "It is impossible for me to send you cash now. . . . For cash grows scarcer every day." (Oct. 30, 1786, Vt. WL.) In Lyon's petition for a state loan in 1789, he also comments on the increase in the value of the state's paper money over its previous "doubtful value." *SPV*, 9: 117.

27. *VRGC*, 3: 359–62. Describing the state of agitation of the population, Chittenden remarked: "For a remedy one cries a Tender Act, another a bank of currency and others kill the lawyers and deputy sheriffs." Pointing out that the number of lawsuits had doubled in the last year, he recommended a tax on lawyers' fees as one of several additional remedies to the emergency.

28. *Nathaniel Chipman*, pp. 67–69. Quotations in this paragraph are from these pages.

29. These members were: Gideon Olin, Elijah Dewey, Lemuel Chipman, and Thomas Johnson. *VRGC* 3: 364.

30. Neither the vote on this resolution nor its wording are recorded in the Assembly Journal of October 31, 1786 (possibly because the referendum had been printed and circulated before the Assembly Journal was printed). Therefore it cannot be ascertained whether or not Lyon opposed this resolution for a referendum.

31. *Vermont Gazette*, Jan. 5, 1786; Aug. 31, 1786.

32. *SPV*, 3, part 3: 284–85.

33. *VRGC*, 3: 365.

34. Ibid., p. 373.

35. *SPV*, 3, part 3: 317.

36. Ibid.

37. *FL*, Aug. 19, 1794.

38. John Spargo, "Isaac Tichenor," Vt. WL.

39. Williamson, *Vermont in Quandary*, p. 110.

40. Fischer, *American Conservatism*, p. 251.

41. Most of these men voted against the Betterment Act of 1784, proposed by Lyon's Committee, *SPV*, 3, part 3: 86–87.

42. Slade, *Vermont State Papers*, pp. 537, 533.

43. Hemenway, *Vermont Historical Gazetteer*, 2: 907; 3: 1154–59; 1: 174–75.

Chapter 5 (pages 55–63)

1. This analysis is a summary of the detailed treatment of the influence of economic geography on the foreign policies of the various Vermont factions, found in Williamson, *Vermont in Quandary*.

2. Chipman, *Nathaniel Chipman*, pp. 37–38.

3. *VRGC*, 2: 382.

4. Ibid., pp. 374–75.

5. Ibid, 1: 435. As early as 1779, the settlers of the Connecticut River Valley region had passed resolutions charging Ira Allen with misappropriating funds derived from the "illegal" sale of confiscated land. Shortly thereafter, Lyon served on a committee appointed by the Assembly which examined Ira Allen's accounts.

6. Wilbur, *Ira Allen*, 1: 476.

7. Ibid., p. 478.

8. Ibid., p. 471.

9. Slade, *Vermont State Papers*, pp. 531–44.

10. *VRGC*, 3: 81.

11. *Spooner's Vermont Journal*, July 31, 1798.

12. *VRGC*, 3: 93.

13. Ibid., p. 83.

14. *Spooner's Vermont Journal*, July 31, 1798.

15. *VRGC*, 1: 23, editor's note: "At the close of the records Secretary Fay left five blank pages 'for the purpose of recording the remainder of the Journals of Council at the Westminster session, which by some mistake in the Transfer of the books from Mr. Tolman to me were not recd.' This is dated April 7, 1789, and shows that the Journal was not recorded until that time." *VRGC*, 1: 107, editor's note: "The first volume in manuscript of the Records of the Council of Safety and of the Governor and Council of the State of Vermont, has the following statement prefixed: 'The first twenty pages in this book is left blank for the purpose of Entering the Minutes of the Council of Safety of the State of Vermont from Jan. 1776 [to] the 15th August 1777, during which time Col. Ira Allen was Secretary and has the minutes of sd. Council in his possession.' . . . Other evidence is found that the early records of the Council of Safety, of the Conventions, of the Governor and Council, and of the General Assembly, had been loosely kept and were not in a fit state of preservation."

16. *SPV*, 3, part 3: 250.

17. Williamson, *Vermont in Quandary*, p. 178.

18. Adams, *History of Fairhaven*, p. 514.

19. Levi Allen to Ira Allen, Aug. 18, 1786 [Letter marked "Bearer Col. Lyon"], N.Y. SL, Stevens Papers. See also note 20.

20. Levi Allen to Ira Allen, 1784, N.Y. SL, Stevens Papers, Ira Allen Papers. This collection was badly burned and the date of this particular letter is barely legible. Levi refers to "the bearer Col. Lyon" in the body of this letter.

21. Lyon to Monroe, June 7, 1817, Pa. HS, Gratz Collection.

22. Levi Allen to Ira Allen, Aug. 18, 1786, N.Y. SL, Stevens Papers.

23. Ira Allen to Frederick Haldimand, Sept. 10, 1784, cited in Williamson, *Vermont in Quandary*, p. 138.

24. Williamson, *Vermont in Quandary*, p. 155.

25. Draft of a Petition to the Archbishop of Canterbury, Oct. 26, 1790, N.Y. SL, Stevens Papers, Levi Allen Papers.

26. Levi Allen to Rev. Dr. Morrice, May 29, 1789, N.Y. SL, Stevens Papers, Levi Allen Papers.

27. Levi Allen to Ira Allen, 1784, N.Y. SL, Stevens Papers, Ira Allen Papers.

28. *SPV*, 3, part 3: 105.

29. Lyon to Timothy Pickering, May 24, 1797, reprinted in Wilbur, *Ira Allen*, 2: 123–25.

30. *VRGC*, 3: 423–24.

31. Chipman, *Nathaniel Chipman*, pp. 70–71.

32. Williamson, *Vermont in Quandary*, p. 164.

33. *VRGC*, 3: 450.

34. Chipman, *Nathaniel Chipman*, p. 81.

35. *VRGC*, 3: 513 and 4: 40; Williamson, *Vermont in Quandary*, pp. 186–87. Among those Vermont friends were John Kelley, a Yorker land speculator with close ties to such important New York leaders as John Jay, Alexander Hamilton, and William Duer. Kelley used the Vermont lands granted to him to repay debts owed Hamilton and Livingston, and this transaction was agreed upon by the commissioners from Vermont and New York in 1790. Nathaniel Chipman and John Kelley submitted a petition to the Vermont Assembly to honor John Jay for his role in supporting Vermont's independence by granting him a town in the

state. Unfortunately, the holdings were in an inhospitable area, and Williamson surmises that Jay probably didn't realize on them as he had hoped.

36. Williamson, *Vermont in Quandary*, pp. 179–80.
37. Ibid.
38. Adams, *History of Fairhaven*, p. 69.
39. Levi Allen to Ira Allen, Aug. 20, 1789, quoted in Hemenway, *Vermont Historical Gazetteer*, 1: 572. Hemenway records this letter as having been written on August 20, 1779. However, this is clearly an error since the letter mentions "our deceased brother," meaning Ethan who died in February 1789 (Wilbur, *Ira Allen*, 1: 521). Ira wrote Levi of Ethan's death on June 5, 1789 (Ibid.). The foregoing leads to the inevitable conclusion that the date August 20, 1779, should have read August 20, 1789. Further evidence supporting this conclusion is that Levi was in London on August 20, 1789, while in August 1779, during the American Revolution, Levi was in east Florida.
40. Williamson, *Vermont in Quandary*, p. 155.
41. *FL*, June 10, 1793.
42. Ibid., June 3, 1793.
43, Wilbur, *Ira Allen*, 2: 3.
44. *SPV*, 3, part 4: 228.

Chapter 6   (pages 64–75)

1. Adams, *History of Fairhaven*, p. 419.
2. See pages 49–52 of chapter 4. Lyon's article, "Twelve Reasons Against a Free People's Employing Practitioners in The Law as Legislators," was published in *FL*, Aug. 19, 1794.
3. *FL*, Sept. 5, 1796.
4. *Vermont Gazette*, Sept. 26, 1791.
5. Lyon to Ira Allen, July 28, 1791, Vt.WL, Ira Allen Papers. Quotations in the following paragraph are from this source.
6. Levi Allen to Ira Allen, Aug. 20, 1789, quoted in Hemenway, *Vermont Historical Gazetteer*, 1: 572.
7. Lyon to Ira Allen, July 28, 1791, Vt. WL, Ira Allen Papers.
8. Wilbur, *Ira Allen*, 2: 8; Montagno, "Matthew Lyon," p. 92.
9. Lyon to Timothy Pickering, May 24, 1797, reprinted in Wilbur, *Ira Allen*, 2: 123.
10. Lyon to Mrs. Jerucha Allen, Sept. 25, 1797, Vt. HS.
11. Montagno, "Matthew Lyon," p. 39.
12. Lyon to Ira Allen, July 28, 1791, Vt. WL, Ira Allen Papers.
13. Montagno, "Matthew Lyon," p. 39.
14. Throughout this work, the designations Republican and Republicanism will be capitalized on the grounds given by Noble E. Cunningham: "Since only an arbitrary decision can determine when, in its evolutionary growth, the party is entitled to have its name capitalized, the proper form Republican has been used throughout to refer both to the well-defined party of 1800 and its more rudimentary structure during the process of development in the 1790's." Cunningham, *Jeffersonian Republicans*, p. ix.
15. Lyon to Armisted Mason, Jan. 16, 1817, JMMF.
16. Williamson, *Vermont in Quandary*, p. 179.
17. *VRGC*, 2: Appendix K.
18. Ibid., 3: 476; Starr, *Dictionary of American Biography*, 9: 283; Hemenway, *Vermont Historical Gazetteer*, 3: 223. Montagno ("Matthew Lyon") states that Smith was known to have antifederalist leanings at the time of the election of 1791, but his remarks in the ratifying convention indicate the contrary to be the case.
19. Since the *Vermont Gazette* did not publish Lyon's articles in their entirety, Lyon later reprinted the complete exchange between himself and Chipman in his own newspaper, *Farmers' Library*. The following citations are from this source.
20. Lyon to Gallatin, Dec. 4, 1803, N.Y. HS, Gallatin Papers, 1803, #74.
21. Montagno, "Matthew Lyon," pp. 39–41.
22. *Annals*, 4, 1 (Dec. 8, 1795): 128.
23. Ibid. (Feb. 4, 1796): 296–97.
24. Cunningham, *Jeffersonian Republicans*, p. 272.

25. *Annals*, 4, 1 (Feb. 4, 1796): 296.

26. Cunningham, *Jeffersonian Republicans*, p. 69.

27. *Annals*, 4, 1 (Feb. 11, 1796): 315–16. The following discussion of the debate is based on pp. 316–24.

28. Speech of William B. Giles, Ibid., p. 319.

29. Ibid. (May 30, 1796): 1497.

30. Cunningham, *Jeffersonian Republicans*, pp. 77–80. See notes citing correspondence between Madison and Monroe, Giles and Jefferson, and Madison and Jefferson over the urgency of winning adherents to the Republican position on the Jay Treaty.

31. Ibid., Table 1, p. 267: "The Voting Record of Members of the House of Representatives on Principal Roll Calls During the First Session of the Second Congress, Oct. 1791–May 1792."

32. Ibid., p. 77.

33. The chief exception to this Federalist position was taken by Representative Daniel Buck from eastern Vermont, who, from inside knowledge of Vermont politics, apparently viewed Lyon as a more dangerous Republican than Smith. He strongly contested Lyon's petition, insisting that the deprived voters were not dissatisfied: "It is Mr. Lyon who complains." *Annals*, 4, 1 (Feb. 5, 1796): 316–17.

34. Cunningham, *Jeffersonian Republicans*.

35. The discussion of this election is based on information from *FL*, Dec. 21, Nov. 23, and Oct. 5, 1796.

36. Despite Tichenor's poor showing in this and previous elections for Congressman from western Vermont, he shortly afterwards was appointed U.S. Senator by the Federalist state legislature (*FL*, Jan. 11, 1797). Nathaniel Chipman, who also polled poorly in western Vermont, similarly managed to ascend politically via appointments by the state legislature. In the fall of 1796 he was appointed Chief Judge of the State Supreme Court (*FL*, Oct. 5, 1796) and in 1798 the legislature elected him U.S. Senator.

37. Montagno, "Matthew Lyon," pp. 76–77; *FL*, Jan. 18, 1797.

38. Hemenway, *Vermont Historical Gazetteer*, 1: 590.

39. *Vermont Journal*, Mar. 10, 1797.

Chapter 7   (pages 76–89)

1. Lyon to Gallatin, Dec. 4, 1803, N.Y. HS, Gallatin Papers, 1803, No. 74.

2. Lyon to Armisted Mason, Jan. 16, 1817, JMMF.

3. Lyon to Gallatin, Dec. 4, 1803, N.Y. HS, Gallatin Papers, 1803, No. 74.

4. Ibid.

5. Lyon to Armisted Mason, Jan. 16, 1817, JMMF.

6. "OFFICIAL LETTER From the French Republic to the United States of America, dated Paris, Dec. 21, 1792," *FL*, Apr. 1, 1793.

7. *FL*, Aug. 8, 1796. Samuel Adams used this precise phrase in 1784 when he protested against attempts to replace the Boston Town Meetings with organized, incorporated town government. He charged that there were many men in America and Europe who "continue such a hankering for the leeks and onions of Great Britain." *Massachusetts Centinel*, May 12, 1784.

8. In his message to Congress of November, 1794, Washington used this epithet in denouncing the Democratic Societies. Miller, *Federalist Era*, p. 160.

9. In a letter to Mathew Carey, written in 1800, Lyon indicates that, at this date, not only was he familiar with "Rossou's *Social Compact*" but that he sold it and had run out of copies. Lyon to Carey, Dec. 20, 1820, Pa. HS, Gratz Collection.

10. Diary of Thomas Robbins, 1: 17, quoted in Ludlum, *Social Ferment in Vermont*, p. 29.

11. Adams, *Defense of the Constitutions*, 3: 56, 57; 4: 284–85; 6: 8–9; N. Chipman, *Principles of Government*, pp. 115–16, 138; Dauer, *Adams Federalists*, pp. 35–47; Link, *Democratic-Republican Societies*, p. 103.

12. Miller, *Federalist Era*, p. 117,

13. Gibbs, *Administrations of Washington and Adams*, vol. 1, p. 413.

14. Herrick, "Matthew Lyon," p. 111.

15. The following quotation from the preface to Benjamin Franklin's *Works*, published in 1793, is of particular interest: "It is a little extraordinary that, under these circumstances, interesting as they are, from the celebrity of the character of which they treat, and from the critical situation of the present times, they should so long have been with-held from the public. A translation of them appeared in France near two years ago."

16. Ludlum, *Social Ferment in Vermont*, p. 251.

17. Minutes of the Rutland Democratic Society, July 4, 1794, *FL*, July 15, 1794. The promotion of schools and libraries became one of the primary activities of local Democratic and Republican Societies in the 1790s. Link, *Democratic-Republican Societies*, p. 169.

18. Petition to Vermont General Assembly, Oct. 2, 1799, quoted in Adams, *History of Fairhaven*, p. 124.

19. "Stated Principles and Regulations of the Associated Democratic Societies, *FL*, Apr. 16, 1794.

20. Miller, *Federalist Era*, pp. 128–31.

21. In October 1794 Lyon reprinted in the *Farmers' Library* a letter from a "gentleman from Quebec," who reported that "all ranks of people in Canada were apprehensive of a war with the United States—that Gov. Simcoe expected to be attacked, had written for reinforcements, and that light Companies of British troops at Quebec, had marched for Montreal, to relieve the troops there who were destined to Detroit."

22. *FL*, Apr. 29, 1794; Miller, *Federalist Era*, p. 152.

23. Brebner, *North Atlantic Triangle*, pp. 66–67.

24. *FL*, Nov. 25, 1793; reprinted in *Independent Chronicle*, Dec. 12, 1793.

25. Brymner, *Canadian Archives*, pp. 57–84.

26. Ibid., pp. 81–84. In July 1801, Graham presented himself as a British agent to Lieutenant Governor Milnes and Major General Burton in Canada. After offering proof of his past services to the Duke of Portland, he supplied the names and descriptions of Vermonters engaged in insurrectionary activities among the Canadians. Burton commented, "He appeared to me to magnify matters, in the hope of some advantage that he seems to point at for himself."

27. Ibid., p. 63.

28. *Spooner's Vermont Journal*, July 31, 1798. This denial was made in response to a blistering attack upon Lyon's entire political career which appeared in *Spooner's Vermont Journal* on May 28, 1798, and in all likelihood was written by Lyon's archenemy, Nathaniel Chipman.

29. Brymner, *Canadian Archives*, p. 66.

30. Levi Allen to Reverend Doctor Morrice, May 29, 1789, N.Y. SL, Stevens Papers, Levi Allen Papers.

31. A mob of patriots in Hebron, Connecticut, enraged by the Reverend Samuel Peters' scathing attacks upon the Connecticut Whigs, forced him to read a prepared confession of his Tory sympathies in August 1774; shortly afterwards he fled to England. During the Revolution, Peters claimed that fifty-six thousand acres of his property were confiscated. Matthew Lyon, as clerk of the Board of Confiscation, was instrumental in confiscating Samuel Peters' farm in Pownal, Vermont, on July 30, 1779. Brush, *Diocese of Vermont*, pp. 27–28; *SPV* 6: 28, 31; Williamson, *Vermont in Quandary*, p. 75.

32. Draft of Petition to Archbishop of Canterbury, Oct. 26, 1790, N.Y. SL, Stevens Papers, Levi Allen Papers. The fact that Vermont is spelled "Verdmont" throughout the petition indicates that Peters himself probably wrote this draft. He had always insisted that Vermont should be spelled Verdmont if it were to be an accurate Latin rendition of the words "Green Mountain." Wilbur, *Ira Allen*, 1: 93.

33. *Episcopal Church in Vermont*, p. 16.

34. Ibid., p. 20.

35. Ibid., pp. 18–20. Graham used the term "English American" to describe himself in the introduction to his book, *A Descriptive Sketch of the Present State of Vermont*, dedicated to his relative, the Duke of Montrose.

36. *Episcopal Church in Vermont*, p. 20.

37. Williamson, *Vermont in Quandary*, p. 211.

38. Ibid., pp. 212–13.

39. Ibid., p. 212.

40. *Episcopal Church in Vermont*, p. 55.
41. Lyon to Peters, Nov. 14, 1795, N.Y. HS, Peters Correspondence.
42. Williams to Noah Webster, July 18, 1795, N.Y. PL, Noah Webster Papers. For an appraisal of the *Rutland Herald* as an influential standard-bearer of Federalism in western Vermont, see Isaac Tichenor to Noah Webster, Dec. 14, 1795, N.Y. PL, Noah Webster Papers.

Chapter 8   (pages 90–107)

1. *Annals*, 5, 1 (May 15, 1797): 55.
2. Miller, *Federalist Era*, pp. 195, 205–6.
3. *FL*, Apr. 13, 1798.
4. *Annals*, 5, 1: speech of Albert Gallatin, May 25, 1797, p. 145; speech of Edward Livingston, May 24, 1797, p. 125.
5. Ibid. (May 30, 1797): 194.
6. Ibid. (June 3, 1797): 234–35.
7. Chipman to Cephas Smith, Nov. 24, 1797, Vt. HS, Nathaniel Chipman Collection. In this letter Chipman referred to Lyon's motion concerning John Adams' second presidential address, delivered November 23, 1797. On this occasion Lyon moved that the House make no formal reply to the president's address, but merely thank him and then proceed with its business. Twenty members of the House, including Albert Gallatin, Nathaniel Macon, and Abraham Venable, voted for Lyon's motion. *Annals*, 5, 2 (Nov. 24, 1797): 635–37.
8. Fischer, *American Conservatism*, pp. 290–91, 308.
9. *Annals*, 5, 1 (June 2, 1797): 232.
10. For discussion of the possibility that Nathaniel Chipman may also have been a student of Tapping Reeve's, see chapter 4, note 2.
11. *Annals*, 5, 1 (June 3, 1797): 235. It was in this same speech that Lyon made his derisive remarks about the Puritans, proudly acknowledging that he was not a descendant of "the bastards of Oliver Cromwell" or those who "hanged" the witches. For complete quotation, see chapter 1, page 12.
12. The entire poem was copied by Matthew Lyon and enclosed in a letter to Stephen Jacobs, Dec. 13, 1804. Vt. HS.
13. *Porcupine's Gazette*, June 6, 1797.
14. Quoted in Adams, *History of Fairhaven*, p. 100.
15. *Annals*, 5, 2 (Nov. 30, 1797): 657. The following discussion of the debate is based on pp. 657–62.
16. *Annals*, 5, 1 (June 28, 1797): 400.
17. Ibid. (June 27, 1797): 394.
18. Ibid. (June 26, 1797): 390.
19. Ibid. (June 4, 1797): 333.
20. Ibid. (July 1, 1797): 425.
21. Ibid., p. 430.
22. Ibid., p. 425.
23. *Porcupine's Gazette*, Aug. 1, 1797.
24. "Deposition of Nathaniel Chipman," *Annals*, 5, 2 (Feb. 6, 1798): 1023.
25. "Testimony of Jonathan Dayton," Ibid. (Feb. 5, 1798): 1011.
26. N. Van Schaack to Theodore Sedgwick, Jan. 14, 1798, Mass. HS, Sedgwick Collection.
27. "Report of the Committee on Breach of Privilege," *Annals*, 5, 2 (Feb. 2, 1798): 961.
28. Ibid.
29. Griswold to an unnamed correspondent, Feb. 25, 1798, YUL.
30. "Testimony of David Brooks," *Annals*, 5, 2 (Feb. 5, 1798): 1015.
31. Ibid. (Jan. 30, 1798): 955.
32. The members of the committee were: Representatives Rutledge (chairman), Venable, Kittera, I. Parker, R. Williams, Cochran, and Dent.
33. *Annals*, 5, 2 (Feb. 9, 1798): 1002.

34. Ibid. (Feb. 1, 1798): 959.
35. Bowers, *Jefferson and Hamilton*, p. 273; and *SA*, Nov. 1, 1798.
36. Gallatin to his wife, Feb. 13, 1798, quoted in Adams, *Albert Gallatin*, p. 193.
37. Jefferson to Madison, Feb. 15, 1798, quoted in Ford, *Thomas Jefferson*, 7: 202.
38. *Annals*, 5, 2 (Feb. 12, 1798): 1007.
39. "Testimony of Matthew Lyon," Ibid. (Feb. 1, 1798): 1025–29. See chapter 2 for the contents of Lyon's narrative.
40. Gallatin to his wife, Feb. 3, 1798, quoted in Adams, *Albert Gallatin*, p. 191.
41. *Annals*, 5, 2 (Jan. 30, 1798–Feb. 12, 1798): 955–1008.
42. McLaughlin, *Matthew Lyon*, pp. 212, 227, 241–42; *Porcupine's Gazette*, Jan. 31, 1798, and Feb. 9, 1798.
43. Quoted in Adams, *History of Fairhaven*, pp. 420–21.
44. Van Schaack to Sedgwick, Feb. 19, 1798, Mass. HS, Sedgwick Collection No. 540.
45. Jonathan Mason to Harrison Gray Otis, Feb. 19, 1798, YUL, Lane Papers (photostat; original in Harvard University).
46. Griswold to an unknown correspondent, Feb. 25, 1798, YUL.
47. McLaughlin, *Matthew Lyon*, p. 228. The photograph facing this page is of a cartoon depicting the Griswold-Lyon affray and contains this handwritten statement: "The cane was purchased at John McCallister's, Phila."
48. Griswold to an unknown correspondent, Feb. 25, 1798, YUL.
49. Ibid.
50. Starr, *Dictionary of American Biography*, 4: 10; *Connecticut Courant*, Nov. 3, 1812.
51. Griswold to an unknown correspondent, Feb. 25, 1798, YUL.
52. *Annals*, 5, 2 (Feb. 21, 1798): 1006.
53. Kittera to Rutledge, Feb. 17, 1798, N.C. SHC, Rutledge Papers No. 948.
54. Lyon to Monroe, Mar. 5, 1816, N.Y. PL, James Monroe Papers.
55. *Porcupine's Gazette*, July 3, 1797; *Aurora*, July 17, 1797; Albert Gallatin to his wife, June 30, 1797, in Adams, *Albert Gallatin*, p. 187.
56. Dauer, *Adams Federalists*, p. 135.
57. *Annals*, 5, 2 (Mar. 5, 1798): 1200; (Mar. 19, 1798): 1271.
58. Dauer, *Adams Federalists*, p. 141.
59. *Independent Chronicle*, Mar. 26, 1798.
60. Smith, *John Adams*, 2: 953.
61. Jefferson to Madison, Apr. 5, 1798, in Ford, *Thomas Jefferson*, 7: 23.
62. *Annals*, 5, 2 (Apr. 6, 1798): 1380.
63. Ibid.
64. Miller, *Federalist Era*, p. 212.
65. *Albany Centinel*, Oct. 12, 1798; *Porcupine's Gazette*, July 27, 1798; and *Pennsylvania Herald and York General Advertiser*, Aug. 1, 1798.
66. *Porcupine's Gazette*, July 27, 1798.
67. Smith, *John Adams*, 2: 965.
68. *Annals*, 5, 2: 1682, 1925, 2120, 1824.
69. Allen, *Naval War with France*, pp. 58–59; Godfrey, "Organization of the Provisional Army," pp. 130–32.
70. Sedgwick to unknown correspondent, Mar. 7, 1798, Mass. HS, Sedgwick Papers.
71. *Annals*, 5, 2 (Apr. 20, 1798): 1482, 1485.
72. Peters, *Statutes at Large*, 1: 596–97.
73. *Annals*, 5, 2 (July 10, 1798): 2148.
74. Ibid., pp. 2167–68, 2097, 2112.
75. The opening lines of the first issue on Oct. 1, 1798, stated: "The public are presented with No. 1, of *Lyon's Republican Magazine* entitled *The Scourge of Aristocracy and Repository of Important Political Truths.*" In the following three issues, "Lyon's Republican Magazine" is dropped from the title.
76. *Spooner's Vermont Journal*, July 31, 1798.
77. *Annals*, 5, 2 (July 5, 1798): 2093, 2100; similar views were expressed by Robert Goodloe Harper on the same date, pp. 2102–3.
78. Ibid. (July 10, 1798): 2162.
79. *Carey's U.S. Recorder*, July 12, 1798, quoted in: Montagno, "Matthew Lyon," p. 187.
80. *Annals*, 5, 2 (July 10, 1798): 2140–41.

81. Ibid., p. 2153.

82. Levy, *Legacy of Suppression*, pp. 264–67. The quotations in this paragraph are from these pages.

83. Jefferson to Madison, July 7, 1798, in Ford, *Thomas Jefferson*, 7: 266–67.

84. *Annals*, 5, 2 (July 10, 1798): 2160.

85. Ibid., 16, 2 (Dec. 4, 1820): 478.

86. Ford, *Hugh Gaine*, 2: 200–1.

Chapter 9   (pages 108–118)

1. The description of Matthew Lyon's trial in this chapter is based on a variety of sources described below (previous descriptions have relied primarily upon Wharton): Wharton, *State Trials of the U.S.*, pp. 331–44. Wharton based this account of the trial on two newspaper reports, one Federalist—*Spectator*, Oct. 24, 1798—the other Republican—*Aurora*, Nov. 15, 1798. Judge Paterson prohibited notes being taken even by reporters during the trial, according to Wood, *Suppressed History of Adams*, p. 163. Wood claims that the report "printed in most of the public papers was by one of the jurors." Wharton's account, based on newspaper reports, cannot be regarded as a wholly accurate reproduction of the trial. It is useful for its outline of the sequence of events, summaries of testimony, and summaries of Judge Paterson's charge to the jury and closing remarks to Lyon. Where Wharton is cited, these are not direct quotations from the trial but a reporter's recollection and summary.

The original court record of the trial had disappeared from the U.S. District Court Records in Burlington, Vermont, by the time Wharton wrote his book in 1849. However, he overlooked a certified copy of the official court record, compiled by Jesse Gove, Clerk, Vermont District, which was published in *Annals*, 16, 2 (Dec. 4, 1820): 479–86, in support of a petition to refund Lyon's fine. The official court record contains the wording of the indictment, the verdict of the jury, and the sentence of the judge, but does not contain a record of the testimony during the trial.

A list of bondsmen, witnesses, and jurors, as well as a brief chronological summary of the trial proceedings, is contained in a document entitled, "Copy of Trial of Matthew Lyon for Sedition, Oct. 1798, copied by Moses Hawkes from the Docket of the Clerk in 1858," Vt. WL. Fragmentary notes on the testimony of the witnesses, the summation of the defendant, and the opinions of Justice Paterson are contained in Notes, U.S. v. Mr. Lyon, N.Y. PL, Paterson Papers, Bancroft Collection.

A more detailed description of the proceedings of the trial from the point of view of the defendant is contained in a letter from Matthew Lyon to General Stevens T. Mason, in jail at Vergennes, Oct. 14, 1798, in *The Scourge of Aristocracy*, Oct. 15, 1798. Succeeding issues of *The Scourge of Aristocracy* contained further material relating to the trial.

2. N. Van Schaack to Sedgwick, Jan. 3, 1798, Mass. HS, Sedgwick Collection.

3. *Spooner's Vermont Journal*, July 31, 1798; Wharton, *State Trials of the U.S.*, p. 333; "U.S. v. Lyon," *Annals*, 16, 2 (Dec. 4, 1820): 480.

4. Wharton, *State Trials of the U.S.*, p. 334; "U.S. v. Lyon," *Annals*, 16, 2 (Dec. 4, 1820): 482–84.

5. "U.S. v. Lyon," *Annals*, 16, 2 (Dec. 4, 1820): p. 480.

6. Ibid.

7. Copy of the Trial of Matthew Lyon for Sedition, Oct. 1798, Vt. WL.

8. *Spectator*, Oct. 24, 1798.

9. Fischer, *American Conservatism*, p. 243.

10. Montagno, "Matthew Lyon." Montagno merely offers this suggestion as a plausible conjecture and does not claim any proof of it, nor have I found any.

11. Ibid.

12. Fischer, *American Conservatism*, p. 290.

13. Wharton, *State Trials of the U.S.*, p. 334.

14. Ibid.

15. Paterson to Nicholson, Feb. 23, 1801, N.Y. PL, Paterson Papers, Bancroft Collection.

16. Nicholson to Paterson, June 20, 1801, N.C. SHC, Hagner Papers #3117.

17. *Annals*, 11, 1 (May 22, 1810): 124.
18. Notes, U.S. v. Mr. Lyon, N.Y. PL, Paterson Papers, Bancroft Collection.
19. Wharton, *State Trials of the U.S.*, p. 335.
20. *Annals*, 11, 1 (May 22, 1810): 125.
21. William Paterson to Joseph H. Nicholson, Feb. 23, 1801, N.Y. PL, Paterson Papers, Bancroft Collection.
22. Wharton, *State Trials of the U.S.*, p. 335.
23. Ibid., pp. 335–36.
24. Notes, U.S. v. Mr. Lyon, N.Y. PL, Paterson Papers, Bancroft Collection.
25. Ibid.
26. Wharton, *State Trials of the U.S.*, p. 336.
27. *Spectator*, Oct. 24, 1798.
28. Wharton, *State Trials of the U.S.*, p. 335.
29. Ibid., p. 336.
30. Ibid.
31. Ibid. In a footnote, Wharton quotes the report in the *Spectator* as follows: "It is said that eleven of the jurymen were ready to find a verdict immediately on leaving the bar, but that one doubted."
32. Ibid., pp. 336–37.
33. A thorough examination of many of these editors' trials appears in Smith, *Freedom's Fetters*.

Chapter 10   (pages 119–130)

1. *Annals*, 11, 1 (May 22, 1810): 122.
2. Lyon to a member of Congress in Philadelphia, Nov. 22, 1798, in SA, Dec. 15, 1798.
3. Mason to Lyon, Nov. 17, 1798, in SA, Dec. 15, 1798.
4. *Annals*, 11, 1 (May 22, 1810): 125–26. In an earlier letter to Albert Gallatin, Lyon stipulated that he received $200 from this subscription, the balance of which was distributed among the other Republican publishers who had been sentenced to jail under the Sedition Act. Lyon to Gallatin, Dec. 4, 1803, N.Y. HS Gallatin Papers 1803, No. 74.
5. Capt. John Wood's LOTTERY.
6. Ibid.
7. Adams, *History of Fairhaven*, p. 111.
8. *Annals*, 11, 1 (May 22, 1810): 125–26.
9. Mason to Lyon, Nov. 17, 1798, in SA, Dec. 15, 1798.
10. Ibid.
11. Unidentified newspaper clipping, Sheldon's Notebook No. 15, Sheldon Museum.
12. *Rutland Herald*, Oct. 29, 1798; Jan. 14, 1799.
13. This anecdote was reported to me by Charles L. Parker, Secretary of the Poultney Historical Society, in a letter dated May 21, 1962.
14. *Rutland Herald*, Jan. 13, 1799.
15. Jefferson to Madison, Jan. 3, 1799, quoted in Ford, *Thomas Jefferson*, 7: 314–15.
16. Quoted in Montagno, "Matthew Lyon," p. 271.
17. Rutland County Citizens, *To the Representatives of the Freemen*.
18. "Petition from the Freemen of the Western District of Vermont," *Aurora*, Jan. 14, 1799.
19. *Episcopal Church in Vermont*, pp. 15, 18, 30 *et passim*.
20. Lyon to John Adams, Mar. 4, 1801, reprinted in McLaughlin, *Matthew Lyon*, p. 404.
21. Jefferson to Madison, Jan. 3, 1799, in Ford, *Thomas Jefferson*, 7: 315.
22. Lyon to Adams, Mar. 4, 1801, reprinted in McLaughlin, *Matthew Lyon*, p. 404.
23. Frederick Wolcott acted as his brother's representative in Litchfield on this occasion. Six months later, he released Ogden from jail upon receipt of a note payable on demand to Oliver Wolcott, noting that it is "not worthwhile to be at the expense of supporting in jail so worthless a fellow. . . Unless he immediately quit this part of the Country, I will again attach and confine him." Frederick Wolcott to Oliver Wolcott, June 10, 1799, Connecticut Historical Society, Oliver Wolcott, Jr., Papers.

24. Ogden to Ephraim Kirby, Mar. 7, 1799, Duke University Library.

25. Kirby apparently attended the Vermont Episcopal Church Convention in 1795. His name is written in ink on a copy of John Graham's report to that convention, located in the Vt. HS.

26. Ogden to Ephraim Kirby, Mar. 19, 1799, Duke University Library.

27. Ogden, *Ecclesiastical Oppressions*, pp. 3, 7, 8, 9, 12, 13. That Matthew Lyon also had favored distribution of the Glebe Lands before his active involvement in the Episcopal Church Conventions does not seem to have perturbed Dr. Ogden. It is possible that he did not know of this earlier phase of Lyon's activities.

28. Isaac Tichenor to Mr. Jacobs, Feb. 14, 1799, Vt. WL.

29. Ibid.

30. Reprinted in Smith, *Freedom's Fetters*, p. 245.

31. "U.S. v. Haswell," in Wharton, *State Trials of the U.S.*, p. 684.

32. White, *Matthew Lyon*, p. 22.

33. *Annals*, 6, 1 (Feb. 22, 1799): 2959. The following discussion of the debate is based on pp. 2959–74.

34. Lyon to Armisted C. Mason, Jan. 16, 1817, JMMF.

35. Lyon to Albert Gallatin, Dec. 4, 1803, N.Y. HS, Gallatin Papers; James Lyon to Jefferson, Dec. 8, 1801, and Jan. 28, 1802, Library of Congress, Jefferson Papers.

36. Lyon to Carey, Dec. 14, 1800, Pa. HS, Gratz Collection.

37. Lyon to Carey, Dec. 20, 1800, Pa. HS, Gratz Collection.

38. Lyon to Carey, July 25, 1802, Pa. HS, Gratz Collection.

39. Adams, *Life of Gallatin*, pp. 255–57.

40. Stevens Thos. Mason to unknown correspondent, Feb. 17, 1801, Duke University Library.

41. Quoted in Benjamin H. Hall to Pliny White, Sept. 14, 1858, Vt. HS, Pliny White Papers. The author of this letter copied these verses from a volume of political poems entitled *Echo*, which was published anonymously in 1807.

Chapter 11   (pages 131–151)

1. Lyon to Adams, Mar. 4, 1801, reprinted in McLaughlin, *Matthew Lyon*, p. 398.

2. Lyon to Jackson, Feb. 28, 1800, Library of Congress, Jackson Papers, Series 6.

3. Lyon to John Messenger, Mar. 27, 1800, Ill. SHL Messenger. The party with whom he made this "bargain" was Edwin Douse of Dedham, Massachusetts. Adams, *History of Fairhaven*, p. 116.

4. Adams. *History of Fairhaven*, p. 113.

5. Lyon to Messenger, Mar. 27, 1800, Ill. SHL Messenger.

6. Roe, *Aunt Leanna*, pp. 17–18.

7. Lyon to Messenger, Mar. 27, 1800, Ill. SHL Messenger.

8. Roe, *Aunt Leanna*, pp. 15–17.

9. Lyon to Messenger, Nov. 16, 1800, Ill. SHL Messenger.

10. Quoted in McLaughlin, *Matthew Lyon*, p. 408.

11. Roe, *Aunt Leanna*, p. 18.

12. McLaughlin, *Matthew Lyon*, p. 414; Roe, *Aunt Leanna*, p. 18.

13. Roe, *Aunt Leanna*, p. 22.

14. Galusha to Messenger, Aug. 10, 1802, Ill. SHL Messenger.

15. *Portfolio*, Aug. 13, 1803.

16. Lyon to Carey, Sept. 8, 1802, Pa. HS, Gratz Collection.

17. Lyon to Carey, July 25, 1802, Pa, HS, Gratz Collection.

18. Lyon to Carey, Dec. 20, 1800, Pa. HS, Gratz Collection; Lyon to Carey, Feb. 15, 1810, Pa. HS, Lea and Febiger Collection.

19. James Lyon to John Messenger, Dec. 23, 1804, Ill. SHL Messenger; Matthew S. Lyon to Pliny White, Sept. 12, 1858, Vt. HS; Lyon to Carey, Mar. 5, 1805, Pa. HS, Lea and Febiger Collection.

20. James Lyon to Jackson, Jan. 25, 1805, Library of Congress, Jackson Papers.

21. Lyon to John Messenger and George Cadwell, Aug. 25, 1805, Ill. SHL Messenger.

22. *Annals*, 8, 1 (Feb. 1, 1805): 1124.

23. Ibid., p. 1126.
24. Fox, "Col. Matthew Lyon," p. 176.
25. Lyon to Carey, July 25, 1802, Pa. HS, Gratz Collection.
26. Roe, *Aunt Leanna*, pp. 62–87. The ensuing discussion of slavery is based on these pages.
27. *Annals*, 8, 1 (Oct. 8, 1803): 543–44.
28. Malone, *Jefferson and His Time*, 4: 448.
29. *Annals*, 8, 2 (Mar. 10, 1804): 1154.
30. Malone, *Jefferson and His Time*, 4: 450–51.
31. *Annals*, 8, 2 (Mar. 10, 1804): 1153.
32. Ibid., p. 1158.
33. Beveridge, *John Marshall*, 3: 569.
34. *Annals*, 8, 2 (Mar. 10, 1804): 1158. The following discussion is based on pp. 1157–59.
35. Transcript Letter, Lyon to Stephen Jacobs, Dec. 12, 1804, Vt. HS.
36. *Annals*, 8, 2 (Mar. 10, 1804): 1157.
37. Malone, *Jefferson and His Time*, 4: 449.
38. *Annals*, 8, 2 (Jan. 31, 1805): 1106.
39. Ibid.
40. *Annals*, 8, 2 (Feb. 1, 1805): 1125. The following discussion is based on pp. 1121–26.
41. Lyon to Edwards, Feb. 18, 1804, Chicago Historical Society, Edwards Papers.
42. Morris, *Fair Trial*, p. 124.
43. Lyon to Jefferson, Aug. 12, 1801, Library of Congress, Jefferson Papers.
44. "Matthew Lyon's Deposition to Committee Appointed to Inquire Into the Conduct of Brigadier General James Wilkinson," in Wilkinson, *Memoirs*, 2, App. 68: 15–24. The following account is based on this deposition.
45. Carter, "Burr-Wilkinson Intrigue," pp. 449–50.
46. Lyon to John Messenger, Mar. 20, 1806, Ill. SHL Messenger.
47. Carter, "Burr-Wilkinson Intrigue," p. 453.
48. Lyon to Jefferson, Apr. 22, 1806, Library of Congress, Jefferson Papers.
49. Jacobs, *Tarnished Warrior*, p. 240.
50. *Annals*, 10, 1 (Jan. 11, 1808): 1400–3.
51. *Annals*, 10, 1 (Jan. 13, 1808): 1458.
52. Lyon to Jefferson, Feb. 22, 1808, Library of Congress, Jefferson Papers.
53. Wilkinson, *Memoirs*, 2, Appendix 68: 15–24.
54. Ibid.
55. Jacobs, *Tarnished Warrior*, pp. 271–72.
56. *Annals*, 10, 2 (Nov. 28, 1808): 551–53; *Annals*, 10, 1 (Apr. 4, 1808): 1934.
57. *Annals*, 10, 2 (Nov. 28, 1808): 551–53.
58. Lyon to Jefferson, Feb. 9, 1808, Library of Congress, Jefferson Papers.
59. *Annals*, 10, 2 (Feb. 7, 1809): 1411–21.
60. Ibid.
61. In 1811, Matthew Lyon beseeched Secretary of State James Monroe to "immortalize" himself by negotiating a treaty with Great Britain as favorable as the one he and Pinckney had obtained in 1806. This stillborn treaty was rejected by President Jefferson and later by President Madison because, despite its most-favored-nation clause, it granted too many concessions to Great Britain. Lyon to Monroe, Sept. 24, 1811, Library of Congress, Monroe Papers.
62. *Annals*, 10, 2 (Jan. 4, 1809): 979.
63. Lyon to Andrew Selden, Jan. 18, 1810, Vt. HS, Ellis Collection.
64. *Annals*, 10, 2 (Feb. 7, 1809): 1420–21.
65. Lyon to Monroe, Mar. 5, 1816, N.Y. PL, Monroe Papers.
66. *An Address of Matthew Lyon.*
67. McLaughlin, *Matthew Lyon*, p. 467.
68. Quoted in McLaughlin, *Matthew Lyon*, pp. 467–68.
69. Lyon to Monroe, Apr. 16, 1816, N.Y. PL, Monroe Papers.
70. Finis Ewing to Messrs. Worsley and Smith, Mar. 14, 1818, Wis. HS, Draper Collection 6CC72, Kentucky Papers.
71. Lyon to Monroe, Mar. 5 , 1816, N.Y. PL, Monroe Papers.
72. Lyon to Monroe, Apr. 16, 1816, N.Y. PL, Monroe Papers. In this letter Lyon explained

that since nothing of a private nature was contained in his previous letter of Mar. 16. 1816, he published its contents.

73. Ibid.

74. Roe, *Aunt Leanna*, pp. 198–204; R.R. O'Hara to Pliny White, Aug. 13, 1858, Vt. HS, Pliny White Papers. According to this letter, Chittenden Lyon eventually discharged all of his father's debts, paying a large sum out of his own pocket, "not willing that his father's memory should rest under any reproach."

75. *Revolutionary War Pension File of Matthew Lyon S36 689*, National Archives, Veterans Records.

76. Lyon to Monroe, June 17, 1817, Pa. HS, Gratz Collection.

77. Peake, *Indian Factory System*, p. 3.

78. Account Current of U.S. Factor at Spadre Bluffs, Arkansas, Jan. 1–Mar. 31, 1822, National Archives, Record of the Office of Indian Trade, Spadre Bluffs Factory, Bureau of Indian Affairs, Record Group 75.

79. Roe, *Aunt Leanna*, p. 210.

80. Ibid.

81. Lyon to Jackson, Aug. 20, 1816, Library of Congress, Jackson Papers, Series 1.

82. Bassett, *Correspondence of Andrew Jackson*, 1: 259.

83. McKinney to Lyon, May 18, 1821, National Archives, Bureau of Indian Affairs.

84. Ibid.

85. Roe, *Aunt Leanna*, p. 209.

86. McKinney to Lyon, Jan. 10, 1822, National Archives, Bureau of Indian Affairs.

87. Peake, *Indian Factory System*, p. 9.

88. Chittenden Lyon to John Messenger, Oct. 31, 1821, Ill. SHL Messenger.

89. Roe, *Aunt Leanna*, p. 219.

Conclusion   (pages 152–155)

1. Hofstadter, *The Idea of a Party System*.

2. Jefferson to Henry Lee, May 8, 1825; Ford, *The Writing of Jefferson*, 10, p. 343.

3. Wills, *Inventing America*.

4. For an indication of the lines along which this debate may run, see Hamowy, "Jefferson and the Scottish Enlightenment."

Bibliography

Primary Sources

A. Manuscripts

Vermont
Sheldon Museum (Middlebury)
University of Vermont, Wilbur Library
    Ira Allen Papers.
    John Spargo Collection.
Vermont Historical Society
    Nathaniel Chipman Collection.
    Ellis Collection.
    Matthew Lyon Collection.
    Pliny White Papers.
Vermont Public Records Division
    Arlington Land Records, Vols. 1–3, 1780–1798 (microfilm).
    Land Records of Wallingford, Vermont, Vol. 1 (microfilm).
Vermont Secretary of State's Office
    MSS State Papers of Vermont.
    Stevens Papers.

Massachusetts
Massachusetts Historical Society
    Sedgwick Collection.
    Pickering Papers.

Connecticut
Connecticut Historical Society
    Oliver Wolcott, Jr., Papers.
Connecticut State Library
    Connecticut Probate Records, No. 2951.
    Litchfield County Court Records, Books 3–5.
    Proprietors Records, Town of Litchfield, 1723–1807
        (microfilm).
Litchfield Historical Society
    Ransom Collection.
Yale University Library
    W.G. Lane Papers.

New York
New York Historical Society
  Gallatin Papers.
  Genet Papers.
  Protestant Episcopal Church Archives 6, Reverend Samuel Peters
    Correspondence (microfilm).
New York Public Library, MSS Division
  Matthew Lyon Miscellaneous Papers.
  William Paterson Papers, Bancroft Collection.
  Noah Webster Papers.
  James Monroe Papers.
New York State Library
  Phelps Gorham Papers.
  Stevens Papers.
      Ira Allen Papers.
      Levi Allen Papers.
  Zephaniah Platt Papers.

Pennsylvania
Pennsylvania Historical Society
  Gratz Collection.
  Lea and Febiger Collection.

Washington, D.C.
Library of Congress
  Andrew Jackson Papers.
  Thomas Jefferson Papers.
  James Monroe Papers.
National Archives
  Records of Division of Veterans Records.
  Records of the Bureau of Indian Affairs.

Virginia
James Monroe Memorial Foundation (Fredericksburg)

North Carolina
Duke University Library
  Ephraim Kirby Papers.
University of North Carolina, Southern Historical Collection
  Peter Hagner Papers.
  John Rutledge, Jr., Papers.

Illinois
Illinois State Historical Library
  John Messenger Papers.
Chicago Historical Society
  Ninian Edwards Papers.

Wisconsin
State Historical Society of Wisconsin
  Draper MSS.
    Kentucky Papers.

B. Newspapers

Aurora (Philadelphia, Pennsylvania)
Banner (Bennington, Vermont)
Camden Gazette (South Carolina)

Connecticut Courant (Hartford)
Elizabethtown Gazette (Tennessee)
Farmers' Library (Fairhaven, Vermont)
Independent Chronicle and Universal Advertiser (Boston)
Massachusetts Centinel (Boston)
Mobile Gazette (Alabama)
Portfolio (Philadelphia, Pennsylvania)
Pee Dee Gazette (Cheraw, South Carolina)
Pennsylvania Herald and York General Advertiser (York, Pennsylvania)
Porcupine's Gazette (Philadelphia, Pennsylvania)
Rutland Herald (Vermont)
Spectator (New York, New York)
Spooner's Vermont Journal (Windsor)
Vermont Gazette (Bennington)
Washington Republican (Jonesboro, Tennessee)

C. Government Publications

Biographical Directory of the American Congress 1774–1961.
   Washington, D.C.: United States Government Printing Office, 1961.
Circuit Court of Caldwell County. *Proceedings.* Caldwell County, Kentucky,
   July 12, 1820.
Force, Peter, ed. *American State Papers.* 38 vols.
   Public Lands, vol. 1. Washington, D.C.: Gales and Seaton, 1832–1861.
Index to the Act or Grant Books of the Diocese of Dublin.
   Appendix, 26th Report, Reports of the Deputy Keeper of the Public Records
   in Ireland. Dublin: 1893.
Peters, Richard, ed. *The Statutes at Large of the United States, 1789–1873.*
   17 vols. Boston: Charles C. Little and James Brown, 1845–1873. vol. 1.
U.S. Congress. *Debates and Proceedings in the Congress of the United States
   (Annals of Congress).* Washington, D.C.: Gales and Seaton, 1849–55.
   4th Cong., 1st Sess., Dec. 7, 1795, to June 1, 1796. 1849.
   4th Cong., 2nd Sess., Dec. 5, 1796, to Mar. 3, 1797. 1849.
   5th Cong., 1st and 2nd Sess., 1850.
   6th Cong., 1st and 2nd Sess., Dec. 2, 1799, to Mar. 3, 1801. 1851.
   8th Cong., 1st and 2nd Sess., Oct. 17, 1803, to Mar. 3, 1805. 1852.
   9th Cong., 1st and 2nd Sess., Dec. 2, 1805, to Mar. 3, 1807. 1852.
   10th Cong., 1st and 2nd Sess., Oct. 26, 1807, to Mar. 3, 1809. 1853.
   11th Cong., 1st and 2nd Sess., May 22, 1809, to May 10, 1810; 3rd Sess.,
      Dec. 3, 1810, to Mar. 3, 1811. 1853.
   16th Cong., 2nd Sess., Nov. 13, 1820, to Mar. 3, 1821. 1855.
Vermont Secretary of State, ed. *State Papers of Vermont.* 14 vols. Bellows Falls,
   Vt.: Wyndham Press, 1918–65.
   Walter H. Crockett, ed., vol. 3. *Journals and Proceedings of the General
      Assembly of the State of Vermont . . .* with explanatory notes,
      1781–1791.   4 parts.
   ———, ed., vol. 4. *Reports of Committees to the General Assembly of the
      State of Vermont,* March 9, 1778, to October 16, 1801, with explanatory
      notes.
   Mary Greene Nye, ed., vol. 5. *Petitions for Grants of Land 1778–1811.*
   ———, ed., vol. 6. *Sequestration, Confiscation and Sale of Estates
      (Loyalist material. —1777–1822).*
   Edward A. Hoyt, ed., vol. 8. *General Petitions: 1778–1787.*
   ———, ed., vol. 9. *General Petitions: 1788–1792.*

Allen Soule, ed., vol. 10. *General Petitions: 1793–1796.*
———, ed., vol. 11. *General Petitions: 1797–1799.*
———, ed., vol. 12. *Laws of Vermont, Constitution of 1777, Laws of 1778–80.*
John A. Williams, ed., vol. 13. *Laws of Vermont, 1781–1784.*
Walton, E.P., ed. *Records of the Council of Safety and Governor and Council of the State of Vermont,* to which are prefixed the records of the General Conventions from July, 1775, to December, 1777. 4 vols. Montpelier, Vt.: Steam Press of J. and J.M. Poland, 1873–76.
Wharton, Francis. *State Trials of the United States during the Administrations of Washington and Adams.* Philadelphia: Carey and Hart, 1849.

D. Books, Magazines, Pamphlets

An Address of Matthew Lyon, to his Friends and the Citizens generally, of the First Electoral District in Kentucky. September 29, 1812. (Broadside) Worcester, Mass.: American Antiquarian Society.
Bassett, John Spencer, ed. *Correspondence of Andrew Jackson,* 7 vols. Vol. 1, *To April 30, 1814.* Washington, D.C.: Carnegie Institute of Washington, 1926–35.
Boyd, Julian P., ed. *The Papers of Thomas Jefferson,* 19 vols. Princeton, New Jersey: Princeton University Press, 1950–.
Capt. John Wood's LOTTERY, assigned to Matthew Lyon, Rutland, Nov. 18, 1798. (Broadside) Microcard, Evans No. 35048.
Circular: Matthew Lyon to his Fellow Citizens of the counties of Christian, Muhlenburg, Ohio, Brackenridge, Grayson, Henderson, Union, Hopkins, Livingston and Caldwell. 1811. Worcester, Mass.: American Antiquarian Society.
Clark, Samuel A. *The History of St. John's Church, Elizabethtown, New Jersey: From the Year 1703 to the Present Time.* Philadelphia: J.B. Lippincott, 1857, and New York: Thomas N. Stanford, 1857.
Cobbett, William. *The Political Censor or Monthly Review of the Most Interesting Political Occurrences . . .* Philadelphia: May 1796.
The Documentary History of the Protestant Episcopal Church in the Diocese of Vermont including the Journals of the Conventions from the year 1790 to 1832 inclusive. New York: Pott and Amery; Cooper Union, 1870.
Farrand, Max, ed. *The Records of the Federal Convention of 1787.* 4 vols. Rev. ed. New Haven: Yale University Press, 1937. Vol. 1.
Ford, Paul L., ed. *The Journals of Hugh Gaine, Printer.* 2 vols. New York: Dodd, Mead, 1902.
———, ed. *The Writings of Thomas Jefferson.* 10 vols. New York: G.P. Putnam, 1892–99. Vols. 7 and 10.
Gibbs, George. *Memoirs of the Administrations of Washington and Adams from the Papers of Oliver Wolcott, Secretary of the Treasury.* 2 vols. New York: W. Van Norden, 1846.
Graham, John A. *A Descriptive Sketch of the Present State of Vermont. One of the United States of America.* London: For the Author by H. Fry at the Cicero Press, Finsbury Place, 1797.
Harrington, Estelle Messenger. *A History of the Messenger Family.* 2 vols. St. Louis: Mound City Press, 1948.
Lyon, James B. *The Lyon Family.* Jacksonville, Fla.: By the Author, 1923.
Lyon's Vermont Calendar: Or a Planetary Diary for the year of our Lord, 1795. Rutland, Vt.: Printed and Published by James Lyon, 1795. Microcard, Evans No. 29123.

Ogden, John Cosens. *A Short History of the Late Ecclesiastical Oppressions in New England and Vermont.* Richmond: By James Lyon at the office of the *National Magazine*, 1799. Microcard, Evans No. 36006.

Perkins, Nathan. *A Narrative of a Tour through the State of Vermont from April 27 to June 12, 1789.* Rutland, Vt.: C.E. Tuttle Co., 1964.

Perry, William Stevens, ed. *Journals of General Conventions of the Protestant Episcopal Church in the United States 1785-1835.* 4 vols. Vol. 1, *1785-1821;* vol. 3, *Historical Notes and Documents.* Claremont, N.H.: Claremont Manufacturing Co., 1874.

Roe, Elizabeth A. *Aunt Leanna; or, Early Scenes in Kentucky.* Chicago: For the Author, 1855.

———. *Recollections of Frontier Life.* Rockford, Ill.: Gazette Publishing House, 1885.

Rutland County, Vermont, Citizens. *To the Representatives of the Freemen of the United States of America; in Congress Assembled . . . January, 1799.* Rutland, 1799. (Broadside) Microcard, Evans No. 36434.

The Scourge of Aristocracy (and Repository of Important Political Truths), Nos. 1-4 (October 1, 1798, to December 15, 1798). Printed and published at Fairhaven, Vt., by James Lyon.

Slade, William, compiler and publisher. *Vermont State Papers;* being a collection of records and documents, connected with the assumption and establishment of government by the people of Vermont. . . . Middlebury, Vt.: J.W. Copeland, printer, 1823.

Wilkinson, General James. *Memoirs of My Own Times.* 3 Vols. Philadelphia: Abraham Small, 1816.

Young, Thomas. *Some Reflections on the Disputes Between New York, New Hampshire and Col. John Hay Lydius of Albany.* New Haven: Benjamin Mecom, 1764. Microcard, Evans No. 9889.

Secondary Sources

Abernathy, Thomas P. *The South in the New Nation.* Baton Rouge: Louisiana State University Press, 1961.

Adams, Andrew N. *A History of the Town of Fairhaven, Vermont.* Fairhaven: Leonard & Phelps, 1870.

Adams, Henry. *History of the United States During the Administrations of Jefferson and Madison.* Abridged edition. Englewood Cliffs, New Jersey: Prentice Hall, 1963.

———. *The Life of Albert Gallatin.* New York: Peter Smith, 1943.

Adams, John. *Works of John Adams,* 20 vols. Edited by Charles F. Adams. Vol. 3, *Autobiography;* Vol. 4, *Novanglus;* Vol. 6, *A Defense of the Constitutions of Government of the United States of America.* Philadelphia: Hall and Sellers, 1787-1788.

Adelson, Judah. "The Vermont Democratic Republican Societies and the French Revolution." *Vermont History,* 32 (Jan. 1964): 3-23.

Albion, Robert Greenhalgh. *Forests and Sea Power: The Timber Problem of the Royal Navy, 1652-1862.* Hamden, Connecticut: Archon Books, 1965.

Alden, John Richard. *The American Revolution 1775-1783.* New York: Harper and Row, 1954.

Andrews, Charles M. *Our Earliest Colonial Settlements.* 4th ed. Ithaca, N.Y.: Cornell University Press, 1964.

Aronson, Sidney H. *Status and Kinship in the Higher Civil Service: Standards of Selection in the Administration of John Adams, Thomas Jefferson, and Andrew Jackson*, Cambridge, Mass.: Harvard University Press, 1964.

Austin, Aleine. "Vermont Politics in the 1780's: Emergence of Rival Leadership." *Vermont History*, 42, No. 2 (Spring 1974): 140–65.

Baumann, Roland M. "John Swanwick: Spokesman for 'Merchant-Republicanism' in Philadelphia, 1790–1798." *The Pennsylvania Magazine of History and Biography*, 97 (April 1973): 131–82.

———. "The Democratic Republicans of Philadelphia: The Origins, 1776–1797." Ph.D. Dissertation, The Pennsylvania State University, 1970.

Beard, Charles A. *Economic Origins of Jeffersonian Democracy*. New York and London: The Free Press, Collier-Macmillan Ltd., 1943.

Beveridge, Albert J. *The Life of John Marshall*, 4 vols. Vol. 3, *Conflict and Construction 1800–1815*. Boston and New York: Houghton, Mifflin Co., 1919.

Bigger, Frances. "Captain Lyon, Bishop of Cork," *Cork Historical and Archeological Society Journal*, 3, No. 33 (September 1894): 192–93.

Bining, A.C. *British Regulation of the Colonial Iron Industry*. Philadelphia: University of Pennsylvania Press, 1933.

———. *Pennsylvania Iron Manufacturing the Eighteenth Century*. Harrisburg: Pennsylvania Historical Commission, 1938.

Bishop, J. Leander; A.M., M.D. *A History of Manufactures from 1608 to 1860*. 2 vols. Philadelphia: Edward Young & Co., 1864.

Borden, Morton. *The Federalism of James A. Bayard*. New York: Columbia University Press, 1955.

Bowers, Claude G. *Jefferson and Hamilton: The Struggle for Democracy in America*. Boston: The Riverside Press, and New York: Houghton Mifflin Co., 1925.

Brant, Irving. *James Madison: Secretary of State, 1801–1809*. Indianapolis and New York: Bobbs-Merrill, 1953.

Brebner, John Bartlet. *North Atlantic Triangle: The Interplay of Canada, the United States, and Great Britain*. New York: Russell and Russell, 1970.

Bruce, William Cabell. *John Randolph of Roanoke, 1773–1833*. New York and London: G.P. Putnam's Sons, 1922.

Brunhouse, Robert. *Counter-Revolution in Pennsylvania*. Harrisburg: Pennsylvania Historical and Museum Commission, 1971.

Brush, Rev. George Robert. *St. James' Parish, Arlington, Vermont and the Diocese of Vermont*. Burlington, Vt.: Free Press Printing Co., 1941.

Brymner, Douglas, Archivist. *Report on Canadian Archives 1891*. Ottawa: S.E. Dawson, 1891.

Carter, Clarence E. "The Burr-Wilkinson Intrigue in St. Louis." *Missouri Historical Society Bulletin* 10 (1954): 447–64.

Cassell, Frank A. *Merchant Congressman in the Young Republic: Samuel Smith of Maryland, 1752–1839*. Madison: The University of Wisconsin Press, 1971.

Charles, Joseph. *The Origins of the American Party System*. New York: Harper and Row, Harper Torch Books, 1961.

Chipman, Daniel. *The Life of Hon. Nathaniel Chipman*. Boston: Little and J. Brown, 1846.

Chipman, Nathaniel. *Sketches of the Principles of Government*. Rutland: From the press of J. Lyon. Printed for the author, 1793.

Clark, Victor S. *History of Manufacturers in the United States*. Vol. 1, *1607–1860*. 3 vols. New York: McGraw Hill, 1929.

Cole, Arthur Harrison. *Industrial and Commercial Correspondence of Alexander Hamilton.* Chicago: A.W. Shaw Company, 1928.

Cothren, William. *History of Ancient Woodbury.* 3 vols. Waterbury, Ct.: Bronson Brothers, 1854.

Cunningham, Noble E. *The Jeffersonian Republicans, The Formation of Party Organization, 1789–1801.* Chapel Hill: University of North Carolina Press, 1957.

Dauer, Manning J. *The Adams Federalists.* Baltimore: The Johns Hopkins Press, 1953.

Davis, Joseph Stancliffe. *Essays in the Earlier History of American Corporations.* 2 vols. New York: Russell and Russell, Inc., 1965.

Falley, Margaret D. *Irish and Scotch Irish Ancestral Research.* 2 vols. Strasburg, Va.: Shenandoah Publishing House, 1961.

Fay, Bernard. *The Revolutionary Spirit in France and America.* Translated by Ramon Guthrie. New York: Harcourt Brace, 1927.

Fischer, David Hackett. *The Revolution of American Conservatism.* New York: Harper and Row, 1965.

Fisher, William Edward Garrett. "Paper Manufacture." *Encyclopedia Britannica,* 11th ed., vol. 20.

Fox, Loyal Stephen. "Colonel Matthew Lyon, Biographical and Genealogical Notes." *Vermont Quarterly* 12, No. 3 (July 1944):163–80.

French, Allen, *First Year of the American Revolution.* New York: Octagon Books, 1968.

———. *The Taking of Ticonderoga.* Cambridge, Mass.: Harvard University Press, 1928.

Freud, Sigmund. "Further Remarks on the Defense Neuro-psychoses." In *Collected Papers,* vol. 1, pp. 155–182. New York: Basic Books, 1959.

———. "On Narcissism: An Introduction." In *The Standard Edition of the Complete Psychological Works of Sigmund Freud,* vol. 14, pp. 67–107. London: The Hogarth Press, 1955.

Godfrey, Carlos E. "Organization of the Provisional Army." *Pennsylvania Magazine of History and Biography* 38 (1914): 130–32.

Goodman, Paul. *The Democratic-Republicans of Massachusetts: Politics in a Young Republic.* Cambridge, Mass.: Harvard University Press, 1965.

Greene, Jack P. "Changing Interpretations of Early American Politics." In *The Reinterpretation of Early American History: Essays in Honor of John Edwin Pomfret.* Edited by Ray Allen Billington. San Marino, California: Huntington Library, 1966.

Hall, Benjamin. *History of Eastern Vermont from its Earliest Settlement to the Close of the 18th Century.* New York: D. Appleton and Co., 1858.

Hall, Hiland. *History of Vermont from its Discovery to its Admission into the Union in 1791.* Albany: J. Munsell, 1868.

Harris. P.M.G. "The Social Origins of American Leaders: The Demographic Foundations." *Perspectives in American History* 3 (1969): 159–344.

Hamowy, Ronald. "Jefferson and the Scottish Enlightenment: A Critique of Garry Wills's *Inventing America: Jefferson's Declaration of Independence,*" *The William and Mary Quarterly,* October 1979, pp. 503–523.

Hartley, E.N. *Ironworks on the Saugus: The Lynn and Braintree Ventures of the Company of Undertakers of the Ironworks in New England.* Norman: University of Oklahoma Press, 1957.

Hartman, H., and Lowenstein, R. "Notes on the Theory of Aggression." In *The Psychoanalytic Study of the Child,* 4: 9–36. New York: International University Press, 1949.

Haskins, Charles H. "The Yazoo Land Companies." *American Historical Association Papers* 5 (1891): 395–437.

Hawke, David, ed. *U.S. Colonial History: Readings and Documents.* Indianapolis: Bobbs-Merrill, 1966.

Heimert, Alan. *Religion and the American Mind.* Cambridge, Mass.: Harvard University Press, 1966.

Hemenway, Abby Maria. *The Vermont Historical Gazetteer: A Magazine Embracing A History of Each Town.* 5 vols. Burlington, Vt.: By the Author, 1868–1891.

Herrick, Hudee Z. "Matthew Lyon, The Vermont Years." M.A. Thesis, University of Vermont, 1952.

Hindle, Brooke, ed. *The Narrative of Colonel Ethan Allen.* New York: Corinth Books, 1961.

Historical Collections Relating to the Town of Salisbury. 2 vols. Litchfield County, Ct.: The Salisbury Association, Inc., 1913.

Hofstadter, Richard. *The Idea of a Party System; the rise of legitimate opposition in the United States, 1780–1840.* Berkeley: Univ. of California Press, 1969.

———. *The Paranoid Style in American Politics and other Essays.* New York: Random House, Vintage Books, 1967.

Hunter, Dard. *Papermaking: The History and Technique of an Ancient Craft.* 2d ed. New York: Alfred A. Knopf, 1957.

Jacobs, James Ripley. *Tarnished Warrior: Major-General James Wilkinson.* New York: Macmillan, 1938.

James, Thomas. *Three Years Among the Indians and Mexicans.* Philadelphia and New York: J.B. Lippincott Co., 1962.

Jameson, J. Franklin. *The American Revolution Considered as a Social Movement.* Princeton, N.J.: Princeton University Press, 1940.

Jellison, Charles A. *Ethan Allen: Frontier Rebel.* Syracuse: Syracuse University Press, 1969.

Jensen, Merrill. "Democracy and the American Revolution." *Huntington Library Quarterly* 20 (August 1957): 321–41.

Jones, Herbert S. "America's First Law School." *My Country* 2, No. 3 (Sept. 1968): 2–7.

Kaplanoff, Mark D. "From Colony to State: New Hampshire, 1800–1815." Scholar of the House Thesis, Yale University, 1970.

Kilbourne, Payne K. *A Biographical History of the County of Litchfield, Conn.* New York: Clarke, Austin, 1851.

King, C.R., ed. *Life and Correspondence of Rufus King. Comprising His Letters, Private and Official, His Public Documents, and His Speeches,* 6 vols. New York: G.P. Putnam's Sons, 1894–1900. Vol. 2.

Koch, Gustav Adolf. *Republican Religions, The American Revolution and the Cult of Reason.* New York: Columbia University Press, 1932.

Levy, Leonard W. *Freedom of Speech and Press in Early American History; Legacy of Suppression.* New York: Harper and Row, Harper Torchbooks, 1963.

Link, Eugene P. *Democratic-Republican Societies, 1790–1800.* New York: Columbia University Press, 1942.

Loveland, Clara O. *The Critical Years, The Reconstruction of the Anglican Church in the United States of America 1780–1789.* Greenwich, Ct.: The Seabury Press, 1956.

Ludlum, David M. *Social Ferment in Vermont 1791–1850.* New York: Columbia University Press, 1939.

McBride, Rita. "Roger Griswold: Connecticut Federalist." Ph.D. Dissertation, Yale University, 1948.

MacLysaght, Edward, ed. *Irish Families, Their Names, Arms and Origins.* Dublin: Hodges Figgis & Co., Ltd., 1957.

Main, Jackson Turner. *The Social Structure of Revolutionary America.* Princeton, N.J.: Princeton University Press, 1965.

———. *The Upper House in Revolutionary America, 1763-1788.* Madison: University of Wisconsin Press, 1967.

Malone, Dumas. *Jefferson and His Time.* 4 vols. Vol. 3, *Jefferson and the Ordeal of Liberty;* Vol. 4, *Jefferson the President: First Term, 1801-1805.* Boston: Little, Brown, 1970.

Martin, James Kirby. *Men in Rebellion: Higher Government Leaders and the Coming of the American Revolution.* New Brunswick: Rutgers University Press, 1973.

McLaughlin, J. Fairfax, LL.D. *Matthew Lyon, the Hampden of Congress.* New York: Wynkoop Hallenbeck Crawford Co., 1900.

Miller, John C. *The Federalist Era, 1789-1801.* New York: Harper and Row, Harper Torchbooks, 1963.

———. *Crisis in Freedom: The Alien and Sedition Acts.* Boston: Little, Brown, 1951.

Mittelberger, Gottlieb. *Journey to Pennsylvania.* Edited and translated by Oscar Handlin and John Clive. Cambridge, Mass.: Harvard University Press, Belknap Press, 1960.

Montagno, George Lucien. "Matthew Lyon, Radical Jeffersonian, 1796-1801." Ph.D. Thesis, University of California, 1954.

Morris, Richard B. *Government and Labor in Early America.* New York: Columbia University Press, 1965. (reprint)

———. *Fair Trial.* New York: Harper and Row, Harper Torchbooks, 1967.

Palmer, R.R. *The Age of the Democratic Revolution: A Political History of Europe and America, 1760-1800,* 2 vols. Princeton, N.J.: Princeton University Press, 1964.

Parker, Charles L., Secretary of the Poultney Historical Society, to Aleine Austin, May 21, 1962.

Peake, Ora Brooks. *A History of the United States Indian Factory System, 1795-1822.* Denver: Sage Books, 1954.

Pell, John, *Ethan Allen.* Boston: Houghton Mifflin, 1929.

Perrin, Gale Porter. *The Life and Works of Thomas Green Fessenden, 1771-1837.* University of Maine Studies, Second Series, No. 4. Orono, Me.: University of Maine Press, 1925.

Pierce, Arthur D. *Iron in the Pines: The Story of New Jersey's Ghost Towns and Bog Iron.* New Brunswick, N.J: Rutgers University Press, 1957.

Pole, J.R.. "Historians and the Problems of Early American Democracy." *American Historical Review* 68 (April 1962): 626-46.

Selsam, Paul. *The Pennsylvania Constitution of 1776.* Philadelphia: University of Pennsylvania Press, 1936.

Smelser, Marshall. *The Democratic Republic, 1801-1815.* New York: Harper and Row, Harper Torchbooks, 1968.

Smith, James M. *Freedom's Fetters: The Alien and Sedition Law and American Civil Liberties.* Ithaca, N.Y.: Cornell University Press, 1956.

Smith, Page. *John Adams: 1735-1826.* 2 vols. New York: Doubleday, 1962.

Starr, Edward C. *A History of Cornwall, Connecticut, A Typical New England Town.* New Haven: Tuttle, Morehouse and Taylor Co., 1926.

Starr, Harris E., ed. *Dictionary of American Biography,* 20 vols. New York: C. Scribner's Sons, 1928-67. Vols. 4 and 9.

Swank, James M. *History of the Manufacture of Iron in All Ages, and Particularly in the United States from Colonial Times to 1891.* . . . Philadelphia: American Iron and Steel Association, 1892.

Tyhurst, James S. "Paranoid Patterns." In *Explorations in Social Psychiatry,* edited by J.A. Clausen and R.N. Wilson, pp. 31–76. New York: Basic Books, 1958.

Wheeler, William Bruce. "The Baltimore Jeffersonians, 1788–1800: A Profile of Intra-Factional Conflict." *Maryland Historical Magazine* 66 (Summer1971): 153–68.

White, Pliny H. *The Life and Services of Matthew Lyon—An Address.* Burlington, Vt.: Times Job Office Printers, 1858.

Wilbur, James B. *Ira Allen, Founder of Vermont, 1751–1814.* 2 vols. Boston: Houghton Mifflin, 1928.

Williams, Samuel. *Vermont during the War for Independence.* (Being Three Chapters Taken from the Author's "Natural and Civil History of Vermont," Published in 1794). Burlington, Vt.: Free Press Printing Co., 1944.

Williamson, Chilton. *Vermont in Quandary, 1763–1825.* Montpelier: Vermont Historical Society, 1949.

Wills, Garry. *Inventing America: Jefferson's Declaration of Independence.* Garden City, N.Y.: Doubleday, 1978.

Wood, Gordon S. *The Creation of the American Republic, 1776–1787.* Chapel Hill: University of North Carolina Press, 1969.

Wood, John. *Suppressed History of the Administration of John Adams (from 1797 to 1801) as printed and suppressed in 1802.* Edited by John Henry Sherburne. Philadelphia: For the editor, 1846.

Young, Alfred Fabian. *The Democratic Republicans of New York: The Origins, 1763–1797.* Chapel Hill: University of North Carolina Press, for the Institute of Early American History and Culture, Williamsburg, Virginia, 1967.

Index